From Anthropometry to Genomics: Reflections of a Pacific Fieldworker

From Anthropometry to Genomics: Reflections of a Pacific Fieldworker

Jonathan Scott Friedlaender
As told to Joanna Radin

iUniverse, Inc.
New York Bloomington

From Anthropometry to Genomics: Reflections of a Pacific Fieldworker

iUniverse books may be ordered through booksellers or by contacting:

iUniverse
1663 Liberty Drive
Bloomington, IN 47403
www.iuniverse.com
1-800-Authors (1-800-288-4677)

ISBN: 978-1-4401-7672-2 (sc)
ISBN: 978-1-4401-8288-4 (dj)
ISBN: 978-1-4401-7673-9 (ebk)

Library of Congress Control Number: 2009937133

Printed in the United States of America

iUniverse rev. date: 10/20/2009

Foreword

Jonathan Friedlaender has devoted much of his professional life to studies of human population variation in Pacific Islanders. His anthropology and pioneering genetics research was conducted largely with what are known as Melanesian peoples on the islands of Bougainville, Malaita, Ontong Java and the Bismarck Archipelago in the Southwestern Pacific. This work began in June 1966 when he was a graduate student at Harvard University and it spans more than a forty-year career that continues to the present. His most recent publications draw on fieldwork conducted in north Bougainville, New Britain, New Ireland, and New Hanover during a series of genetics surveys conducted between 1998 and 2003. His collaborator on this memoir of his life and experiences in the Pacific is Joanna Radin, a young but remarkably knowledgeable historian of science currently conducting graduate studies at the University of Pennsylvania. These two professionals weave a fascinating fabric of complex texture that incorporates the educational, political, governmental, and research climate of the 1960s, 1970s, and 1980s with the trials and tribulations of a young researcher and academic trying to make his way in a highly competitive arena. The book is much more than a series of recollections about one man's life; rather, it is a history of an important era in the development of anthropological genetics and the dramatic transition in this science that took place in the early 1980s.

The book is largely chronological but with some movement forward and backward in time when ideas were being developed. It begins with Friedlaender's youth in North Carolina and the transformation of his intellectual life when he attended Phillips Exeter Academy and, later, Harvard College. He came from a family in which the pursuit of learning was not only encouraged but was also supported educationally. His first experiences in an alien field situation were under the umbrella of the Harvard Solomon Islands Project (HSIP) where he worked with a large professional research team. In many ways, working with a team is an excellent means of introduction to socially-, culturally-, and physically-demanding field conditions (similar to my own experience). Later that same year (1966), after gaining some knowledge of the area and its people, he began to work on his own with Bougainville villagers, who, until the Second World War, had had very little contact with Western peoples. His success, during this independent research conducted under challenging conditions, resulted from a combination of hard work, honesty and sensitivity in dealing with his research subjects, good luck, and good judgment. Also, Friedlaender has a cheerfulness and pleasant nature (which might not be totally apparent from the interview commentary), and this personality attribute probably served him well in working with the people he studied. Those who know Jonathan Friedlaender recognize this good nature, but one overlying a powerful determination and creative ability.

Following this initial fieldwork in 1966-67, Friedlaender made ten more trips to conduct research in the South Pacific. As he notes, the early work in population genetics focused on blood constituents (blood groups and serum proteins). He also took anthropometric measurements, and gathered information on language distributions which were found to parallel the patterns of genetic diversity (extraordinary language and genetic diversity on New Guinea and Island Melanesia characterizes this region of the South Pacific). Between 1975 and 1985, the field of population and anthropological genetics was transformed by the development of techniques to identify DNA directly – both mitochondrial (mtDNA) and nuclear (nDNA) DNA. Friedlaender and most other geneticists had to make this transition from the genetics of phenotypic inference to the genetics of DNA analysis. Friedlaender also provides insightful commentary on the failed Human Genome Diversity Project and the politics of the time, the changing conditions of field research in Melanesia from the mid-1960s to the present, the ethical challenges that were presented early on and how they have changed through time, and how the roles of women students and professionals in the field have changed over the past half century. The final section of this work discusses in some detail both the theoretical and material outcomes of this important research and the prospects for future investigation of genomics.

Friedlaender's book should have appeal to a number of audiences – students, professional anthropologists, and lay readers, alike. It might serve as a primer for all those about to embark on research in the South

Pacific, and as a valuable text on field research, particularly the practical aspects and ethics of field research. Perhaps, the book's most valuable contribution is as a chronicle of the history of the small, but significant, science of human population genetics and its development. Much of human population genetics today has arisen from anthropological interests in human biobehavioral evolution. Jonathan Friedlaender's *Reflections* is a valuable addition to the historical record of this important science. This is also a worthwhile book to read for anyone with interests in the history of science or the history of *a* science.

Michael A. Little

Anthropology Department
Binghamton University
September 2009

Preface

The genesis of this publication was an interview of Dr. Jonathan Friedlaender I conducted over two days in December 2008. Earlier that fall, I had approached Dr. Friedlaender with the hope that he might be willing to reflect upon his career for the benefit of my research as a doctoral candidate in the history and sociology of science at the University of Pennsylvania. I was interested in fieldwork practices of biological anthropologists who had been influential in incorporating the techniques of population genetics. He sat with me for over eight hours of interviews in a quiet corner of Temple University's Anthropology Lab. Following the interviews, Dr. Friedlaender and I worked together as I transcribed portions for him to review. Reading these recollections stimulated new memories and insights and these were added to the transcript, which Dr. Friedlaender reorganized to enhance clarity and readability. The resulting document retains the conversational tone of the oral history interview, but may be more practically considered a scientific memoir.

When he learned of it, Dr. Michael Little, who has major interests in the history of biological anthropology, strongly encouraged us to formally publish this manuscript. We are grateful for his suggestion and enthusiasm.

Dr. Friedlaender's career was of particular interest to me because its arc reflected important changes in the application of genetic, and later genomic, techniques to the study of human history. This document, which he adapted from our interview, situates those changes in the context of his early life in an assimilationist Jewish family in the segregated South, numerous fieldtrips among South Pacific villagers, his intellectual development at Harvard and Wisconsin during the Vietnam and post-Vietnam War period, and subsequent controversies concerning Sociobiology, Non-Darwinian evolution, the Human Genome Diversity Project, and gene patenting, among others.

Because this document is intended for a heterogeneous audience, readers may wish to focus on those sections that best satisfy their interests.

The first two chapters include details about Dr. Friedlaender's formative years with particular attention to his family, childhood interests, and schooling. The next several chapters consider his relationship to his teachers at Harvard and his early experiences as an anthropologist in the field and the classroom. This portion focuses on personal, intellectual, and practical considerations of profound influence on the trajectory of his career. In the final few chapters, readers will find reflections on the practice, politics, and contemporary societal and ethical implications of anthropological genomics as it has emerged over the last several decades.

The process of producing this memoir motivated Dr. Friedlaender to begin gathering up letters, photographs, and video from his time in the field. The Melanesian Archive at the University of California, San Diego has now accepted the donation of Dr. Friedlaender's materials, including the raw transcripts and original audio files from the interview, which will make them accessible to a wide audience.

All proceeds associated with the sale of this book will be donated to the Library Fund of the Institute of Medical Research in Goroka, Papua New Guinea.

It has been a special experience to take part in the production of this document and I thank Dr. Friedlaender for his enthusiasm, candor and thoughtfulness.

Joanna Radin

Department of the History of Science and Sociology
University of Pennsylvania
Philadelphia, PA
Summer 2009

Acknowledgement

Muriel Kirkpatrick was an indispensable source of assistance throughout the preparation of this document. In particular, she helped to prepare many of the images that illustrate the text and provided editing support. She has also curated the Friedlaender family's Melanesian art and artifact collection which was donated to Temple's Anthropology Department. She strongly encouraged the making of an accompanying video interview filmed and produced by Gordon Gray, illustrating the uses of those artifacts, entitled "Forty Years in the Making: Jonathan Friedlaender's Solomon Islands Collection."

Photo Credits

Figures 2 and 6 by Howard Bailit

Figure 7 courtesy of Jesse Page

Figure 13 by Hillary Arlaw

Figures 13, 16, and 17, – Source: Patterns of Human Variation: The Demography, Genetics, and Phenetics of Bougainville Islanders, by Jonathan S. Friedlaender, pp. 82, 114, 116, Cambridge, Massachusetts,: Harvard University Press, Copyright © 1975 by the President and Fellows of Harvard College.

Figures 18, 28, 34, 38 by Bilgé Friedlaender

Figure 34 by Jay Pearson

Figure 36 by Rebecca Lewis

Figures 1, 5, 14, 26, 31, 32: Unknown photographers

Jonathan Scott Friedlaender

Vital Statistics

Born August 24, 1940, New Orleans, LA

Father – Marc Friedlaender (born 1905)

Mother – Clara May Beer Friedlaender (born 1906)

Brother – J. Stephen Friedlaender (born 1935)

Marriages and children.

Married to Bilgė Civelekoglu Friedlaender from 1971-1984

Daughter – Mira Asli Friedlaender (born March 29, 1972)

Adopted – Banu Hummel

Married to Rebecca Elizabeth Lewis from 1986-2000

Son – Benjamin Lewis Friedlaender (born January 7, 1988)

Married to Françoise Rubinstejn Friedlaender from 2004-present.

Education.

1946-1955 (primary until 9th grade) Curry School, Greensboro, North Carolina

1955-1958 (10th until 12th grade) Phillips Exeter Academy, Exeter, New Hampshire

1958-1962 Harvard College, Cambridge Massachusetts, received B.A. in Classical Art History, *magna cum laude,* Phi Beta Kappa

1962-1963 University of Pennsylvania, M.A. in General Anthropology

1963-1968 Harvard, PhD in Biological Anthropology

1968-1969 University of Wisconsin, Population Council Postdoctoral Fellow

Professional positions.

1969-1970 University of Wisconsin, Assistant Professor

1970-1974 Harvard University, Assistant Professor

1974-1976 Harvard University, Associate Professor (untenured)

1976-1982 Temple University, Associate Professor

1982-2004 Temple University Professor, retired as Professor Emeritus of Biological Anthropology

1992-1995 National Science Foundation, Director, Physical Anthropology Program

Table of Contents

Chapter 1.

Family Background and Early Education

JR (Joanna Radin): We're going to do a biography of you and start at the beginning. So let's start by talking a little about where you were born, your childhood, your family and we'll move on from there.

Family and Childhood

JF (Jonathan Friedlaender): Good. I do think those are important.

I came from a southern Jewish background – very assimilationist. I was born in 1940, in New Orleans, where my mother had been born and raised (my father was from Columbus, Georgia, and they were second cousins). I grew up in Greensboro, North Carolina, where my father was a professor at the Woman's College of the University of North Carolina (now UNC-Greensboro). I was a second child – my brother, Stephen, is five years older. As children we were very close, and spent a great deal of time together in our family's modern house, built in 1941 overlooking a pond in the woods, 10 minutes' drive outside town. We were expected to do well in school, and we took music lessons as well (my mother's influence). My brother was the star and somebody I relied on as a child to play with, learn from, and emulate. We were classic first and second sons. I happily followed in his footsteps. We rarely quarreled. I remember he once snapped at me and being very deflated by it – and this was when I was 17 or 18! It was not until my college years that I began to think of myself as possibly his intellectual or physical equal, nor did my parents, particularly my father. In grade school, I was a somewhat above-average student, hardly outstanding, and was a poor athlete – I was fat. I was not a leader in any way, but I did have a small circle of friends.

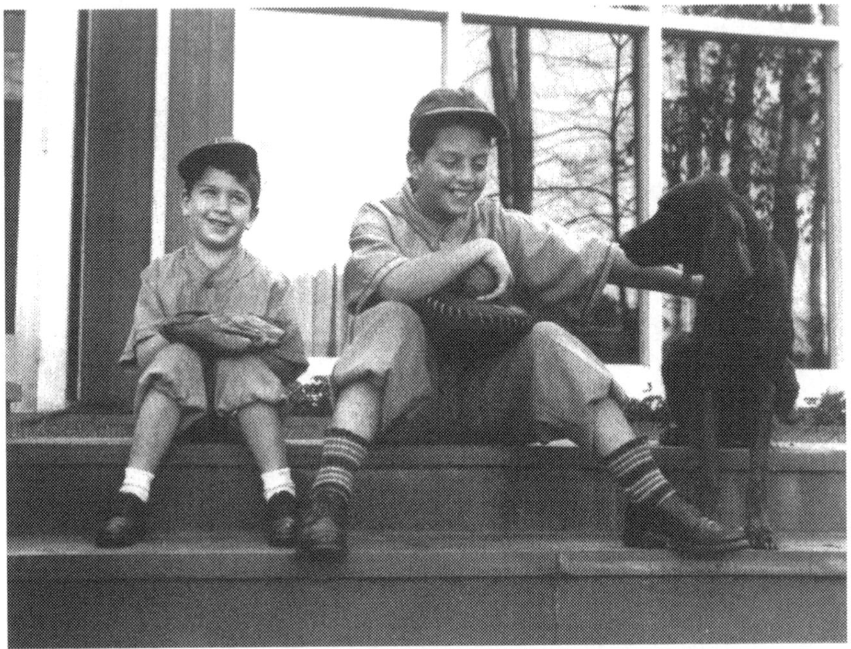

At home in Greensboro, with older brother Stephen and Lucy. 1946.

My mother was trained as a pianist (she graduated with all sorts of honors from H. Sophie Newcomb, the women's college of Tulane, including Phi Beta Kappa and being the class president – there was a great obituary of her in the Boston Globe when she died two years ago). She was beautiful, gracious, and warm, though demanding as a mother. People were instinctively attracted to her, and she was an acute judge of others. Her father was a lawyer with an honorable reputation, but without my father's family resources. She oversaw our music practicing every school night right after dinner (I played the flute, my brother the violin). Then we did our homework, which she and my father often helped us with.

My father was not a radical, but he had socialist sympathies in the '20s and '30s. He had a strong sense of moral rectitude. The family story goes that he didn't want to take over his father's mill in Georgia that bailed cotton because it was making money off non-union, and poor black, labor. He wanted to go into academics, a career path which was just opening up for Jews. After graduation from Princeton and majoring in art history, he tried Harvard Law

School for a short time as a sort of compromise with his father, but didn't do well and dropped out to pursue English literature. He had gone to a southern high-school, and in the early 20th century, those were academically poor, which put him at an intellectual disadvantage as a freshman at Princeton. The public schools in Greensboro were not much better in the 1950s, either. Because of his own experience, he wanted us to go the best schools he could find, so he sent us both away to Phillips Exeter Academy in New Hampshire (my mother was not so excited, but went along) – I still was following my brother's footsteps there – and subsequently to Harvard as well.

My father's love was the arts, English literature in particular, and Shakespeare most specifically. He won prizes as a teacher. He was an admirer of creative artists, but lacked the spark himself – he was too thorough and critical. Later in life, after being involved in unsuccessful and contentious attempts to reform the college curriculum, he helped found a publishing house in New York (Atheneum Publishers) and, finally, when a difficult situation also developed there, he became an associate editor of the Adams family papers at the Massachusetts Historical Society, where he was happiest. That's why they moved first to New York and then to Cambridge.

My parents were preoccupied with our family and with my brother's and my development and education. We spent a great deal of time together, went on long trips, watched ballgames of different sorts, attended concerts, and so forth. I always felt fortunate to be their child, although it certainly had its stifling aspects as the youngest.

I began to learn how to write decent sentences at home because of my father's almost nightly corrections of my homework assignments, which were difficult for me to endure. His involvement in my homework continued for a long time. My first research paper was for a course in American history in the 12th grade, and he urged me to do it on the civil rights movement as it affected Greensboro in the mid-1950s. When I showed him my draft, he didn't think it was satisfactory, and he (with my brother's help) rewrote it heavily. I felt badly about that entire experience, very inadequate.

When I wrote my senior thesis at college, he again wanted to see the drafts. It was hard for me to let him do that, given our history. One of the things I liked about going away to prep school was that I didn't have to show my homework to my father, because that's what would happen every night at home, when I was in 7th, 8th, 9th grade. He looked at the first chapter draft of my thesis and made all kinds of stylistic corrections. I was just like, "Oh no . . ." It was so painful. Almost every sentence had red pencil marks and revised sentence structures. I was upset about it and I didn't show him any of the other chapters. When he asked to see them, I would say, "They're not ready yet." In the end, my thesis was given a *summa cum laude* evaluation by the faculty readers. The only criticism they had was that the first chapter was not well written; it was complex and Germanic in its sentence structure, but the style improved dramatically in later chapters, so you bet I let him know that!

JR: I bet you did!

Early Environment

There was always an understanding in the South, especially during my parents' childhood, that the Ku Klux Klan and others had it in not only for blacks, but for Jews on occasion if they got out of line (the operative phrase was "too uppity"). In the 1920s, the famous lynching of Leo Frank, who'd been pardoned after he was convicted in a questionable case of rape and murder of a 13 year old girl, sent tremors through the southern Jewish community. I only learned of this a few years ago – these sorts of things weren't discussed in my childhood home. Much later, my father told me he remembered being chased home from school in Columbus, Georgia, by boys yelling "Christ-killer", but I was not aware of any anti-Semitism at my school – only one minor incident that I can recall, that the student (a preacher's son) apologized for the next day. Nevertheless, it was important to be above reproach or criticism from others, to be good examples, to avoid controversy. We were taught to be morally responsible, to be considerate of others, and to be truthful (the Principal at my school once told my father I was "the most honest boy he ever knew," which certainly pleased my father but also somewhat amused him, I think). At Exeter, I was appointed a chapel monitor by the Dean. The chapel monitors were students who were somehow supposed to be of especially good character (it meant we had to report those students who were late or absent from the daily morning assemblies, called morning chapel).

Because of its five colleges, Greensboro was unusually liberal for a southern town. Many of the leading members of the business community were Jewish as well. It was no accident that the most important early sit-ins occurred there, led by black college students. Ours was a liberal southern background, but my parents were also financially secure because of my grandfather's mill in Columbus. Like everyone else in the South of any means during that period, we had black servants – a cook who had grown up in my mother's house in New Orleans, and a series of others who were college students earning their way through one of the two black colleges in Greensboro. This created interesting situations as integration began to occur during the 1950s, when my parents started inviting their first black guests to the house (some of them ex-employees).

JR: I want to probe a little bit more. You've mentioned and definitely given cues about how your upbringing prepared you for your later ease in the field and I wonder if you could elaborate about your childhood early memories. Are there certain books or specific experiences you had growing up that you identify with your interest in anthropology or your later career pursuits?

Camp

JF: My early camping experiences made the idea of fieldwork in the Pacific jungles an appealing prospect for me, and not overly intimidating (I think of myself as a cautious person). My father's sister lived in Milwaukee and had sent her two sons to a camp in northern Wisconsin that emphasized a lot of canoe trips in the northern forests. My father was taken with the idea of sending us there as well (as a boy, he'd gone to a summer camp in northern Maine). So my brother and I spent four or five summers each there (that was for two months, with perhaps four camping trips each summer). It was unusual to be from so far away – most of the boys were from the Chicago-Milwaukee area, and a few from Iowa, and a handful from Saint Louis. I was nicknamed "Southie," but when I came home, I would be teased about my freshly acquired mid-western accent. We often traveled alone on trains to and from camp. We only overlapped there one year, but many of the camp staff had known my brother, who had been particularly well-liked and a successful camper and leader. I was more solitary, but I enjoyed the camping a great deal. I was a strong canoe paddler (we had a canoe at home, and I spent a great deal of time exploring the woods around the pond behind our house), and I got to go on special canoe trips, one to Canada for 10 days, as I recall.

Books

As for influential books, I liked pre-histories, ancient histories, and adventures. Some of my favorites had to do with either going back in time or with origins of different cultures. I was always interested in the origins of western civilization, which meant Greek archaeology and myths. My interests also included 'primitive' peoples. I remember Mark Twain's book *A Connecticut Yankee in King Arthur's Court* where the mechanic hero is transported back into time to Arthur's Tintagel, and he makes critical differences by introducing modern inventions, rivaling Merlin. I thought, "Wow, that's neat! That would be a wonderful experience!"

In a certain way, going into Melanesian cultures that had had limited experiences with the modern world made me feel a little bit like that. I had to spend lots of time – which I liked doing – giving explanations for how America had recently put a man on the moon, for example. "How did you do that?" [The people would ask]. I would then take a couple hours to outline the situation as I understood it. Other typical questions had to do with the manufacture of special items. I remember being asked how glass bottles were made (if it wasn't just magic). My response was perhaps too simple ("If you take some sand and heat it in a hot fire, it will melt and turn into glass when it cools"), and often not entirely satisfactory, since they knew they couldn't make that happen in their fires. Other times, things flopped. I remember that the comet Kohutek was supposed to become visible while I was in Bougainville, and I confidently predicted its arrival, rather like a scene from the old movie *King Solomon's Mines* that starred Stewart Granger. Unfortunately,

Kohutek didn't put on a big show. In any event, it was an empowering kind of situation where I knew a great deal about the outside world that these people didn't know and wanted to know. So that was one thing.

I liked a series of anthropological books, for example, *The Mute Stones Speak*, or *Gods, Graves, and Scholars*, by C.W. Ceram, which you may have heard of. They were about early archaeological discoveries in different areas; Heinrich Schliemann's excavations in Troy, early Maya discoveries in the Yucatan peninsula, and so on. I loved those sorts of adventure stories about early archaeology and discovery. I remember being taken with a book about exploration in the Amazon called *Journey to the Far Amazon*, by Alain Gheerbrandt. So those were early; 8, 10, 12 years old, and they sparked my interest in anthropology and prehistory, along with real adventure accounts like those of Jacques Cousteau and his early underwater archaeology in the Mediterranean.

Phillips Exeter Academy (1955-1958)

Getting back to my education, I went away to Exeter beginning in the second year of high school. In fact, my entry test scores were so poor that I had to go there for summer school to qualify (this was not uncommon, but my brother had avoided that). I plugged away and did creditably, but again I was not outstanding in any way. While my brother made the honor society, I didn't. I did greatly enjoy wrestling, lost a lot of weight and got into shape, which was important for my self-esteem. The wrestling coach, Ted Seabrook, was an important character for many boys there. He was a hero in John Irving's early novel about Exeter, *The World According to Garp* (Irving was an Exeter faculty child and wrestler 3 years behind me – his father was my English teacher in summer school, and when I wrote a theme saying I expected to follow my brother through Exeter and Harvard, he commented that I might be aiming too high). I had an interesting course in biology with a lab that I much enjoyed, as well as one in ancient (meaning Greek and Roman) history. However, my SAT[1] scores and recommendations were

1 The SAT, or Scholastic Aptitude Test, consisted of two multiple choice tests in mathematics and English. It was essentially mandatory for college entrance. A combined perfect score for the two tests was 1600. I had a score of about 1400, about the 95th percentile of college applicants.

good enough so that I didn't have to apply anywhere but Harvard, which I recall was something of a surprise to me, and also to my father. At Exeter during that period, that was not highly unusual, though (as I recall, about 60 of our class of 210 went to Harvard, with lesser numbers to Yale and Princeton – something like 40 and 20 – yet my Harvard College class of 1962 was the first one to have a majority of graduates from public schools).

Harvard College – 1958-1962

When I entered Harvard, I didn't know whether I wanted to study classical Greek archaeology or biology. I was assigned a Freshman Advisor whose name was Carl Seltzer. I met with him once, in my first week, and he said "Well, given your background and interests, you have to go into biological anthropology." He was trained as a biological anthropologist, but was making a living as a shoe salesman, since, I was told, he couldn't get a good academic job, but wanted to stay in the Boston area. He said "These are the courses you have to take, Anthro 1A, 1B, and 1C" [taps on table to emphasize]. I said "Oh, O.K. . . ." Of course, my father had already been through the Harvard course catalog with me before I left home and had said "*this* is what you ought to do . . ." He knew the reputations of all these grand old men, such as Clyde Kluckhohn and Henry Murray – they were all major figures in this period in the social sciences. He thought I should take their courses – a more general selection. You can see I was easily influenced one way or another, so I did what Seltzer said because he was the last one I talked to, and emphatic! Besides the Kluckhohn and Murray course, I ended up taking a course with W.W. Howells, and with Douglas Oliver in cultural anthropology, which was pretty dry. I also took an elementary behavioral biology course co-taught by Edward O. Wilson, who was quite young then, which I thought was dull, too, at the time (perhaps too elementary? It also met early in the morning; I think 9 am, as did Oliver's). I did take first year chemistry, but was slow to grasp the concepts – I had to get some tutoring over Christmas vacation to get a satisfactory mark. While I had done well enough in math at Exeter, taking integral calculus and getting advanced placement for college, and scoring over 700 on the math SAT, I wasn't particularly interested and didn't pursue it in college, which, looking back, I regret.

I ended up majoring in art history because that's where classical archaeology lay at Harvard (I had no Latin or Greek, so Classics was out – I tried elementary Greek in my sophomore year, which met at 8 am – I hardly made it to class, and I believe I ended up with a C or maybe a C-). The archaeology part of the anthropology department at Harvard didn't include the classical world – only non-literate or at least non-western societies. Majoring in art history also wasn't threatening. The concepts in cultural anthropology seemed new and different and difficult to grasp. Kluckhohn's course opened up entirely new ideas and fascinating perspectives to me – Freudian psychology, psychological interpretations of ancient Greek culture and religions, cultural relativism, and more. There was so much I didn't know! I discussed majoring in anthropology with Kluckhohn in one meeting I had with him during his office hours. In fact, he suggested majoring in something else if I thought I might eventually end up being an anthropologist (to become knowledgeable in a specific area). So my undergraduate interests suddenly headed off in the direction of Greek archaeology while I also took some biology courses along the way.

Towards the end of college, I began to do well academically for the first time. Of course, I found most art history classes that I had to take easy – studying was mostly memorizing pictures or statues and their accompanying descriptions, a day or two before a scheduled test or exam. My best learning experience was having individual weekly tutorials in my junior and senior years with the major professor there of Greek archaeology, George Hanfmann.

After my junior year, at his suggestion, I went to Greece for the summer to work on my dissertation project, the stylistic development of the Corinthian capital. I had a wonderful time – but I didn't like the classical archaeologists! They were all dry and dull Brits and preppy Americans. I had much more fun traveling around on local buses to different towns and archaeological sites. When people on the bus would realize I was an American, they'd often introduce me to some elderly well-dressed English-speaking gentleman at the next stop, often sitting in an open-air café sipping Greek coffee, who had retired from working in the U.S. and had returned to Greece, living on social security payments. It was also fun dancing in the tavernas in the evening.

When I came back to Cambridge in the fall to my first tutorial meeting, I said, "Professor Hanfmann, I collected all the data we planned, but I've decided I don't want to go into this as a career." I didn't think I could do much that would make any difference in what was known about ancient Greek civilization – so much has been done it was almost literally like no stone had been left unturned there. Besides, the classical archaeologists seemed to be a snooty bunch. After a moment to digest it all, he said, "Well, I understand, Jonathan, but do you still want to do this project?" I said, "Sure." I was surprised and relieved at his response. So we went ahead and did the thesis, and it was well received. While the thesis was graded *summa cum laude*, I graduated *magna cum laude* because my overall grade average wasn't outstanding. That's how I backed into getting elected to Phi Beta Kappa the week before graduation (when I called my parents to tell them, my father said, "Are you sure?"). I had written a nice paper with Hanfmann's guidance, and I had learned how to do a library research paper, even though it was not on something I wanted to continue. So that was an important experience for me.

At Hanfmann's urging, after graduation I submitted a revised version of my thesis to *The Journal of Architectural History*. The reviewers said, "It would be fine if you cut it down more, and of course you have to get various permissions for all the figures from different authors." And so I never did it – it seemed like a put-down and a lot of work at the time, and I was crestfallen, even if that would have been a typical experience for publishing a peer reviewed academic paper. I didn't know any better at the time.

Two years later when I was an anthropology graduate student, Hanfmann wanted me to come back to his excavations in Sardis, Turkey and be the bones analyst, which I did.

Chapter 2.

Graduate School: Deciding What to Do (And Where)

University of Pennsylvania, 1962

So, coming out of college at 21, I felt more confident in my own abilities as a potential academic. Since I didn't want to continue classical archaeology, I decided then that I'd go back to anthropology. What kind of anthropology, I didn't know – most likely, cultural anthropology. Penn, at the time, seemed to have broad coverage of anthropology, in terms of biological, cultural, and archaeology. I went down to Philadelphia and frankly, the cultural anthropologist, at least the one who taught the graduate student introductory course, was extremely dull and strange. He was a fine scholar who was in the National Academy of Sciences, and he worked in the Pacific (Ward Goodenough). He was nicknamed Dr. Sominex by the undergrads. He made no bones about the fact that he didn't prepare for his lectures. He told us that he just looked at the title he'd listed for that day's lecture in the syllabus, thought about it for a couple of minutes beforehand, and then went into class.

I was drawn to the physical anthropologists at Penn. It also became clear that year that the physical anthropology part of the program was falling apart. Wilton Krogman taught the graduate introductory course, and he was an engaging lecturer and a great raconteur – a big, garrulous man. He was based in the medical school (Anatomy) and was a classic osteologist sort. His course convinced me to go into biological anthropology (I got the best grade, which reinforced my interest). Another famous biological anthropologist there had just retired (Carleton Coon) and another one had left the department to become Provost (Loren Eiseley). Frank Johnston was just coming onto the faculty as a junior person, so it wasn't an attractive situation there.

Since Penn was in transition, I had to choose where to go to pursue biological anthropology. Also there was a girl involved, and she was going up to Cambridge to graduate school, and so I thought maybe I'd just go back to Harvard, too! I had had that introductory course as a freshman with Howells, which was good. The other possibilities included the University of Wisconsin, which had three faculty members in biological anthropology – that was a lot in those days – and there was also the outside possibility of going to the University of Michigan because of their strength in genetics.

JR: Do you mean to work with James Neel?

JF: That was problematic, since he was at the medical school. It would have meant being in anthropology and it would have been working with Frank Livingstone, someone who had himself worked with Neel. He was an early worker in sickle cell anemia because of Neel's pointing him in that direction. Afterwards I sometimes thought I should have gone there. Other people in my age cohort went that route; Ryk Ward – maybe you know him (he recently died, just having been appointed professor at Oxford a few years ago), and Ken Weiss, another excellent person, still at Penn State. Rich Spielman at Penn in the medical school was another (he also recently passed away). So they were working either with Livingstone or Neel. Ward and Spielman went to the Yanomami with Neel. Those were the places to go if you were interested in genetics and anthropology. But I went to Harvard so . . . Not only was there the love interest, but I knew and liked Cambridge, and I had never been to Michigan. Going to Michigan would have meant committing to genetics, which I wasn't ready to do. I wasn't that certain. Human paleontology was a possibility in my mind, as well – Krogman's osteology was, too.

JR: There were a lot of factors in your choice of Harvard. I'm interested to know what your background in genetics was at the time when you were making this decision. You said you'd taken some biology in college. . .

JF: Right. Well, as I mentioned, at Exeter I had a good evolutionary biology course with a dissection lab. There was some genetics included, rudimentary, of course, with Hardy-Weinberg equilibrium equations. In college, I did take a genetics course, as a junior. It would have been in 1960 or 61. It was still fairly soon after the DNA revolution began with Watson and Crick's paper in 1954. The lecturer was named Howard Levine. There was still considerable excitement about the double helix structure. How the DNA code actually worked – how it corresponded to RNA and then determined amino acid sequences and proteins was still unknown. Gobind Khorana's important early discoveries on that came just afterwards, in the early 1960s. So I was interested, but I didn't do particularly well as I recall. We did some fruit fly crosses, but the connection to human evolution and explaining human variation was distant. It was exciting but it didn't pertain too much . . . I couldn't make the connection with my other interests and it seemed separate from anthropology and human origins at that point.

Transferring back to Harvard: Courses and Professors, 1963

When I went back to Harvard as a graduate student in biological anthropology, I took a human genetics course in the Anthropology Department taught by Edward Hunt. It was heavily clinical, with lots of examples of genetic drift such as Ellis-van Creveld Syndrome[2] among the Amish, that sort of thing. It was that kind of idiosyncratic, disease-oriented genetics. The text was Curt Stern's *Human Genetics*, which was rather encyclopedic. Examples of genetic drift cited were single isolated populations that diverged in red cell antigen allele[3] frequencies such as the inhabitants of Tristan da Cunha or the Hutterites. It was not compelling. During this period, Stern gave an invited lecture at Harvard, and that was impressive. The promise that human genetics would develop as a more explanatory discipline was there, but it was

2 This syndrome involves dwarfism and 6 fingers on each hand. It is a recessive disease and is far more common among the Amish than elsewhere. This was because one man of the small founding Amish group in the USA carried a single copy, and since there was inbreeding in following generations, dozens of subsequent Amish carried 2 copies of the disease gene.

3 "Red cell antigen allele" refers to the different parts of the red blood cell coat that are determined by different gene forms. Examples are the ABO and Rh blood types. An allele is one of a number of forms a gene can have, such as the alleles for the type A or B or O blood type.

understood that biochemistry (which I had no clue about) was going to be central.

A fresh breath of air came during my graduate work in the 1960s – Luigi Luca Cavalli-Sforza's work on the distribution of gene frequency variation across a series of populations in the Parma Valley in Italy. That opened up what people were calling "micro-evolutionary" studies, how human populations slowly become different from one another in allele gradients and as shown in calculated genetic distances. There were predecessors, such as William Boyd, who wrote a book called *Genetics and the Races of Man* in 1950, which was based on gene frequency distributions. It was different from the approaches that biological anthropologists had been using before that, since Boyd characterized population differences by simple allele frequency gradients in the ABO and Rh red blood systems, for example, rather than talking about discrete racial distinctions in morphology, the way Carleton Coon and Stanley Garn and almost all the other physical anthropologists were still doing in the 1950s and 1960s. What I was learning in graduate school that seemed to be, on the face of it, much more sophisticated statistically, was W.W. Howells' handling of morphological variation with multivariate statistics. I think I showed you that . . .

JR: And just for the record, "that" was the biographical memoir you wrote of William Howells.

JF: Right. It was a biographical memoir for the National Academy of Sciences (I also did a shorter version for the *American Anthropologist* that got heavily edited – not as good). That was his major contribution, besides his well-written popular books in anthropology. He had a population-based sense of normal variation, and he used that as a critique, in the first place and most famously, I think, of Carleton Coon's notion of separate and discrete races of humans.

There was a clear tension between population geneticists and traditional physical anthropologists at that period around 1960. I recall Coon derisively referring to Theodosius Dobzhansky as "that fly boy," for example (Dobzhansky had written a book similar to Boyd's, *Genetics, Evolution, and Man*, in 1955, that downplayed any possible discreteness of human racial distinctions). Known human population genetic data at that time were still rudimentary, with only a few genetic variants widely tested – mostly a hand full of blood groups. By comparison, a century of measuring people around the world had been conducted by "*rassengeschichte*"-oriented physical anthropologists. Coon and others dismissed the early genetics work as inadequate by comparison to the masses of morphological data they'd been collecting and examining, even though their racial preoccupation had been discredited by the end of the Second World War (German physical anthropology never really recovered from its identification with Nazism until this century).

Howells ended up sharply critiquing his own teacher Earnest Hooton (who had died by that point), and also William Sheldon, who had developed the technique of somatotyping. Sheldon's idea was that there were discrete elements of physique derived from the primary fetal tissues that people had in different amounts: ectomorphy, endomorphy, and mesomorphy (from the ectoderm, endoderm, and mesoderm). Using principal components or factor analysis[4], Howells statistically tested if Sheldon's three "components" of physique had any validity. He found people varied on a first component of size (simply whether they were big or little); and a second component, which contrasted whether they were fat or skinny. There was no significant third component. So his results didn't fit with Sheldon's three categories of physique – the only possible correspondence was between endomorphy and the second principal component, of fatness. I thought that was insightful and powerful.

Later on, he applied sophisticated statistics and a population-based approach to his cranial studies. The best of these were accomplished in his retirement. He made a major effort to find particular cemetery populations from a specific period where he could say with confidence,

4 Factor analysis, as well as principal components analysis and multiple discriminant analysis, are popular multivariate statistical techniques. They all take a set of many measurements on individuals and identify the most important measurements, or combination of measurements, that describe variation or distinctions among the individuals. They take account of the redundancy among many measurements (i.e., through their correlations). While the techniques were conceived before the Second World War, their applications to anthropological data only became practicable with the advent of high-speed computers around 1950.

"These people died in this area at one time period, within about 100 years," whether it was an African population or a European population, or a Pacific population. He then categorized them by sex. In some cases, he knew their sexes from cemetery records. Where he didn't, he had to try to establish sexes from the skull, which is problematic (if the pelvis is recovered, it is far more certain). In any case, he had a "male" and a "female" set for each population, and then he applied multivariate statistics to the cranial measurements (multiple discriminant function analysis in the first instance). He achieved a nice array of population variation for both sexes. He had two multi-dimensional spaces – a male plot and female plot, which acted as checks – and they did show similar distributions or population relationships. In the original study in the early 1970s, he had information on 18 populations, as I recall, and at least 1,000 skulls, each with something like 30 measurements – a lot of data!

Then he fit earlier fossils into this modern human morphological space he'd constructed. He used skulls from the European Mesolithic, late Pleistocene Java, or even earlier periods, and when he got back to Neanderthals, they were just way off in outer space; they didn't fit in his modern cranial space at all. He used that result to argue that there was no evidence that Neanderthals could be the direct ancestors of modern Europeans or other modern groups. The recent genetic evidence also suggests a similar result. I thought that was a powerful way of looking at these things – he had begun doing this sort of analysis while I was taking graduate courses – Michael Crichton's undergrad thesis was another example of this discriminant function analysis that he championed.

On the other hand, I also thought about becoming a paleontologist and going to the African Rift Valley to dig up early materials, as the Leakeys were doing. However, that was clearly extremely difficult to set out to do. There was nobody at Harvard who was digging in Africa at that time, and almost no Americans (Clark Howell was the only one I can recall). I didn't have any contacts. It seemed much more feasible to go in this other direction in modern human variation and micro-evolution. There were a couple of Harvard expeditions in this area that had gained funding, so they were the best opportunities for me to pursue. So that's how that developed – it was what was available at the time.

JR: This is interesting. Could you talk more, before we delve into the fieldwork, which I'm interested in, about your personal relationships with the faculty that you worked with as a graduate student at Harvard? I know you've mentioned Howells. Albert Damon is also someone whom you worked with, and Douglas Oliver. Could you say a little about your experiences with them?

JF: Sure. I chose Howells as my advisor at the beginning, and I liked him and respected him. He was the professor. He was a formal but charming gentleman of the old school. I learned much later that he came from a mid-Western abolitionist background on his mother's side which may well have affected his approach to the question of race. Everybody thought of him simply as a "Boston Brahmin" (he grew up in New York, but he had very strong Harvard family connections).

One story that was attributed to him (correctly, I'm almost certain) concerns a distressed married grad student who came to his office, saying, "Dr. Howells, my wife is pregnant, I only have a teaching assistantship, and things are getting extremely hard financially. What can I do?" According to the story, Howells was sympathetic and said, "Well, in such circumstances, there's really only one thing left to do." The student said, "What's that, Dr. Howells?" "Touch capital."

He was hard of hearing and, especially with my soft voice I had problems communicating with him. When I came into his office he would sit with his hand cupped around his ear trying to hear, and I would raise my voice unnaturally. A lot of times he understood what I was saying, but a lot of times he didn't. It was not always clear. I was hardly alone in that. There were a lot of stories about it – may I tell one?

JR: Please!

JF: One undergraduate, Bridget Kelleher, was a faculty brat and thought she knew how to work her way around everyone. Bridget would come into Dr. Howells' office for her weekly tutorial and he would say, "Bridget, read this book by Coon and be ready to discuss it next week." The following week he would ask her questions. "What do you think about Coon's book?" and she would answer, "Well, Dr. Howells, [mumbles inaudibly]." And he would answer, "Uh..., O.K.," as if he understood. He wouldn't acknowledge that he couldn't understand. But then apparently he got a new and better hearing aid. She came in for another tutorial and he asked "Bridget, what did you think about this week's assignment?" And she said "Well, Dr. Howells [mumbles inaudibly]." And he said, "Bridget! What are you doing?! You're not making any sense! Speak up! Speak up!" Everybody thought that was just hilarious.

Still, everybody had the sense that he knew what he was doing, and he was a major figure. He described a lot of cranial material systematically, and we all respected him. Some people thought osteology[5] was dull, of course, and he was non-directive in terms of developing dissertation projects with students. I remember at one point fairly early on asking him for advice on developing a thesis project, and he was little help. I think he expected it was the student's job to follow his or her interests. I wasn't drawn to osteology except as it related to early fossil studies, so that meant looking elsewhere for a thesis project.

I thought about working with Irv DeVore after I took his primate behavior course my first year. He had been a student of Sherwood Washburn's at Chicago, and followed him to Berkeley. They had done new, more sophisticated, baboon behavior studies and films. It was the best primate behavior study done at that time, way after the films out of Penn State done by Raymond Carpenter decades earlier – that was in the 1930s and 1940s. DeVore and Washburn's study was supposed to have direct implications for understanding or recreating models of early hominid behavior (Carpenter's didn't make that overt claim). DeVore became closely associated with E. O. Wilson in the Biology Department. Irv was charming, almost too charming a guy, a handsome young guy, and his background apparently included a stint as a Texas radio announcer for H. L. Hunt's conservative radio station, Life Line, I believe. He was an excellent speaker and a real showman. The students, especially the women, just loved him. He would bring little prosimians to lecture, and of course he showed lots of good primate

5 Osteology is the study of bones, and Howells specialized in the subdiscipline of craniometry – the measurement of skulls.

behavior films. He had everybody eating out of his hand. I did well in that course in primate behavior and liked it as well (I was second in a class of about 80).

I don't know why I didn't switch, but I certainly thought about going into animal behavior studies. I took a subsequent course with E. O. Wilson in animal behavior. Of course it was much better than that earlier elementary course I'd had with him as a freshman, when I missed a lot of classes, as I mentioned. I hadn't gone to all the labs, either (I can't believe I did that – I must have been feeling superior as an Exeter grad as a freshman to cut so many classes!). Now this was before Wilson published *Sociobiology*, but he was certainly headed in that direction. We read a lot of early ethology[6] by Irnäus Eibl-Eibesfeldt, Niko Tinbergen, Konrad Lorenz and all those people, vs. Daniel Lehrner, who wanted to explain everything behavioral as being mostly learned. The overriding question was whether behavior was primarily learned or inherited, and of course Wilson and DeVore emphasized inheritance, and innate patterns of behavior. This was always the nature of these courses. While I was taken with behavior studies, I think that, in the end, I felt safer with Howells.

There was something about Irv, I don't know, that I distrusted. He was a little too facile. I recall an evening talk he gave as a new faculty member during my first term (to the undergraduate Anthro Club), making all sorts of hypothetical connections between animal behavior studies, African Bushman social structure, and reconstructions of proto-human society, that was enormously appealing in its sweep. However, Thomas Beidelman (another new faculty hire in cultural anthropology) became upset and attacked him sharply, literally foaming at the mouth, basically saying "You can't make these simple associations and analogies between monkeys and hunter-gatherers – there's considerably more going on specific to each that makes comparisons and analogies among them very misleading." I remember DeVore didn't say much in his own defense at all. It was embarrassing, and the other senior members of the faculty in attendance instinctively jumped to defend DeVore before the students. DeVore got tenure, and Beidelman left. I found that meeting quite instructive.

6 Ethology is the study of animal behavior in the natural setting.

Irv developed the Kalahari Desert project a couple of years later with Richard Lee, and I thought that would be a fine thing to get involved with. The African Bushmen, or more properly the San, were the "archetypal" primitive hunter-gatherers. I had a reading course with Richard Lee, trying to learn something about African ethnology, since I'd decided that was going to be my area of examination on the general exams we had to take as graduate students (this was the equivalent of qualifying exams in many departments). At one point, I asked Lee, "I'm looking for a thesis project – could I possibly come on your Kalahari study?" Richard Lee said "Jonathan, we're not ready to pick anybody this year – it will be next year." At least, that's what I was told. Perhaps he wasn't impressed with me – the reading course was rather elementary.

I also went to Al Damon before my general exams, and I said, "Dr. Damon, can I come on your expedition to the Solomons?" I was getting worried that I didn't have a thesis project. I had a half-baked idea of doing something like Cavalli's Parma Valley project, except in the mountain valleys of Switzerland, but I had no contacts there. Damon said, "We don't have any extra money. We're taking physicians, we're taking people who are already professional physical anthropologists, and graduate students only in *cultural* anthropology." They were the ones who were going to go a year before the surveys to get everything set up.

The General Examination

So, when I took my general exams, I still didn't have a dissertation project, which you wouldn't be allowed to do these days. You sat at a table with five professors and they could ask you whatever they fancied for two to three hours, including guessing what they'd had for lunch or whatever. I did well, in part because I had tried to figure out what everybody was going to ask me, rather than just trying to learn everything under the sun. I knew who was going to be on my committee, which helped me prepare (this was not technically allowed, but everyone asked the department secretaries, and they told us). Besides the basics I'd been taught in formal classes, which I assumed they'd cover, I made sure to review what they were teaching that particular week or the week before, so I had some idea of what was on their minds.

JR: And this was an oral exam?

JF: Yes, it was open-ended and free-form, and while that terrified everyone, I ended up enjoying the experience a great deal. It was a great moment for me. I won the "Bobbs-Merrill Prize" for the best general exam that year in the Anthropology Department. Of course, I was happy to get the award, but the prize itself wasn't much, just two big binders filled with reprints of anthropological articles published in various journals that Bobbs-Merrill was trying to promote for course adoption to grad students and faculty. My girlfriend at the time, an archaeologist, thought I was poorly prepared and would probably fail (she knew I didn't know more recent African archaeology very well, for example, even with her help). The point was that I knew it was impossible to know "everything" well, but I had made and memorized about 10 pages of outlines on different topics I thought I would absolutely need to know. This is generally the best way to prepare for any test, anyway, to try and anticipate the questions your examiner is likely to ask.

I never had a course with Douglas Oliver. He was the department chairman then so he was *de facto* the cultural anthropologist on this group of five, even though I was being asked questions about Africa (come to think of it, he never asked me a question about ethnology that I can recall – I don't recall *any* question he asked me! Perhaps by that time, about an hour and a half into the exam, he decided to end it, since I was doing well).

JR: Who were the five people in the room?

JF: There was Oliver, Damon, and Howells. The requisite outside biologist was Charles Lyman, a physiologist, and then there was Clifford Lamberg-Karlovsky. He was a young archaeologist then who seemed to me at the time to be off-beat, riding a motorcycle and wearing leather jackets to work at Peabody Museum when the men on the faculty all wore coats and ties, but anyway he helped me on that day and beforehand. When I had discovered he was going to be one of the examiners less than a month before the exam, I went to his office and said to him, "What should I know?" And he said, "I'll ask you questions on this subject, and this, and this, and you should read these references" – all very specific. I had had a reading course in African archaeology with another more famous senior professor named Hallam Movius, who was just a terror. I'd had a terrible time with him, as well. That was mostly my fault, but I'd learned very little from that reading course even though he ended up thinking what I did was fine. That was another story. I could tell you about if you'd like me to tell it.

JR: I would like to hear whatever you'd like to tell.

JF: O.K. Movius had done his major work, but my no means his only work, in southwestern France, on a site that covered the transition between the Neanderthals and early modern humans (the Cro Magnon) at a site called the Abri Pataud in the village of Les Eyzies, in the Dordogne region. I think he was the only American archaeologist allowed to work in France after the war. He had also worked in Asia (there's a distinction in stone tool traditions between India and Southeast Asia he recognized that became known as Movius' Line), and had done some work in Israel as well – Mt. Carmel, I think. He was a prominent figure, but he was difficult to work with. Few of his graduate students ever got through, and if they did, it took forever. He was always demanding new things and had a ferocious temper. When I thought that Africa might be my area of preparation, I signed up for a reading course with him in my first semester. I met with him once early on, and he gave me a long reading list and told me to come back when they were done (I'm rather vague on this – I knew it was my responsibility to schedule the next meeting, which was a novel idea to me and suggested he didn't care much about the reading course at all). It was my first reading course and I thought it would be something of a lark – pass/fail, and unstructured. Then, I had more serious romantic issues going on that took up a great deal of time and emotional energy that semester. They were upsetting and a great drain. I let the reading course languish and I didn't go back to see Movius for a long time. I believe I finally showed up again just before Christmas break and he said, "Well, young man, you've clearly been neglecting this and you can't expect that I'm going to pass you." I had thought it would be the simplest thing in the world to slip through. He was so abrupt and angry with me (and appropriately so) that my legs began to shake uncontrollably. I could hardly stand up. I was terrified. He said, "If you want to pass this course, you're going to have to read these 7 books, and you're going to have to write summaries of each." Some of them were in French because Northern Africa was included in the coverage.

It was a great deal to have to do over vacation and before the end of the term in mid-January. I went running to one of his advanced students I happened to know well. I had been on an excavation in Colorado and Wyoming run by him along with his sister. They were Henry and Cynthia Irwin. I was 18 at the time, just about to enter college, and it had been great fun digging in the West. I said "Henry, Dr. Movius is going to ruin me! I'm going to flunk that course and flunk out of grad school! What am I going to do?" He said, "Take it easy Jonathan. We're going to work this all out. What he wants is the translations of these French books – not word for word, just a summary. Can you do that?" I said, "I think I can do it for one or two of them." He said "Fine. Type it out, triple spaced and with big margins – he likes lots of pages. Then summarize these other archaeology books in the Penguin paperback series (in English) to fill things in from East and South Africa. If you turn in something that's close to 100 pages long, everything will be alright. And remember to make a carbon copy, because he'll want to keep one for himself." So, I showed Henry what I was doing for two or three days and did the rest over vacation. I showed up at Movius' office after Christmas with this big pile of paper. I'm sure he didn't read it, but he seemed more than satisfied as he thumbed through the pages. He said "Good work; this will do fine, Friedlaender. I will keep this for my records – hope you have a copy."

Certainly I didn't want him on my general exam committee, and Lamberg-Karlofsky had been hired in the interim. He knew more about African archaeology than Movius, I believe, so he was the archaeology committee member. His expertise was in Iranian archaeology, and he subsequently got tenure and became the head of the museum and a major figure himself.

The other twist on the general exam was that I developed a mild case of mononucleosis a week or so before the exam. They said "Do you want to go through with this exam now, or wait until you recover?" I said "I've studied so long I might as well do it now." As a result, they were solicitous at the beginning of the exam. Dr. Howells said "You know Jonathan, my wife had mono and it was dreadful." And I said, "Well, I'll just see what I can do." So, they were aware I wasn't feeling the best, but they still asked me a lot of, you know, good questions – except for, really, Dr. Damon.

I thought Damon had no imagination and was focused on details. He wasn't interested in evolution that I could see. He didn't seem to be trying to look at human variability and understand what was causing it. He only wanted to see what was associated with his somatotypes, or what normal variants might be correlated with behavioral or clinical features. On my general exam, he asked me a lot of straight anatomical questions that seemed to have no functional context, which I had trouble with. One I answered, because we had had to take human anatomy at the medical school. He said "Some people say you have not two lungs but three. What would that mean?" I said, in a way that made it seem a simple-minded question, "You mean the lingula, Dr. Damon?" And he sort of visibly squirmed and said, "Yes, I mean the lingula." It was easy to make him feel uncomfortable. He then said, "What if you take someone's blood pressure on the arms, and it's quite high, 150 over 120, and then you take blood pressure on the legs, and it's 110 over 70. How can you explain that?" I promptly said, "I have no idea, Dr. Damon" (implying he was asking a pointless sort of question). He said, "There might be a blockage in the aorta." And I said "Oh O.K." I just essentially refused to answer or take it seriously. I didn't think about it very hard. Specific clinical information wasn't what I was interested in – I wasn't training to be a physician. I don't remember him asking many more questions after that.

Dr. Damon and I had a strained kind of relationship. He was also often cutting but he thought he was just being witty. For example, I had asked him for a recommendation for my NSF fellowship (and I'm sure it was perfectly fine – it must have been very good, in fact), and what he said, when I asked if he mailed it in (since he was often late and forgetful), was, "I did get the letter off for you. Of course it was filled with the usual mendacities." He thought that was funny. I didn't think it was funny at all! It was probably a line he remembered from Groucho Marx, whom he was always quoting.

Charles Lyman, a physiological biologist was the fifth examiner. I knew that he was lecturing that week on counter current systems. These provide a way to retain heat in many animals (for example, the vein and artery arrangements in chicken legs help keep the feet cold and the body warm), and he asked me about that, and I was able to answer that. Of course, he also pulled a total surprise, plopping a big bone on the table for me to identify (it was the cervical complex of a porpoise). At first, I was surprised and taken aback, but with a little prompting, I figured out that it belonged to a marine mammal (seven compressed cervical vertebrae into one), so that was satisfactorily dealt with as well. His questions might be thought to be superficially similar to Damon's anatomical details, but that's missing the point. Counter-current systems are functionally successful adaptations that a variety of animals had independently developed to regulate or prevent heat loss in their extremities. It wasn't just a simple quirk of anatomy. That was the difference. The same was true of the shortened neck bones from the diving mammal – apparently most diving mammals have that as an adaptation to their return to the water, but they retain the diagnostic mammalian seven cervical vertebrae.

So I passed the general exam in about an hour and a half.

Getting on the Harvard Solomon Islands Expedition (with a NSF Fellowship)

I saw Doug Oliver the following day in the infirmary, in the waiting room of the infirmary (they admitted me for a few days of rest for the mononucleosis – I think three or four, that was all). He said, in his deep formal voice, "You know Jonathan, you performed very well on the general exam. Now, what are you going to do for your thesis?" And I said, "Well, Dr. Oliver, I honestly don't know!" And he said, "Why don't you go on the Harvard Solomon Islands Project? Al Damon is getting it together for this summer." I replied, "Dr. Oliver, I asked him some time ago and he said that there was no room." Also, about a week before the exam, I had been notified that I had received an NSF graduate fellowship. Only about 40 were awarded each year in all of anthropology nationwide, perhaps even less – it had about a 10% success rate. Oliver had announced my award at the start of my general exam. So he continued, "Now that you have your own funding from the NSF, I'm sure Dr. Damon will be happy to have you along."

When I got out of the infirmary I went back to Dr. Damon and said "Dr. Oliver said I should ask you again, now that I have a NSF Fellowship." He said, "Well Jonathan, I hesitated to bring it up, I would love to have you on now that you have your own funding. Since I'd told you 'no' before, I didn't feel I could ask you again, because . . ." Whatever – he was abashed or ashamed. That was typical of him. He was not only critical of others, but was especially self-critical in a way that curtailed his own abilities. He felt he'd made a mistake, but it kept him from asking me under the new circumstances – he could have said "I know I refused you before, but if you still haven't made other plans, now that you have your own funding, of course you are welcome to come along. . ." So that's how I got on that expedition – because of Oliver.

JR: Can you say a little bit about what this NSF fellowship was, what motivated you to apply for it and what you were applying for?

JF: This was the standard NSF Graduate Fellowship application of only about three pages. It still exists. These days you have to apply within the first year or even before entering grad school, and obviously this was in my third or fourth year – I'd already been a teaching assistant. It was not necessarily for a particular research topic, it was for general support during your graduate work. In my case, it was essentially a stipend for about $3,200, which was a lot of money in those days. That was enough to cover my expenses to go out for at least the summer to the Solomon Islands, though that hadn't been written in originally. I think I had said something vague in the application about going to the Swiss isolates, similar to Cavalli's study in the Parma Valley. They didn't care about the subject. It was more important to write a couple of coherent paragraphs about a potential project, and to have good references, grades, and GRE[7] scores. Much later, I was on the committee that awarded those fellowships (The National Research Council) – that was interesting to see it from the other side.

JR: So you were already thinking then about doing a population genetics-type project at the time?

JF: Right. This was after I'd taken most of my classes and had turned to this direction. Whether it was going to be with the African San or with the Solomon Islands, it was going to be a project on contemporary human variation, which included genetics, because clearly that was important even though we were still dealing with the ABO and Rh blood groups and not too many other gene frequency variants. It would deal with variability across a series of populations (not simple studies of genetic drift in one population, like the Amish, Hutterites, or Dunkers that had been done previously). The African San hunter-gatherers were much more appealing kind of, a more sexy population than the Solomon Islanders . . .

JR: Can you say more about that?

JF: There has always been this sense in anthropology that the San might represent a relic population from a much earlier period (of course, a lot of cultural anthropologists would be uncomfortable with this characterization – the debate over DeVore's talk I mentioned is an example of that).

In contrast, in the 1960s, nobody had any idea how long people had been in the Pacific islands. The archaeological record was extremely poor. I remember when I came back with all of my materials that showed these remarkable and significant differences between North and South Bougainville, I asked John Terrell, an archaeology grad student who worked in the area, "What is the earliest time of settlement in New Guinea and Australia and this part of the Solomon Islands? These distinctions I'm finding look like they grew up in place over an extremely long period of time." He

7 Graduate Record Examination – the standardized test taken by graduate student applicants, equivalent to the SAT for entering college students.

said, "Maybe 8,000 or 10,000 years, max." I said, "That's amazing, it just doesn't seem those divergences could have happened so fast. That's about the same time period people were thinking the whole settlement of the New World took place, in an equivalent 10,000 year interval, and the distinctions among American Indians, say in skin color, are nowhere near as great as what you see in these different islands." So I wrote at the end of my monograph that the distinctions I found within Bougainville must have grown up over thousands of years, maybe 10,000, *maybe more*. I was just too timid to put down anything longer in my thesis or first book.

What's happened since the 1960s is that the bottom has fallen out of the time frame for the first human settlement in that part of the world. Now we're talking about 40,000 to 50,000 years ago for the initial settlement in this region of the Southwest Pacific, or what's called Near Oceania (a term coined by Roger Green). That would have made it more interesting to me as a graduate student. It now represents a very early migration of anatomically modern humans out of Africa. At that time there was a sense that the Pacific was all recently settled, and didn't have much to do with early origins of modern humanity, unlike the African San. Since my interests were in early human evolution, the San were a much more appealing group, since the time depth in the Pacific seemed so shallow. But the Kalahari Project wasn't open to me for whatever reason.

JR: So, going back to Dr. Damon, you re-approached him and asked him and he subsequently agreed that you could [go to the Solomons]?

JF: Yes. Very quickly, he said, "You could take somatotype photographs, do finger-printing, PTC tasting abilities, do skin reflectance measurements, and test people for color-blindness." I said "Sure." I hoped maybe I could do those rather simple jobs and learn some other techniques, because I had no idea how to take blood or anything, and maybe I could do my own little related project that would fit in somehow.

He was what they called in those days, a human biologist as opposed to a traditional physical anthropologist. His undergraduate major at

Harvard was sociology, and I recall he told me he picked that because it was supposed to be easy to get good grades. Then he won a Rhoades Fellowship to Oxford and went into medicine afterwards (Harvard Medical School). He was interested in biological anthropology of the sort of Sheldonian, somatotyping variety I mentioned that Howells critiqued so effectively.

Incidentally, Peabody had a collection of somatotype photos of (naked) entering Harvard Freshmen (I may be in there), and, more notoriously, some from Wellesley. These were the subject of an article in the *New York Times Magazine* much later. I don't know who collected them, or under what excuse. I believe I read that they were part of some "posture correction" studies in the 1930s and 40s. I don't know Damon's connection to these, but he certainly was aware of them. He loved just to measure and collect data, to my mind without much purpose. He was always talking about anthropometry as the "Queen of the Sciences," which I found truly arcane. He had us all learn somatotyping as well as proper measurement technique.

I don't know exactly what his role was in developing the Harvard Solomon Islands Project with Oliver and who the initial instigator was. From my perspective, I thought it was not well conceived. It seemed to be a big fishing expedition – "We hope to find distinctions in modernization effects among these primitive peoples." Little attention was paid to the historical relationships of the different groups, either in terms of how they might be related, or the languages they spoke, and of course the archaeology was poorly known, as I mentioned. A great deal of medical and bio-anthropological information was to be collected: there was an ophthalmologist, pediatricians, a dentist taking dental impressions, a virologist, infectious disease specialists, and they had a cardiologist, too. Damon and others (Eugene Giles and later Howells) did the anthropometry. Blood genetics was covered, of course. Even cholesterol levels (new at that time). It was a fairly extensive health profile and certainly exhaustive in anthropometry. There were an unbelievable number of measurements and observations taken, including mid-digital hair, ear attachment type, and so forth. To what end, I had no clue. I suppose the general notion was, as with the Yanomami, to contrast "primitive" and "modern" health states across the board, and in this instance, to see if different degrees of modernization had any correspondence in biological or health variables.

I got a little side-tracked . . . In my graduate work I took a course with Damon called Human Biology, or Contemporary Human Biological Variation. The focus of that, besides the somatotyping and so on, was trying to tie worldwide human variation to adaptation to different climates and ecologies. Adaptation was the major theme in human biological studies at that time. It was tied into the Human Adaptability section of the International Biological Program (the IBP). You've done a lot of background on that . . .

Adaptationist Studies, the International Biological Program, and the Harvard Solomons Project

JR: I'd be interested, for the sake of the record, your take on it and how the Harvard Solomon Islands project fit or didn't fit with that broader enterprise (the IBP).

JF: In that course, it became clear to me that it was nebulous to talk about adaptation and differential natural selection affecting different human groups in different ways. The general assumption in biological anthropology then (and before) was that human population differences were the result of differential natural selection favoring different characteristics in different human environments. Human skin color variation was of course the classic example, since everyone has assumed for centuries that there is some sort of adaptation of light skin to temperate environments and dark skin to tropical ones. However, the actual proofs for different adaptations as a general thing turned out to be remarkably weak. We used a book edited by Stanley Garn called *Readings on Race*. The articles tried to suggest that, for example, different nose shapes affected the humidifying of inhaled air, or Australian Aborigines had different physiological responses to cold than did highland Peruvian Indians – to cold desert nights and cold at high altitudes, respectively. I can't remember the other groups that were discussed, but the general theme was that different populations had dramatically different ways of lowering or maintaining their temperature in their extremities, for example, and this purportedly had to do with local adaptations, with differential selective responses.

During the course, Damon had Russell Newman give a guest lecture. Newman was working at the Army physiological center in Natick, Massachusetts and was well trained in this area. In fact, he was a mentor of Paul Baker. The Army's interest in this entire area was fairly obvious – to protect soldiers from extreme environmental effects and to explain why, for example, black soldiers in Korea got frostbite more than white soldiers. Was it hereditary and genetic, or was it because the black soldiers were mostly from the South and had never dealt with such cold? Another possible explanation was that black privates were more likely to be given nighttime guard duty outside. Newman said, "That's just a bunch of nonsense in Garn's book. The Australian Aborigines, for example, are taking drugs (alcohol) that are making them respond differently to cold, having different patterns of vasodialation and vasoconstriction that are different than the Peruvians (chewing coca) and different from the American student-athletes." I said to myself, "You mean this whole adaptationist/differential approach is wrong? What's going on here? These are just local responses to drugs?" It made me question a lot of the notions of localized differential adaptations of groups that were supposed to be the result of selection. We were getting a lot of other questioning of the adaptation hypotheses that were so common in biological anthropology then.

I'll give another example. In skeletal and human biology at that time, everybody assumed the so-called "mongoloid face" was obviously an adaptation to cold because the Eskimos had it and they lived in a cold climate (the association implied a cause-effect relationship, but was hardly a proof of that – it was a tautology). However, Ted Steegman put thermocouples on peoples' faces (graduate students who were working up in Alaska and also some Inuit) and he said, "I don't see any difference in the responses to cold. Yes, the Inuit have flat faces and their noses don't protrude as much, but the warming effect on the inhaled air and cooling of the face surface is basically the same as in Europeans." Steegman argued that what was critical to the Inuit's success in the Arctic cold was their culturally mediated micro-environment; it was their fur boots and fancy parkas that kept them warm, not their flat noses, high cheekbones, and fatty eyelids! You can't prove any differential selection or a different adaptation. The role of culture in modern human successes in colonizing ecologies outside the tropics has simply been overwhelming, and the biological adaptation component has been close to nil, with a few exceptions. It even made me wonder if it could be proven that differences in skin pigmentation were beneficial in terms of survivorship and reproduction, the two components of natural selection.

We were beginning to get a contrary notion – people were basically all the same in terms of their biological or physiological adaptations across the globe, but culture was heavily involved as an intermediary response to local environments, causing a lot of these differences between groups. With regard to differences in size and shape, these old so-called biogeographical laws (Bergmann and Allen's Rules) had argued that round, globular-shaped people up in the northern latitudes were somehow selected for there, versus thin and small people in the tropics. However, contrary studies were showing that a lot of that was simply the influence of diet – that poor people living in the tropics tend to be small and thin, and people in the wealthy societies that live in the temperate zones tend to be big and fat. This sort of conclusion harked back to some early anthropological work done by Franz Boas around the early part of the 20th century.

I remember in the Damon course, I got a D on the hour exam at six weeks. I just hadn't done the reading or paid attention – I can't remember the details. I said, "Oh my god, what am I doing!" So I buckled down, worked hard, and I did the requisite reading. I got an A on the final exam and paper, and an A- for the course. He said "Congratulations, you picked yourself off the mat and did well." And I thought, "Yes, well, because I had to!" I remember that the paper I wrote was on Oceanic pygmies and whether they had a kinship with African pygmies, with lots of pros and cons. Damon asked me afterwards what I thought the simple answer was, after summarizing all the known papers. I said, "I don't know – it remains unclear" (I'd say after our recent work, if there is a connection, it's not direct at all. We can't see any special genetic connection between African and Oceanic populations, in spite of obvious similarities in skin pigmentation – the first settlers of Near Oceania were likely dark-skinned groups like their ancestors in Africa, and their descendants remained so; however, even the genetic determinants of their similar skin color seem different).

As a note, that was about as much attention as I paid to Pacific biological anthropology before I went on the Harvard Solomons Project. As I said, my early problem with the Solomons Project was that I didn't see how they were going to be able to tease apart the effects of modernization and old population distinctions.

I'll give you an example. Probably the paper from the Solomons expeditions that Damon was most pleased with was called "The antecedents of cardiovascular disease," published in *Circulation*. In it, he claimed that differences in blood pressure between Solomon Islands populations were caused by specific differences in sodium (salt) consumption, not just general modernization effects. However, no one had measured the differences among the groups in sodium consumption, to see if they were related to the blood pressure differences – the argument was simply anecdotal (the one group with higher blood pressures boiled their sweet potatoes in salt water). I subsequently argued against their explanation with our longitudinal studies, saying rising blood pressure in some groups was more likely a function of the considerable weight gain associated with new foods heavy in grease and sugars, and that the timed overnight urine samples that I took showed no population distinctions in sodium excretion that could be linked with blood pressure differences. It also turned out that after people boiled their sweet potatoes in sea water, they usually peeled them, getting rid of the sea salt.

That sort of logical laziness bothered me, especially when I went out to the Solomons. Besides increases in weight and larger size, especially in younger people (both of which did seem to be associated with modernizing diets), I found a lot of variation in many measurements, blood genetics, fingerprints, and even tooth sizes across remarkably small areas within Bougainville. These couldn't possibly be the result of differential selection, although John Terrell, the archaeologist who'd worked in Bougainville I mentioned, had suggested there were different "adaptive zones" in Bougainville. That made no sense to me. Bougainville was a small island, only 120 miles long, about the size of Long Island. Any distinctions had to be on account of drift, or migration patterns, or isolation.

Those skeptical concerns of mine were something that I carried out of his Human Biology course as a reaction. This old adaptationist attitude was part of the racist legacy of biological anthropology at that time. Coon and Garn's work emphasized the apparent hereditary biological distinctions among human groups as being the result of adaptations to different environments. It was saying, "Skin color differences are only the beginning – there are biological differences between groups you don't even realize that are beneficial in specific environments." This was true for some other genetic distinctions, especially some related to malaria resistance, but others weren't convincing. As I mentioned, even the specific reasons for skin color differences remained hard to understand – there were serious problems with the early versions of the vitamin D explanation that William Loomis proposed. The outlines of the skin color story are only now beginning to become clear.

Now we can talk about the Harvard Solomon Islands Project. Damon was certainly the field leader of the expedition. I don't know what would have happened in the long run in terms of publication if he had lived. You can see from the bibliography in the 1987 Oxford book that there were a lot of publications, but many were on ephemeral subjects, such as hand-clasping tendencies and tongue rolling abilities. Of course, he developed cancer in the middle of the field expeditions in 1970, I think, and that undoubtedly impacted subsequent publications. The last field season was in 1972. There were a number of following publications, but nothing to kind of pull it all together. Suddenly, there I was back at Harvard in 1971 as someone who had been on the Solomons Expeditions, but not closely involved with the project as it had developed. I was trying to expand my own dataset from my dissertation and write a separate monograph (which appeared in 1975). The Harvard Solomons data were sitting there as a resource, not being taken advantage of. Ultimately, I decided to do a follow up study on those. But that's a story for later.

When Damon was dying in 1973, his wife Selma told me he wanted to see me in the hospital – Mass General. He was extremely emaciated by that point, like a death camp survivor. It was clear he was near death, but he was matter-of-fact and stoic. He said, "Jonathan, I have a project or two I want you to finish off for me." One was a textbook, *Human Biology and Ecology*, and the other was a book he was editing called *Physiological Anthropology*. Of course, I said, "Certainly." Neither was a major effort. For the physiological volume, I think I had to write an introduction and there were one or two incomplete papers that I had to get authors to finish. He also hoped I would do something with the Solomon Islands materials as well. I don't recall how I responded, but at that point, I hadn't given that possibility much thought. I had been busy trying to distance myself from that project. While I had been something of a student of his, I didn't feel close to him. It was a strange situation.

I also felt uncomfortable with Howells in my new position as an assistant professor. I didn't even know how to address him. I didn't know whether I was still supposed to call him Dr. Howells or Bill! That was not an issue with Irv. Irv was always Irv. Howells would go over to the Faculty Club for lunch every day and sit at the "Anthropology Table" (the other regulars were Gordon Willey and some rich archaeologists associated with the Museum who didn't teach or collect a salary). He asked me to come along, and I often did, but I had little to say. It was awkward.

Harvard Personalities: Miscellany

JR: That's interesting. There are two things I want to go back to before we talk about the Solomon Islands and your entry into the field. Going back to Howells, one of the things I noticed when I was reading the festschrift volume that you worked on, *The Measure of a Man*, that I wondered if you might say a little bit about, was Michael Crichton's contribution. Did you know him personally? Could you say something about your relationship with him and how you think he drew upon anthropology in his writing?

JF: His biological anthropology background was important for him (he just died a month or two ago). He was two years behind me, since I went to Penn for that one year, and my first year back at Harvard he was a graduating senior – we were both in an advanced seminar with Howells. Everybody knew he was bright. I think he wrote about his undergraduate thesis experience in the Howells festschrift. He was supposed to go to Egypt the summer before his senior year to do a skull measuring project under Howells' direction. He was going to examine whether ancient Egyptian skulls looked more like sub-Saharan Africans or like Europeans, using Howells' favored technique, discriminant function analysis. He ended up chasing a girl in London, so he spent the summer working on the Egyptian, African, and European skulls that were available in the British Museum, not in Cairo.

JR: Yes, a version of that story is in there.

JF: He mentioned that Howells was mildly miffed he didn't go to Egypt, but let it go. He ended up writing a fine thesis, a *summa*, which was published as a Peabody Museum monograph, on just this subject. It was dry, but it was good. It showed that the Egyptian skulls looked much more European – they didn't look sub-Saharan African. So, it was interesting given what happened subsequently with the debate over just that argument, in the 1990s I guess, with the proposed Afro-centric view of ancient Egyptians.

Michael Crichton was a tall young man, about 6'8." He had to have been a basketball player – I think he played a little basketball, but not seriously. He was quiet, had a baby face, and often blushed. He talked in the festschrift about how Howells treated him. Clearly Howells liked to puncture his balloon a little – he [Crichton] was pretty cocky. Howells corrected every little error he could find in Crichton's papers, even in the citations and their style. He graduated *summa cum laude* and then he went off to medical school. Still, it's clear from his writings that the evolutionary background has a lot to do with his early work, which he initially started to pay for his medical school costs. Some of it was more medically oriented, and of course his successful TV show *ER* came along. But *Andromeda Strain* and some of the other books. . . I haven't read too many, but he was a fantastic writer, easy and facile. Some of his later books are written simply as screen play scripts, rather off-the-cuff. A lot of his later work was, if you will, critical of the scientific establishment in a way that I was surprised about – but I still suggested him as a plenary speaker for the AAAS[8] meeting in California a while back when the AAAS was meeting in Los Angeles, and apparently his address was well received. I think Howells regarded him as probably his best undergraduate student. Howells wasn't going to influence him to go into biological anthropology. Howells knew he was going to do what he damn well wanted. When we were planning the festschrift, I don't know if it was Gene Giles' idea or mine to get in touch with Michael, but as far as I'm concerned, his is the best piece in the festschrift. It was entertaining and revealing, about Howells and himself.

JR: I believe he said he got the idea for the *Andromeda Strain* from a footnote in a G.G. Simpson volume that was assigned to him in an independent reading with Howells. I thought this was an interesting detail.

JF: That's true – I had forgotten that. It was quite a group of faculty who were around Harvard then. In fact, Howells had me take a graduate course in my first year with G.G. Simpson and Ernst Mayr, two of the major architects of the "Modern Synthesis" of evolutionary theory in the 1950s. It was a graduate seminar in evolutionary biology. Two or three of us, that was how many people were in biological anthropology each year, went over and took this seminar with these evolutionary maestros and advanced biology grad students. I had a lot of trouble. I was intimidated by both of them, especially Mayr. He was something, sure of himself, typically Germanic in his attitude. We read his book, *Animal Species and Evolution*, a chapter or two a week with accompanying articles, and read a couple of books by Simpson, who was a retiring man by that point and was also not well.

My biology background was not up to snuff, and my final paper was mediocre – it was on rates of evolution. It's interesting, but I don't recall getting any evolutionary theory during my year at Penn – certainly not the immersion I got at Harvard. Thinking back on that first year or semester at Harvard, it took me a while to find my footing. I recall coming home at Christmas worried that I wouldn't make it,

8 The American Association for the Advancement of Science is the umbrella organization for all science in the U.S., and its annual meetings are meant to present a public face for science achievements.

but ending up with 3 A-s and a B-. In the long run that exposure to Mayr and Simpson was important. Later I was a teaching assistant in a class where Howells was the primary professor, and he had Mayr give about three lectures on evolutionary theory. That summarized and reinforced a lot of the population-based arguments that were important to me later on, about the importance of population variation and its relation to the species concept that was Mayr's major contribution. Mayr was forceful and he was also clear about what he thought. The correct biological perspective was always "population thinking," and the incorrect biological perspective was always the Platonic notion of the ideal type, or "typological thinking." End of story!

Howells was much less didactic. He would present a lot of data and conflicting theories. He was careful not to present his theoretical preference as the only worthy one. It took a long time to see where his ideas fit in. I remember coming to his office and saying, "Dr. Howells, I have to fill in my course schedule for the next term. What else should I take besides these obvious ones that are offered in the department?" He said, "Well, a course in statistics would probably be a good idea." I wouldn't have thought of that. Clearly, when you know what Howells was all about, it was essential. He wanted everyone to have a proper statistical approach to their problem. This was new at the time – the major voice in physical anthropology for decades had been Aleš Hrdlička at the Smithsonian, and he almost forbade the publishing of statistical data in the *American Journal of Physical Anthropology* for years. Howells was understated. Many times, people missed the point he was trying to make, and this was compounded by his deafness. Some anthropologists in his cohort thought he was simply a fool who used his connections to get back to the Harvard professorship (I heard this sort of remark myself).

JR: Could you say more, picking up on Damon and his seemingly sort of problematic place in the field and also a little bit more about Oliver as well and then we'll move into to discussing the Solomon Islands?

JF: I was going to discuss Oliver first because his influence on me was relatively minor to begin with. I didn't take any courses with him, since I was preparing Africa as an area in my general exams. I took only one formal cultural course at Harvard, as a matter of fact, a good one in African ethnology with Tom Beidelman, who left for NYU before I took my exams (he was too brash for Harvard – he told everyone where to get off with great relish, especially DeVore and Oliver). I had taken that elementary course in cultural anthropology with Oliver as a freshman, as I mentioned, which I'd found less interesting than Kluckhohn's. It was kind of a one-ethnography-per-week kind of course. I hadn't read his big Bougainville ethnography, *A Solomon Islands Society*, closely at all, although it was one of the required books – it was incredibly detailed. Of course, when I went to Bougainville, I read it closely, and it was absolutely invaluable there as a guide.

I began to get to know his graduate students when I knew I was going to go on the Solomon Islands expedition that spring of 1966. He had a number of students whom he was supporting by this NIH[9]-funded Solomons Project. He was direct, just like the advice he gave me to talk to Damon. That was typical of him.

Here's another story about his directness and his wry sense of humor. I wanted to analyze my materials with computer programs developed at the University of Hawaii by a well-known population geneticist there named Newton Morton. I had written to him, "I like your approach, can you send me your computer programs so I can analyze my Bougainville data with them?" They were applications of Gustave Malécot's theories. He wrote back, "No, you have to come to my lab in Honolulu." This was in the relatively early days of computing, 1969 or 1970, and moving software was problematic . . . he said, "We've got the software running on our own computer here, we also have funds for researcher support, so you should come for the summer and analyze your data here." I thought that was great, to be paid to go to Hawaii for the summer and get research done at the same time. So, Oliver – who loved Hawaii – he ended up there in the 1970s and spent a lot of time there – said, "Jonathan, I understand you are going to Hawaii." And I said "Yes, Dr. Oliver." And he said, "If you're going to Hawaii you'll have to learn how to surf!" He said, "You can use my surfboard!" So he told me where it was, under somebody's house.

9 The National Institutes of Health, the largest source of federal funding for health research.

When I got there, I bought an old jalopy for $300, found Oliver's surfboard under the house, roped it to the top of the car, and took it out to the beach at Ala Moana. It was a huge old board, about 12 feet long. I didn't want to take a lesson, but I realized after that afternoon that I didn't know what I was doing. All the surfers were clustered where the waves were breaking. I didn't want to get in their way, so I paddled over by the side and, of course, there were no decent waves there and it was impossible to catch anything as a result. I got tired paddling madly on Oliver's big board, trying to catch the small waves. I still wanted to learn how to do it, so I went to Waikiki where they gave lessons. I didn't use the big board, I just rented one of the smaller boards they had, and watched a lesson in progress. It was easy just to stand up if you were in the right place and paddled a couple of strokes at the right moment. Of course Waikiki is one of the easiest places in the world to learn to surf because the waves are generally only two or three feet high and they build up gradually and evenly (that's because the ocean bottom there is flat).

I came back to Cambridge at the end of the summer and saw Dr. Oliver. He said "Well, Jonathan, did you learn to surf?" And I said, "Yes, Dr. Oliver, I did." He said, "Did you use my board?" I said, "Well, I tried, but I could never catch a wave with it. It was too big." He said, "Well, I never did either – I only use it paddle around on!" He was that kind of man – he had a wry sense of humor. He was extremely knowledgeable about the Pacific. Besides his work on Bougainville, he wrote major books on Polynesian society as well. He was an ethnographer of the first order. This continuing interest of his in the Pacific laid the groundwork for the Harvard Solomon Islands Project and all the cultural anthropologist graduate students in the study.

So my relationship with Oliver began after the fact of my joining the Harvard Solomon Islands Expedition, and developed as I worked on Bougainville, which had a special place in his affections. I wrote letters to Oliver and Howells from the field asking for advice and reassurance – I went back to the area where he had worked originally, on the southwest side of Bougainville, and he loved that. He was very helpful. There was also the whole business of my locating men he had photographed and measured in the late 1930s, which was interesting as well. He sent out a large box of photographic portraits of those men. People loved looking at them, and it helped me locate and remeasure many of the surviving men 30 years later.

You also asked something about Damon. What was it? How that developed?

The Transformation of Anthropology during the 1960s and 1970s

JR: Just trying to get a sense of your idea, and understanding of his place in the academic field.

JF: In the *academic* field. When you say that, I immediately think of his place in the Harvard department. I don't have a good perspective on where he stood in the field at large. Especially since he died relatively early, I don't think he came close to attaining the stature of leaders in human biology like Paul Baker and Geoffrey Harrison. The Solomon Islands Project had become his major achievement, but it was already running into funding problems while he was still alive, so it's not at all clear what he could have achieved with that.

At Harvard, in the Anthropology Department he was peripheral. Of course, anthro departments in those days were small. Like so much else, anthropology was transformed by the Vietnam War. That was when departments exploded in size.

JR: Can you say more about why that was?

JF: During the Vietnam buildup, (cultural) anthropology became an alternative major for protestors, because it seemed to offer a critique of (our) ethnocentrism, meaning it was anti-establishment. Enrollments in graduate school generally also ballooned because in the mid-1960s you could still get a student deferment from the draft (I had one). It was clear that when student deferments ended in 1969, the student protests suddenly became intense, with draft card burning and the rest. I'm sure that the reason there's been no major protest about the war in Iraq is that there's no draft now. A lot of protesters and people who were critical of American society became anthro majors. Using the war as taking-off place, they decided that they would major in cultural anthropology, or sociology . . . I think those were the two major beneficiaries – perhaps Government (what Political Science is called at Harvard) as well.

I was back at Harvard as a junior professor in 1971, right at the peak of the Vietnam War demonstrations, and we were watching our undergrad enrollments explode. The faculty member in charge of undergraduate affairs, Mike Moseley, asked me to help put together a graph for an Anthro faculty meeting, trying to predict what the size of the undergraduate anthropology major would finally be. We were trying to extrapolate from what was happening at the time – how many sophomores were coming in compared to the junior and senior classes. There were about twice as many sophomores as there were seniors that year. We had already become one of the 5 largest departments in the College, as opposed to being one of the smallest 10 some years before. Moseley and I were trying to argue that we needed to hire more faculty, of course (we were both assistant professors, who had little to no chance of promotion at Harvard, but things were unsettled then). We were met with some skepticism by the senior anthropology faculty members. They said, "You can't assume that sophomore classes will continue to grow, so what is the steady state based on the current sophomore class size, rather than supposing that, too, may continue to enlarge?" Of course, I knew that was the best assumption, but it still meant anthropology had grown enormously. This was a Vietnam anti-war phenomenon in cultural anthropology and it fed into the whole culture wars controversy later on . . .

In those days, the primary theoretical orientation in cultural anthropology was Claude Levi-Strauss' structuralism. That was later replaced by the new criticism or deconstruction theory coming out of English, which I thought was certainly destructive. Subsequently, there was a definite polarization between those new sorts of cultural anthropologists on the one hand, and the biological anthropologists, archaeologists, and more traditional ethnologists, like Oliver, on the other. The archaeologists were usually caught in the middle, and biological anthropologists were clearly stuck with being hopeless reactionary "positivists."

Cultural anthropology had been the lynchpin of anthropology in the old days, using what was called the comparative method to try to find commonalities in cultures associated with particular technological levels of organization, and then building up a series that was supposed to represent evolutionary stages in the development of complex cultures and societies. Anthropology was originally an historical science, trying to recreate earlier stages of human social and biological evolution. The general notion was that by studying the wide array of cultural diversity of people at different technological levels of development today – the African San, the hunter-gatherers at one extreme, and us urbanites at the other – that you could extrapolate back to reconstruct earlier behaviors in earlier models of human society in the Mesolithic period, among Paleolithic hunter-gatherers, and in pre-historic times generally.

This was undoubtedly too naïve, and was rejected by most contemporary cultural anthropologists. They said that today's so-called hunter-gatherers may just be marginalized populations, and you can't claim what they're doing now has anything to do with pre-historic hunter-gatherers. The new criticism went even further, suggesting the bias of the observer is so great that little objective "fact" could be reliably gathered by an alien ethnographer at all.

It was true that the most extreme proponents of the comparative approach made some rather outlandish claims. Lucien Lévy-Bruhl's old work, such as *The Primitive Mind*, was the easiest of these to critique, since it held that non-cosmopolitan people actually thought differently from urban groups, but other more appealing notions of a general connection between technological levels and cultural practices, such as Robert Redfield's, were also discarded by later generations of cultural anthropologists, and I thought this total rejection was too extreme – throwing out the baby with the bathwater.

That was detrimental to the cohesion of anthropology as a whole. It has never recovered, and many departments have split in two as a result. Now, cultural anthropology is shrinking in its appeal with its claims diminished, even though it still remains the largest portion of the discipline in terms of enrollments and faculty (it remains highly politicized from the experience of the 1970s). That may change in the future, however, if the present trends continue.

So that's a little bit of my take of the recent history of anthropology, and how it was heavily influenced by the politics of the 1960s and '70s.

Perspective on Harvard Biological Anthropology, the IBP, and the Solomon Islands Project

In biological anthropology at Harvard, Howells was the only physical anthropologist who had tenure, a full professor, and he was getting old and was about to retire. In fact he did his best work in retirement, as I wrote in the NAS[10] memoir. There were other people who taught occasional courses who were Lecturers, and one assistant professor position that was never *de facto* tenure track (the one that I held, after Gene Giles). Ed Hunt was one Lecturer and Al Damon was the other. I don't know exactly how poorly they were paid, but they taught occasional courses. Ed Hunt's primary base was at Harvard's Forsythe Dental School. Damon was still involved with the Harvard School of Public Health, but I believe he gave that up at some point and hoped to get a tenured position in the Anthropology Department. They were both peripheral. Hunt taught some genetics and dental anthropology. Damon taught human biology. They still had undergraduate tutorial duties and all the rest. Then there was Irv DeVore – who was, at least at that time, based in a different department, Social Relations (Sociology), and a number of grad students were interested in his work, as I said before.

Generally biological anthropology has always been heavily oriented towards skeletal biology and paleontology, and remains so. Skeletons are easy to obtain and they're cheap to analyze. Over the long haul that means a lot. For example, graduate students can do theses on bones recovered from archaeological sites without much financial aid at all. Departments are reluctant to invest heavily in expensive laboratories for junior hires (now often $500,000 or more) who may not stick around for long. As for human paleontology, it is hard and expensive to develop large-scale expeditions and excavations to Africa and other Old

10 The National Academy of Sciences

World sites from a U.S. base. When I was NSF Physical Anthropology Director in the early 1990s, such expeditions cost well over $100,000 per 6 week field season, so only 2 or 3 American programs (always in the Rift Valley) were adequately supported by the NSF, which was always the primary source of funding.

Although Damon considered himself a new sort of human biologist, in some ways his work derived from some old threads of physical anthropology. A lot of early physical anthropology attempted to relate physique and even cranial shape to behavior – almost like phrenology. Earnest Hooton had dealt in that kind of poor work, as did others in the 1920s and 1930s, and Cesare Lombroso tried to predict criminal behavior from head shapes. I'm not sure exactly where Damon got his interest in this area from, but he worked with William Sheldon for a while at Columbia, who saw a relationship to behavior in his somatotype categories (jolly fat people, nervous skinny people, and so on). Damon was taken with the idea that physique could tell you a lot about disease susceptibility. As an example, he talked about women who were endomorphic, this jingle of "fat, fertile and forty," that was likely to lead to gallstones. He was interested in the effects on clinical health of these biological variables, even if it was totally unclear what was causing the association.

I don't know what his relationship with the founders of the IBP (International Biological Program) was. Chuck Weitz probably knows much more, and also Mike Little – they would know because their teacher was Paul Baker. Other major players were Geoffrey Harrison, who was at Oxford, Joe Weiner, and Derek Roberts – all British. The British physical anthropologists always had more of an anatomical and clinical background. Their notion of physical anthropology and human biology had much more to do with health status and therefore trying to find evidence for differential natural selection. In my impression, the Adaptability Section of the IBP was supposed to be primarily a funding umbrella. They all had their different notions of what they wanted to study – highland Peruvians or whatever – but there was no obvious underlying cohesion among the project aims. I think they hoped it might enhance funding opportunities, but it finally came to rather little.

JR: So was the IBP funding the Solomon Islands Project or was it just supporting it intellectually?

JF: They made the argument that it was intellectually part of the IBP project. The funding for the Solomons Project came from NIH, of course. The objectives of the project were clearly health-related, such as cardiovascular disease and blood-pressure related elements affected by modernization. I believe the IBP had no funds at all to support research projects, although they tried, and ultimately it failed.

JR: I wanted to talk about – part of my thrust of my question about Damon's place in the field comes from the fact that in the final chapter of *Physiological Anthropology* he makes a call for biological anthropology as an applied science but Paul Baker writes an introductory chapter that is somewhat skeptical about this claim. I wondered if you could entertain an "as if" kind of question: if Damon hadn't died untimely, do you think he would have continued to push that agenda – or been able to push that agenda?

JF: Well, I haven't read that in a long time, but what I remember was reading Paul Baker's Introduction and being surprised about how pessimistic it was. Here was the man who had made a major impact on the field promoting human adaptation and adaptability studies. He got major funding for his graduate students and himself – primarily from the Army – on his high altitude adaptation and adaptability studies in Peru. He'd made a big name for himself at Penn State, when Penn State was not much of a place to go, when it was just developing as a major research institution from being an Ag (Agriculture) school. Then he wrote this piece, rather late in his career, maybe in his sixties, that was skeptical about what they had proven, or could hope to prove, in terms of the basis of these adaptations. I recall I did tend to agree with his statement, however.

And then, as you say, Al Damon was always saying biological anthropology was an "applied science." I thought this was dull, since my perspective was always evolutionary, trying to understand how things came to be the way they are. In his courses, Damon was always talking about how you could make better pieces of equipment to fit the human body, better clothes sizing, if you only had more sense of normal variation, and he was talking about all kinds of things that I had absolutely no interest in. Hooton had done some applied work – for example, he helped design the seats in Pullman railroad cars, and they'd donated a dozen or so to the Peabody Museum smoking lounge (it was odd to see this rather bare room in the museum basement with the distinctive looking Pullman car chairs arranged along the walls). He also got a fee and used that, along with his public speaking fees, for support of his lab, I recall. I think Damon could have gone on like that, getting incidental funding. He was getting funding from all kinds of unlikely places, like the Tobacco Institute. I don't remember why – I hope it didn't have to do with the non-effects of smoking!

I was asked to speak at his memorial service at Harvard along with Howells and a couple of his other former students. I felt I should be honest and straight-forward in my reflections, while respectful, and so I talked about his strong critical streak (especially of himself and also of others). I also told the story of my experience in his course where after a terrible start, and his criticism, I ended with some sense of accomplishment (and his praise). His wife Selma told me afterwards that their minister (Damon was an Episcopal convert from Judaism) thought my speech was especially insightful and touched his particular human qualities, and she liked it as well (I learned much later that theirs was not a happy marriage). I remember one speaker, Wynne Burr, who had become a physician. Damon liked to direct his best undergraduate students go into medicine. He thought that medicine was a noble calling, and I felt that he didn't have too much respect for me because I wasn't interested in becoming a physician (I may have been wrong, of course – I may have been just sensitive to his general critical streak). In any case, Wynne was smart, and he gave an impassioned statement at the memorial service about how Dr. Damon had this vision of applied human biology that was going to take over physical anthropology. I was thinking, "O.K., sure." I didn't know where that was going. What I considered mundane applications didn't interest me.

JR: And how interesting then that you wound up having to complete several of his projects.

JF: Yes. There were a number of developments in my career that were simply taking advantage of situations, or almost being presented with situations that I felt I had to do something with. That had also to do with certain choices in my Pacific fieldwork that we'll talk about later on. Many times I couldn't go to particular places because of the politics or civil wars. For example, I was ultimately forced away from Bougainville and the Solomons by internal politics or civil strife, so I went to New Britain and New Ireland in part because they were peaceful places. Fortunately, I was able to take advantage of it. I couldn't just knock my head against a stone wall and give up.

Chapter 3.

The 1966-1967 Harvard Solomon Islands Expedition

Background

JR: There are two topics that I'd like to talk about, and I imagine that they'd be intertwined. One is your experience with the Solomon Islands Project as well as what it was about intellectually. The other is fieldwork, as a subject, and your sense of yourself as a fieldworker and how that formed. How did you learn what to do? I'm particularly interested in the collection of blood samples as a technique in the field. So I'll let you speak as you see fit.

JF: My first year in the Solomons and Bougainville was certainly a personal development story, but could also be seen as something of a period piece. I went with next to no background in Pacific ethnography or prehistory, or expertise in human biology fieldwork techniques. The other graduate student who was along, who had a degree in dentistry, was Howard Bailit (he's mentioned as Howard a lot in my letters to my parents). He'd discovered he hated grinding teeth and inflicting pain, so he was following Ed Hunt's suggestion to switch to biological anthropology.

JR: And you say in your acknowledgements in your first book that he's deserving of a co-authorship.

JF: Right, because he took all the dental casts in 1970 when we went back together. Howard was a hard worker and subsequently did excellent dental anthropology work. We were the young guys, at least among the biological anthropologists, but because of his dental degree, he was more of a professional at that point than I. Then there were also all the physicians, who made up most of the group of about 11. It was a big group, and I thought it was grossly overdone.

We got out to Bougainville and it rained and rained and rained (no surprise there). Gene Ogan was the cultural anthropologist of the first group, the Nasioi. He's still alive and kicking in Honolulu. I just saw him last year at a meeting in Canberra. Gene had already been to the Nasioi area a couple of times. He was student of Oliver's and he was fairly old for a graduate student. He had done things before anthropology, including military service. The Nasioi were the most modernized of all the groups we studied. Bougainville was just about to develop a big copper and gold mine, but the Nasioi had already had a 50 or 60 year contact history with missions and with plantations. They had therefore become distrustful of European motives in general and Australians in particular. Gene had a tough time in trying to persuade people to come in for these medical exams and to be measured and have blood samples taken.

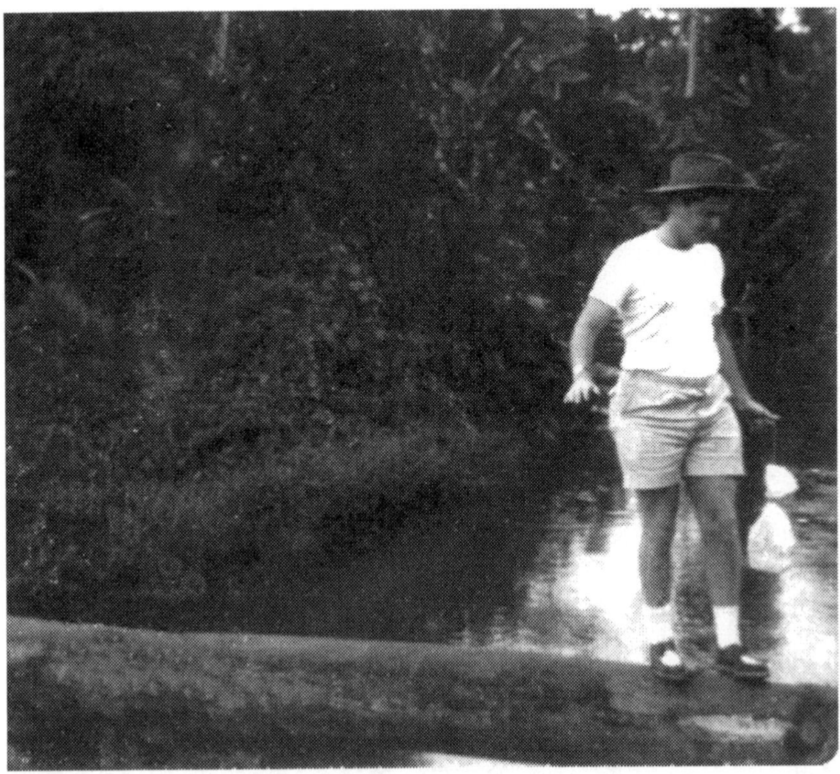

First days in the field. Tentatively crossing a log in clean clothes, with a new Australian digger hat, spiked golf shoes, and holding a camera safely in a plastic bag. June 1966.

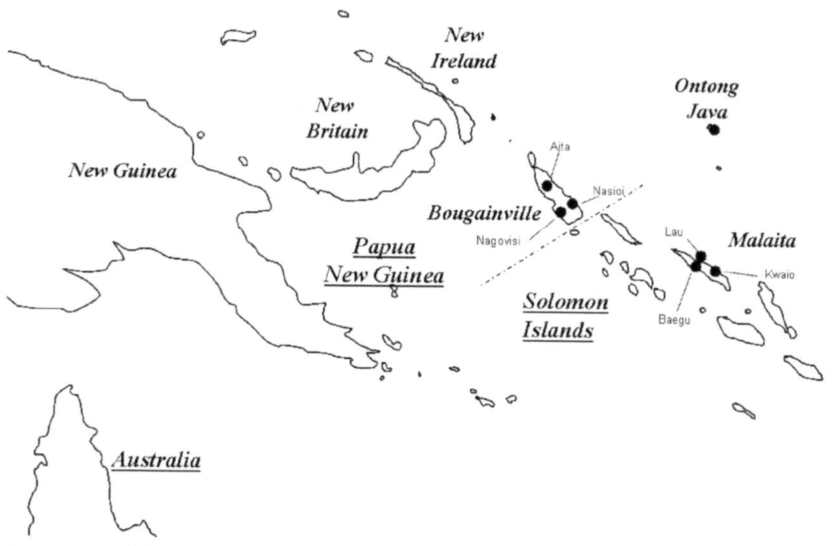

Locations of the Harvard Solomon Island Expedition field sites: the 1966 expeditions were to Nasioi and Kwaio; 1968 to Lau and Baegu; 1970 to Nagovisi and Aita; and 1972 to Ontong Java and Ulawa (not shown, since it was never revisited).

Going up to his house where he lived there was my first experience in the field – how to light a Tilley lamp, what sort of bedding to use, how to use a primus stove, just how to live! Mosquito netting and all that kind of equipment that seems after the fact kind of obvious was not. He was the first anthropologist I saw living like that. He said, "Oh, you'll be fine." It certainly was more comfortable than camping in a tent. The traditional houses were cool and airy; on stilts, with bamboo walls and leaf roofs. The most important thing he stressed was, "You must remember, you're a guest here. These people don't have to tolerate you in their village and they don't have to cooperate. You have to be seen as generous; one of a Melanesian Big Man's attractions is that he's supposed to be magnanimous." That was sound advice. He impressed upon me the way you had to behave in the Pacific, in village life. You couldn't be an old fashioned colonial boss or master ("*Masta*" in pidgin English, or Tok Pisin as it is called there) and command, "Boy, come here and sit down! I'm going to measure you." Sometimes, situations could be extremely exasperating, especially when people wouldn't show up after extensive planning and discussion, but empty threats would do no good. I saw the problems clearly that he had to deal with in the Nasioi situation. It was not easy. It was not simple oftentimes or straight forward.

This was in a period in American history, of what I would call, American triumphalism. We were still in the Cold War; it was the Kennedy or just post-Kennedy era, with the development of the Peace Corps. We sort of assumed that we could go around the world and improve people's lot with our superior knowledge and democratic traditions, in competition with the Soviet Union and Chinese Communists. There's just an echo of that currently with Obama coming in to power, but then we certainly thought we had the answer for everybody. For example, I recall McGeorge Bundy, who had been a dean at Harvard before being recruited by Kennedy and then Johnson, giving a speech back at Harvard, defending American intervention in Vietnam as fulfilling the role of America as the "world's policeman," a phrase he coined, I believe. Such chutzpah! I had thought about going into the Peace Corps or the State Department or something like that when I graduated from college. . .

JR: I had wondered about that…

JF: I can tell you about why that didn't happen. I would come home from college and my father would ask "What do you think you're going to do after graduation?" or "What do you think you're going to do after your major in classical art history?" Once I said, "Well, maybe I'll be a doctor." And he would question me about it from a negative side, but which I think he meant as a constructive thing, sort of like "you have to consider these potential downsides." He said, "A doctor – do you think you want to be around sick people all your life?" I said, "Oh, I hadn't thought of that, maybe not." I was deflated and discouraged. Or another time, "I think I want to go into the Peace Corps" and he said, "What would you do after that?" And I said, "Maybe I'd go into the State Department." He said, "Jews don't get far in the State Department," or something like that. Finally I said, "Well, maybe I'll go into anthropology." He didn't have an answer for that one. He was an academic himself. I don't know what that has to do with what I was saying.

JR: We were talking about the Peace Corps . . . other possibilities of things you might have done.

JF: Oh yes, and American triumphalism. The Pacific was tailor-made for that sentiment, because the Second World War had been a remarkable victory in a just cause, primarily by American forces. The Japanese were about as bad as the Germans. Our soldiers had acted, apparently, marvelously in the Pacific. They had been on good behavior and were greatly admired by the Pacific islanders. The positive attitude towards Americans also was reinforced because of our black troops. The Service was segregated during the war, so black troops were restricted to non-combat tasks like truck driving and stevedore support. The Melanesians were perfectly aware of the segregation, but felt that American blacks were still treated better by American whites than they themselves had been treated by the plantation owners and overseers. I remember one Bougainville man reminiscing that as a little boy, an American G.I. had given him an Army cap and taken him under his wing, almost adopting him. I assume it was a black G.I. Certainly in contrast to the Japanese and to the Australians and British in colonial times, we were seen as the great liberators by the local people in general. True or not, I heard stories in south Bougainville of little boys being cooked and eaten by Japanese conscripts (our submarine service was particularly effective in isolating the Japanese, who were starving and malaria-ridden by the end).

Cargo Cult Issues

A lot of this positive attitude towards Americans also had to do with something called cargo cult that already existed there, but became more common after the war. It was based on the premise that all the wealth of the modern world came by magic from America. As a result, there was an enormous reservoir of goodwill that we capitalized on one way or another in the 1960s. For example, at the war's end, a major chief formally asked an American admiral to take over or "look-out" for (*lukautim*) the Solomons rather than hand it back to the British.

We had to be careful about the American association with cargo cult, but it was certainly relatively easy as an American to walk into villages and be accepted. You still had to act properly, and Kevin Mohr [a graduate student from Wisconsin who ultimately dropped out] did not – you now have his diary – but at least initially we had people's good will.

JR: Can you say more about the history of the cargo cult phenomenon in the region?

JF: Right. Cargo cults are a specific Melanesian form of what are more generally called revitalization movements, or millenarian movements, which occur when one society perceives itself as in an inferior situation vis-à-vis another society or part of society, and can't psychologically cope with that inferiority. There are a couple of things that can happen in such a case. Either they can adopt the dominant group's behavior and try to assimilate and totally forsake their old kinds of belief systems and social, organizational principles, or they can undergo this kind of revitalization/transformation in opposition to this outside influence, which often includes incorporating certain aspects of the outside influence. Usually it involves one person having a vision of how to regain their rightful stature as a worthwhile or even superior culture with some sort of dramatic change, having received word from god or some spirit on some way to get to a better place.

You can see revitalization elements in all kinds of revolutions, even in the rise of Hitler and Nazism in reaction to the German defeat in the First World War. A lot of religions have revitalization elements, like Jesus among the Jews in response to Roman domination. The Ghost Dancers of the American Southwest, with their special shirts that would repel bullets, the Jonestown Cult, and the Boxer Rebellion in China, were all revitalization movements, but in the Pacific, revitalization took on a lot of forms that were seen as sort of amusing, but they were serious.

Everybody had the sense that all the good material things in life came from America. After all, in the Second World War they'd seen the unbelievable power and wealth of the American Navy. The Americans had ships with enormous amounts of "cargo," or *kago* in Tok Pisin. So "cargo cults" were seen as a way to get all this wealth delivered to them, because clearly it was all magic – no one knew how to manufacture any of these things in such incredible abundance.

Some areas were more likely to develop these cargo cults than others and were susceptible to cargo cult movements developing repeatedly. Buka Island, just to the north of Bougainville, was known as one such cargo cult center. One group that formed there was called the Hahalis Welfare Society. A man there said he had a vision. I don't know if it was from Jesus or from some other spirits. It was supposed to be supernatural, and it called for a total transformation of society. They dissolved old notions of the family. They were going to raise a multi-racial, supernatural master race, so all the women were put together in one longhouse. They invited people in from outside to have sex with all these women, married or unmarried. They had Chinese, Europeans, and people from different local groups come in. Also they collected their own taxes, and they refused to pay taxes to the government, and a lot of the money went to the leaders. They felt that this was also going to cause *kago* from America to come in.

The Australian government arrested the leaders of the Hahalis Welfare Society on the basis that they weren't paying taxes and were spreading false rumors. Of course the missions were also upset because people weren't coming to mass and were acting immorally.

In the movie called *Mondo Cane* – that dealt with cargo cults among other curious phenomena in the Pacific – they talked about the President Johnson cult, I believe, which still exists. Do you know about that?

JR: I'm not sure I do.

JF: This was on the island of New Hanover, where we collected a few samples recently. We tried to do some fieldwork in one Johnson cult village there unsuccessfully in 2000 – people weren't interested. In any case, some people there heard on the radio during the Vietnam War that President Johnson was going to fly over their island on the way to Vietnam to meet with the then-President (Thieu, I believe) to try to settle some details of the war. The people in New Hanover decided, since he was the American President, the American "king," they would try and capture him, hold him for ransom, or make him their own king so they could get all the cargo from America. So they made a landing strip . . . now it's starting to ring a bell? They laid out torches to mark the strip and they made large stick models of airplanes like giant duck decoys. When Air Force One "saw" the airstrip, it was supposed to come down and land, and then they'd capture Johnson. Of course, it never landed. But the idea remains. Perhaps it would have been best if he'd gone there! Some people there still raise and salute the American flag every morning and profess their allegiance to President Johnson and that they want to become part of the U.S.

So, we had to be careful and specific in our description of our purposes. In the Solomon Islands, I have a document there [in my letters] that describes "Marching Rule" which was the Solomon Islands version of cargo cult revitalization in the 1950s. So it was a fairly common occurrence.

JR: This is a good background for thinking about the kind of context in which the expedition was happening.

JF: Absolutely.

Funding the Harvard Solomon Islands Project

JR: In our earlier session we ended with talking about how the project was funded; it was NIH funded as opposed to being funded through the military or the Atomic Energy Commission. Could you talk, to the extent that you know, about the process of how the Solomon Islands Project got funding.

JF: You know I'm vague on this, since it happened before I became involved. I think that should become much clearer at Peabody Museum if you find the original grant proposals . . .

JR: They are there.

JF: Good. This was a period in the 1950s and then the 1960s that was the great expansive period of federal funding for science and health research. That included the creation of the National Science Foundation, which I know a lot about, which grew up as a direct result of the Manhattan Project success in the Second World War – are you aware of all that?

JR: Yes.

JF: That was a fine rationale for funding not just nuclear physics but a great deal of science! That's the way it started, with Vannevar Bush's letter to President Truman, urging him to keep up the state of American science as part of our national defense, as shown by the critical development of the A-bomb. Basic science was suddenly important to national defense. Now NIH was always different from NSF, but NIH expanded dramatically during the 1950s as well. Anthropology started to be funded by NSF in the early 1950s. Harvard professors like Gordon Willey, Hallam Movius, and Bill Howells were beginning to apply for their first NSF grants, and being successful by-and-large. You could say it was rationalized for Congress as part of the national defense effort, but NSF was independent in the end, and you could say that about NIH, the Interstate Highway System, and graduate "defense education" fellowships (NDEA), as well. NIH was different because it did not have a national priority or limitation. NSF is a national U.S. science support mechanism. If you are a non-US citizen, you can still get an NSF grant as long as you are associated with a U.S. institution. Conversely, you can't get a NSF grant if you are a professor in France or England or Japan, even if you're an American citizen. The opposite is true of NIH. You can be a foreign national and working with a foreign institution and apply to NIH. So it's much broader in that sense. In the 1950s, representatives from the NSF and NIH would show up at anthropology meetings and essentially plead for decent proposals, saying, "Look, you know, this is what we do, this is what we fund, you should think about applying." They still do that, but with far less sanguine prospects for funding.

It made sense for the Harvard group to apply to NIH as opposed to NSF because of Damon's background in medicine, the emphasis on health consequences, and also the funding was going to be larger than it could have been with NSF. NIH was always much larger than NSF. The leaders of the project thought they had generous support, which they certainly did. I think it was around $70,000 per field season, which was a lot in 1966 dollars. Some expedition leaders would say, "You know, we've been in the military (a few were veterans of the Korean War) and we know how government money gets wasted there – it's better spent this way than on new bombs and aircraft. This is peanuts."

JR: When we had spoken earlier, you talked about Baruch Blumberg's claims for helping get the funding from NIH for the Solomon Islands Project. That's something he has said to me, so it's interesting that you raised that point independently . . .

JF: He said that to you?

JR: Yes. I was just wondering if you could tell me your impression of that particular relationship because he was also involved in publications that came out of the project.

JF: You're going to have to ask him for specifics. My recollection is that he told me he was on the NIH panel that recommended the Solomon Islands Project for funding, and he pushed it strongly. I don't know how well he knew Al Damon – you'd have to ask him about it. I know the expedition had subsequent funding renewal problems. I refer to that in my letters home, I believe. I don't know exactly when the cutoff finally happened. The money ran out shortly after 1972, after the final field season. Then Damon died in 1973. I believe the papers about the Solomons that Blumberg wrote were after the fact, if those were the ones on Australia Antigen that involved me.

JR: That sounds about right.

JF: Again I'm sure that's the kind of thing you'll be finding at Peabody. So in terms of how it happened, how it developed, I am unclear, especially about the role of Damon and Oliver. Hopefully that will be in the records at Peabody.

JR: Yes, I'm curious to find out because the one thing I did notice in the finding aid at the Peabody is a file that says "Letter concerning PI of the project." It seems as though it is something of a puzzle to be determined.

JF: Right, because here you had a man (Damon) who I think came up with the idea of the Solomon Islands Project, who had all the field responsibilities, but who was not a tenured professor, and I know that makes it much more problematic for funding. I know they'd prefer to have someone on the faculty who is going to be there for the duration, rather than somebody who was a year-by-year appointment. So I don't know who was in charge technically.

The personalities on the Harvard Solomon Islands Project, 1966

JR: So let's talk about the Solomon Islands Project and your first experience in the field. We've discussed it already, getting to this point, but just if you could speak about your exposure to the field and what was it like? What did you learn on that expedition?

JF: As I mentioned, I was definitely a junior member and Howard Bailit was kind of a junior member too, and that was made clear to us from the outset, as well as the cultural anthropologist graduate students. So, for example, on our way to the field we were meeting people who were going to be collaborators in Australia, people who were going to be doing lab work, total serum cholesterol and so on.

JR: This would be people like R.J. Walsh?

JF: Not so much Walsh, I believe. I subsequently found him, when I met him, to be open, generous, and hospitable. I can't remember the man's name because I never met him. I believe it was White. He had a party in Sydney and only invited the people with advanced degrees. Perhaps there were just too many of us – I don't know. I thought, "What's this?" It didn't make us feel – it's like making a clear distinction within the field team before we even started. That happened other times. For example, the more senior people got to go on a fancier boat with the British District Commissioner coming back to the capital, Honiara.

We were definitely the junior guys, I especially, and my tasks were minor in my own estimation. I can take decent pictures (maybe the art history training?), and fingerprints were easy. I was sent to Wisconsin to learn how to take fingerprints just before we left. That was a simple technique you could master in 15 minutes. I did care about taking decent photographs, especially since Dr. Damon wanted these somatotype photos, and I thought it might be difficult with especially dark subjects in the tropical light. Apparently he liked mine a lot, even though it was a rather primitive set-up I used – I was surprised. He said I managed to get muscle definition on the subjects particularly well. I had worried about that and sent some trial shots to my parents from Hawaii for them to develop and critique. In the end, I simply pinned up a white sheet on a house wall as background, used a 12 inch square blackboard and chalk to record I.D. numbers, and had a tripod at the specified distance for the full-body shots. For the portraits, I simply took the camera off the tripod and went in close for a hand-held close-up. I tried to wait for sunny conditions, which wasn't always easy, since it usually rained in the afternoons. Perhaps that's what he liked – that I took mine outdoors. Later expeditions had fancier set-ups, with two cameras, one with a telephoto for the portrait, and with indoor set-ups, with flash, etc. I know at least one year where this didn't work at all, as the "automatic" nature of the flash exposures wasn't synchronized properly, or the exposures were totally off, so that everyone looked like big ink blots with two white eyes.

Damon was an odd field leader. He was preoccupied with expense accounting, and keeping to our time schedule. He would get concerned that things like rain delays were keeping from getting us into the field, which was ironic since they all had plans for long leisurely trips home, through the Great Barrier Reef, Iran, or some other exotic place. They had their tickets with return dates they had to keep. True enough, it rained a lot, especially in Bougainville, and with all this equipment it was hard to get it all up to the field site from the hotel in Kieta (a run-down affair with eight rooms, where people got malaria from the mosquitoes swarming in the two shower stalls in the men's room – more of a disease risk there than in the villages). We were delayed 2 or 3 days and people would complain about Ogan – it was his problem as the cultural anthropologist: make people come, have the food ready, make the rain stop, and so on, and he became upset. He felt put upon by this large group of physicians, primarily. This was a constant problem that all the cultural anthropologists had to deal with in the different field sites. Damon hadn't thought through things well – he'd had no prior experience in such uncertain conditions, I suppose, although he'd been stationed in Turkey in the Air Force.

A good example of how this came to hurt the expedition was during the transition between the two groups we surveyed in that first field season, since we had to move everything from the Nasioi area of Bougainville to the Kwaio down in Malaita in the British Solomon Islands Protectorate. We had a great deal of equipment, and Damon had chartered a DC 3 – that's the kind of airplane everybody used then – to fly us and our equipment down from Bougainville to Honiara on Guadalcanal Island in the Solomons. Then we were going to ferry it all across to Malaita. When the airplane came to pick us up at the airstrip in Bougainville, the pilot came out and said, "I can't take you, you've got a passenger list of 11, and I don't know how many thousands of pounds of baggage and equipment." So there we were, ready to go, but the airplane pilot said "you can't do it." Dr. Damon said, "Nobody told me that overweight would be a problem!" He hadn't realized it was a potential issue, and this is exactly the sort of anticipation of problems that an expedition leader must be responsible for. Ultimately they had to hire a separate airplane to come get the rest of the cargo and it meant another delay and much higher expenses. It was that sort of experience that led me to avoid organizing large expeditions like that – my mantra became travel light and be flexible.

After a while there were other people along who began to become, what should I say, not *de facto* leaders, but they were more involved with the planning, connecting with the cultural anthropologists, and so forth. Lot Page was the primary example. Lot was a man of wide interests. He was a great ocarina player, for example, and a mushroom poisoning expert – in Massachusetts, people would call his number if they thought they'd poisoned themselves with an unfamiliar mushroom. He also loved butterflies, was a great birder; all kinds of naturalist interests. He loved being in the field. He would go out with Roger Keesing on hiking expeditions. When we arrived in Kwaio, there was an influenza epidemic in progress, and people were dying from pneumonia complications, Lot would go out with Roger and treat people, giving them antibiotics, and I believe he'd done much more than Al [Damon] on that score.

Also, I was told that when he came on a later expedition, Howells was acknowledged as the expedition "big man" by the local people, probably because of his general demeanor, even though Damon was the team leader. Al was just stiff, and he could only think narrowly in terms of what he was familiar with.

Another example of that – in the field in the tropics, what you wear on your feet is always a problem. The best footgear is native bare feet (I have pictures of those feet), but we didn't have that, we don't have habituated bare feet, with toes widely spaced and strong toe muscles that allow you to dig into muddy hillsides, as if you had eagle claws. Another story – bush Melanesians couldn't wear ordinary shoes because their feet were so broad, and this was used in the late colonial period to keep them out of bars – everyone was required to wear shoes. The rationale was that they didn't want people cutting their bare feet on broken beer bottles. That shoe stipulation was later broadened to include flip-flops, which ended the not-so-subtle discrimination. I'd asked Gene Giles for his advice on footgear, and he suggested buying canvas topped golf shoes with spikes (they didn't work well on rocks especially, and I ended up just using running shoes). Anyway, Damon wore his regular sturdy leather lace-up shoes, with low galoshes covering them, or what were called rubbers then, along with long socks and Bermuda shorts. That was his field outfit. Needless to say, when he was walking in the jungle paths, he simply got muddy, wet, and slipped all over the place, and mold undoubtedly grew inside his leather shoes. I would imagine he changed his field outfit the following seasons.

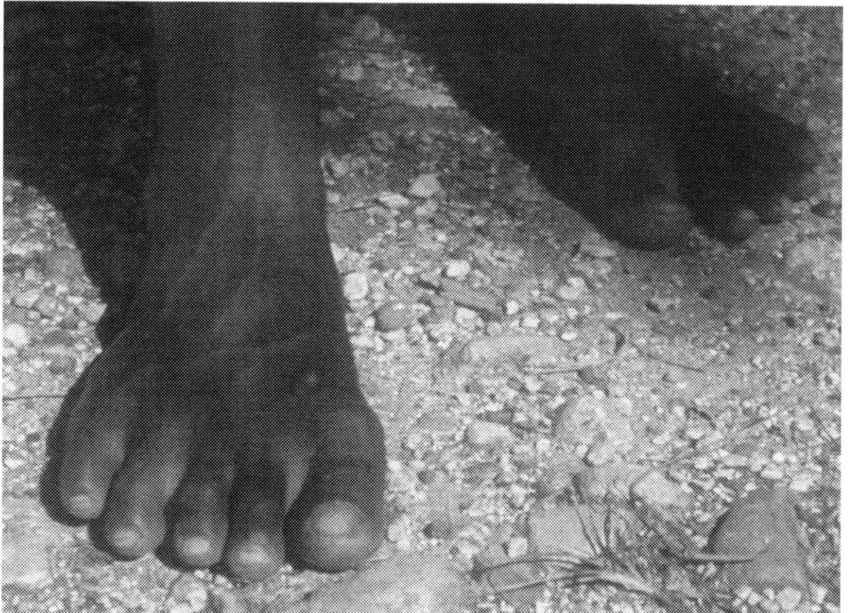

Well-adapted Melanesian feet.

Being at the bottom, I resented the hierarchical aspects of the expedition. I identified with Gene Ogan. I learned a lot from him about what he saw were important interaction issues with the local people. Few in the group bothered to learn much Tok Pisin. As a field language, Ogan first learned Tok Pisin and ultimately learned Nasioi, which is difficult (the Nasioi later told me he spoke it about as well as a six year old child would, which sounded good to me!). It was clear that we could all have spoken to people more directly if we just learned more Tok Pisin, which is easy. Everybody in Bougainville spoke Tok Pisin, although not everybody in Malaita did. As a group, we were totally dependent on Ogan and then Roger Keesing. Of course, everybody learned a little bit of Tok Pisin, like *opim maus* (open your mouth) if you were a dentist, or *sindaun* (sit down) if you were an anthropometrist. I didn't learn a great deal of Tok Pisin then, although I bought a book to study in preparation for the time on my own. It was only after the team left in August that I had to become fluent, and quickly. So that's a kind of a picture of the group dynamic from my perspective.

Harvard Solomon Islands Expedition members. Kwaio, August, 1966. Mentioned individuals in second row, from left; 2nd– Jerry Bloom; 3rd – Gene Giles; 5th – Lot Page; 6th – Albert Damon; 8th – Roger Keesing; 9th – Howard Bailit; 11th – JSF.

In Malaita, Roger Keesing and the Kwaio were an interesting contrast to the Nasioi and Gene Ogan. I'm reminded of the old chestnut that people pick dogs like themselves . . . Well, in a certain sense there was a fit between the anthropologists and the people that they studied. The Kwaio were a wild bunch who had killed William Bell, an early District Officer, after World War I – and that account became almost their origin or identity myth. You'd get that from *Lightning Meets the West Wind*, a fine book Keesing co-authored on that incident. Even though their leaders were eventually hanged and the rest of the Kwaio were totally disrupted by the retribution in the aftermath, it became their heroic struggle. They took a lot of pride in being the people who resisted the power of the Western World. It's like the Iraqi who threw his shoe at Bush the other day – instant hero!

Of all the groups in the Solomons, Roger chose to study them. He was careful. He knew about "Marching Rule" and the other revitalization movements linking America with resistance to the British. He had a sense that if he entered Kwaio from the usual beach on the east coast, from Sinerango Harbor, where Europeans always entered, he was going to be identified as another European with magical qualities, or intent on subjugating them, so he made the effort to hike across the island from the western coast, to cross over the mountains and come down from the "bush" side. He was therefore regarded as a different kind of foreigner, and he tried hard to be an extremely good and conscientious fieldworker, but inevitably, he got caught up in the politics of the situation and the power inequality of his position vis-à-vis the Kwaio.

Napoleon Chagnon is a great example of someone who did get terribly entangled in such a situation . . . however, that's a different story. Incidentally, in the early 1990s, Chagnon, whom I didn't know well, called me up at NSF to ask if I knew of a situation in New Guinea where he might conduct new fieldwork – it had gotten so bad for him in Venezuela and Brazil. I professed total ignorance, which was pretty much the truth.

Unloading cargo at Sinerango Harbor, Kwaio, July 1966.

Roger tried to find ways to make a constructive impact on Kwaio life in ways they wanted. For example, people there were worried that their young people would either stay home and would not make money the way groups around them were doing, or they would go to the towns or boarding schools and not return. If they did, they'd never learned how to build a traditional house or to garden or live comfortably in bush circumstances. So the Kwaio wanted to have a special school in their area. Roger was instrumental in having a Peace Corps couple sent to open a bush school there. That was David and Kate Aiken—they were supposed to teach English and math and a few other subjects in the mornings, and in the afternoon the Kwaio were going to teach the kids bush techniques, how to garden, how to build houses, how make various traditional things. The traditional objects they made were sold by the "Kwaio Cultural Centre" and a lot of the Kwaio artifacts I bought and donated to Temple were from that source. That was the kind of reasonable and well thought-out thing Roger tried to do. However, I believe after the Aikens left, the bush school initiative died.

Roger also set up The Kwaio Development Fund, where the proceeds of at least some of his books went. But, you know, there are always problems in that kind of arrangement, because after a while, arguments arise over real or perceived misuse of those sorts of funds. The Kwaio also felt they were being taken advantage of by the national government, so they resisted the national government dictates. They basically wanted their independence. Roger tried the best he could to be a representative to the national government before they had an actual representative to a national government themselves.

This all became more and more difficult because of the local personalities involved.

For example, one of the Kwaio leaders was, according to Roger, a schizophrenic – Fulafo'u. He was a great diviner, mesmerizing. People knew that he was kind of either in touch with the spirits or just plain crazy, as often is the case. Fulafo'u and others wanted to sue the national government (and the British) for some enormous sum, perhaps $28 million, as compensation not only for the massacre and desecrations associated with the Bell incident 70 years before, but also for the Kwaio suffering pollution from the menstruating women that were constantly being flown over Kwaio land in airplanes. (They were deathly afraid of female pollution, either through menstruation, childbirth, or defecation/urination. They would say, *Mekim body wik* in Tok Pisin – "Makes your body weak.") After a while, Roger threw up his hands and said, "I don't know what to do with these guys." He said to them, "You can find more productive ways to spend your time than this lawsuit, and I refuse to help you on this one."

That was a situation that often happens with cultural anthropologists, no matter how well-meaning they are, or sophisticated their plans. Their special role and backgrounds from dominant cultures raise the expectations that people have for them. Of course, it has to be said that Roger took considerable delight in twitting the British colonial set in Honiara, the capital, which probably didn't do him much good. He was apparently an accomplished tennis player and entered the annual tennis competition at the restricted membership (whites only) Guadalcanal Club. The contestants were supposed to wear all whites in those days. Roger beat the (white) pants off everyone, dressed in his khaki field shorts. However, I don't think he played barefoot!

I can give another example of the difficulties cultural anthropologists faced if you want to hear it. You know Pierre Maranda . . .

JR: There is quite a bit of correspondence with him in the Solomon Islands files [currently stored in the Temple Anthropology Lab] . . .

JF: Yes, he came from a Jesuit background. He left the priesthood to become an anthropologist and he was involved in Levi-Straussian structuralism and still goes back to see Levi-Strauss in Paris, who is now 100 years old. If you go on the web, I saw something the other day, an interesting account about him. Pierre and his wife Ellie were studying the Lau in Malaita, and they were mainly interested in the pagan mythology of the Lau. Pierre became the repository of these myths (the present-day Lau refer to these as "pagan"). The old priests said, "You are becoming the repository of our powerful sacred legends and these are not to be revealed to just anyone, but only to those who will help to perpetuate these myths and to keep them and their spirits strong." There's an article in *The Walrus* magazine about this online. It's an interesting story, what's happened over the years.

Ceremonial funerary canoe. Lau Lagoon. 1968.

He's now accused by the Lau for causing the destruction of a lot of things, because since he knows the pagan myths, he now has their power and he won't reveal them to the new set of Christian Lau. There are no more pagan priests, everybody has become Christian now, and a lot of people want to "convert" the pagan skulls of the ancestors which are kept in the sacred areas by saying the right kind of pagan spells that only Pierre knows. He won't give the spells to them for this purpose of conversion of the dead.

JR: Do you have any sense of what he feels his reasons are?

JF: He feels he was entrusted with these myths by the pagan Lau on the clear understanding that they were not to be used by non-believers for the destruction of the ancestors' spirits, and that's exactly what this new Christian generation wants them for, to destroy any semblance of the old pagan mythology, life, and power. The Christians call pagan ways "the work of the Devil," to be destroyed. It's all on the web . . . Here's the link: http://www.walrusmagazine.com/articles/2006.05-anthropology-pacific-the-octopus/

JR: I will have to look at that . . .

JF: It's another case where a cultural anthropologist with fine motives has gotten into a lot of difficulty because he's seen as having special powers that the local folks didn't have, and they relied on him or expected special things from him in return. He had a special position as an intermediary or, in this case, some sort of repository. It's a difficult situation.

Now, concerning Chagnon, I'm not going to defend him because I don't know the specifics of that particular case, but I'm just saying it's clearly a difficult position to be in. I tried hard myself not to get involved in those kinds of situations.

On the Job Preparation and Training

JR: And what about the actual "doing" of the work on a day-to-day basis, as another layer of the kinds of issues to be negotiated in the field?

JF: First of all there was my practical training for my own project, and deciding what I wanted to include in my survey battery. What I did learn as a new and essential technique during that first couple of months with the Harvard expedition was how to take blood. It was very informal training. The expedition phlebotomist or blood taker, Jerry Bloom, said, "Look Jonathan, this is what you do: you put the tourniquet around the arm, clean the area off with alcohol, and stick with the needle. It's that simple. Now let's see you do it." And I said, "Uhh, O.K." As you can imagine, I was tentative with the needle and sticking it in to somebody's arm, which I had never done before, so at first I might stick someone two or three times and not hit a vein. He said, "Look, you've got to understand that it doesn't hurt. I've taken 20,000 blood samples in my life and it's never hurt *me* once." I said, "Ohhh . . .O.K., I get it!" In other words: don't think about the pain you're inflicting, that will distract you. That's how I learned, from using humans as practice. I don't know exactly what would be acceptable behavior in the U.S. now, but I assume you have to be certified. That was just not even an issue then.

JR: What was the protocol for getting people enrolled? Was that more challenging than getting people to pose for a photograph? Or doing fingerprints or any of the other various measurements going on?

JF: I learned the techniques that I thought I was going to use during that two month period, and I decided what I *wasn't* going to do (I did want to be able to compare results with the Harvard Solomons battery, at least for those things I thought important). Some of that is laid out in my letters home. I wrote to Howells thinking about how many measurements I needed to take, because in terms of who was taking the longest period of time on the big expedition, it was the anthropometry. Al Damon was taking forever because he was taking 40, 50, 60 measurements or observations, and that was split with another person – Gene Giles in 1966. You can see on the anthropometric blanks. I settled on 12 measurements, only doing adult males, not women or children, and that helped a lot with time. The rationale for measuring only adult men vs. women in those days, as in so many medical studies, was that pregnancy and nursing unnecessarily "complicated" matters with women on measurements like weight.

However, I don't think I've answer your question directly; "What was the protocol for getting people enrolled?" This varied from the Harvard Solomons study to me, and at different periods. The Harvard sampling strategy was (finally) based on local residence groups. If you didn't live in a particular area, you were generally excluded (of course, you could come to the open clinic wherever you were from). As they enlarged their samples, they would encourage people from villages further away to come to be part of the survey. It took them a while to settle on whom to include and exclude. That was the main reason the Nasioi sample was smaller than the others.

Developing a Research Plan

JR: I want to hear more about how you decided on objectives.

JF: The most important thing I did during that introductory period was to conceive of my own research plan and design. This happened surprisingly early in my experience in Bougainville, in that first month of fieldwork in July 1966. I saw that in my letters home to my parents. In conversations with Gene Giles and Gene Ogan, I developed a proposal to NSF[11] for a dissertation improvement grant that was based on linguistic variation and intensive sampling, village by village by village along one path, from north to south Bougainville that transected the most diverse set of languages that I could find in one small manageable area. My sampling also had to be within a reasonable distance of a refrigerator and an airport in order to get the blood samples shipped to Walsh's lab in Sydney in good shape.

I hoped to do two things. One was finding an area with a great deal of biological variation within a small region. That's why I used the language diversity, as kind of a guess of where that biological variation might be. Secondly, I wanted to see if I could link biological variation to patterns of small-scale migration across these different villages that I hoped to establish with parish records.

This is the great advantage of working with humans rather than animals – I had some idea of recent migration rates or marital exchange

11 The National Science Foundation

from parish records or direct interviews. That's why I dealt with "marital migration distance" comparisons both in my first book, and in the first chapter of my last book (the 2007 Oxford U Press volume). The only effective way to do that was not to skip over different villages, but to go village by village along a transect – in this case, a real path from one village to the next.

The goal was to tie patterns of hereditary variation to underlying dynamics of isolation and migration. It worked fairly well. Nobody else that I know of had done such micro-sampling in such a small region or found variability like that – including Cavalli's work in the Parma Valley or Neel's with the Yanomami. I used the language map from Jerry Allen and Conrad Hurd's little book, *Languages of the Bougainville District*, put out by the Summer Institute of Linguistics, to plot out my proposal. Gene Ogan showed me his copy and then I bought my own. That's what I subsequently followed.

I found similar variability across that region in both blood typing with ABO blood groups and with the Inv gene, and also with regard to the short set of 12 measurements on the head and body I decided to take. In fact, the anthropometric pattern across villages was the most striking element of the clustering of variability by language group in that area of Bougainville. I certainly didn't need the complete battery they'd used in the full expedition, which took about a half hour per subject.

I was lucky that I hit such an area. I never replicated that hyper-intensive sampling design again, but what I kept with me was the sense that there might be a rough correspondence between linguistic variation and genetic variation, particularly in Melanesia. I think that was the strongest element of my thesis and the first monograph (1975). I've always been preoccupied with the question of whether there was a correspondence of language and hereditary variation in this region. That continues to our most recent work.

Alison Brooks, an important African archaeologist, asked me a couple of years ago, "Jonathan, why is this region so hyper-variable, as opposed to Europe or Asia?" I fumbled around for an answer at the time, but the best explanatory hypothesis, I believe, has been proposed by Daniel Nettle, a cultural anthropologist who worked in West Africa, another region of high linguistic variability. His idea to explain the hyper-variability regions is that these populations lived in ecologically stable tropical areas that didn't have dramatic wet and dry seasons. When they began farming or horticulture in these areas, they became especially self-sufficient. This self-sufficiency meant that there wasn't any reason to develop large-scale networks of trade and marriage exchange, and this in turn would result in local isolation, endemic feuding and tribalism, which would lead in turn to more language (and by extension, genetic) differentiation over larger areas. That was his argument for why these regions were so hyper-variable in language variability and, I say, in terms of biological variability. I think that's about as good an argument as I've seen. While New Guinea and Island Melanesia have many hundreds of different languages, large sections of Australia, Asia, or Africa do not. There are only a few places where this hyper-variability exists.

Chapter 4.

Going Solo: 1965-1966

Setting Out Alone

The Harvard expedition members left in early August, and I returned to Bougainville with the equipment and supplies I decided I needed for my own survey. Whatever criticisms I had of the Harvard expedition, I learned everything in that 2 month stint with the Harvard group that I required to do practical fieldwork, and had gotten the necessary equipment and lab contacts to devise my own derivative project. My projects derived directly from that base.

I picked the Eivo as the beginning area for my survey in Bougainville, as a Northern Papuan speaking population, and I was going to move south from there towards the Nasioi along that one path. I didn't know how much money I was going to have, or how long I could stay, so being able to compare just them with the Nasioi already covered by the Harvard Solomons study would provide a minimum contrast. The NSF proposal that I had just submitted in July was still pending, and there's a copy of an addendum I sent NSF in August from Malaita, that laid out much more in detail what I wanted to do (at a much greater cost).

Manetai, the Catholic mission in Eivo, about 20 or 30 miles north of Kieta, seemed to be a logical base of operations. Gene Ogan had always been on good terms with the missionaries in Nasioi (Marai Mission was close to his house), and I couldn't have done many of these things without them. The missionary I'd met in Keita (Father Miltrup) told me the priest at Manetai with the Eivo was Nicholas Kutulas who was from San Francisco. He had a Greek background (unusual for a Roman Catholic priest). "Oh, Father Nick, he'll be fine." Most of these Catholic missionaries were relatively sophisticated seminary graduates, but Father Nick was just down-to-earth, or rather salt of the earth.

View of Bougainville east coast from copra boat, with Mt. Bagana active. August, 1966.

He didn't know I was coming, although I'd sent a message meant for him over the mission short wave radio from Kieta (he wasn't listening that day). I got on the mission motor launch (an old copra boat about 30 feet long) with my gear and was dropped off on the shore at Vito village, about two miles from the mission. I expected him to be there, as I needed some help with my *kago* to get up to the mission station. This was my introduction to things not going exactly the way you assumed – it happens all the time. After waiting for a while, I left the *kago* on the beach, walked to the mission, introduced myself to Father Kutulas, and fortunately got him to go back with me with his tractor and trailer to get my equipment, most of which was stored and locked in three metal patrol boxes. What if he'd said "No?" This would be my clothes and bedding (cot, mosquito net, foam mattress, and sleeping bag), a box or two of food and cooking and eating utensils, and equipment, including needles and vacutainers, a spring scale, anthropometer, two calipers, a short wave radio, and other odds and ends (measuring forms, ledger books, and so on). It was important to travel light, but I still couldn't possibly carry it all myself. Once I got back to the mission, I talked to him about what I hoped to do in greater detail. I think he thought it was all extremely peculiar, but he wasn't going to be less than helpful, especially since the other missionaries in Kieta had been supportive.

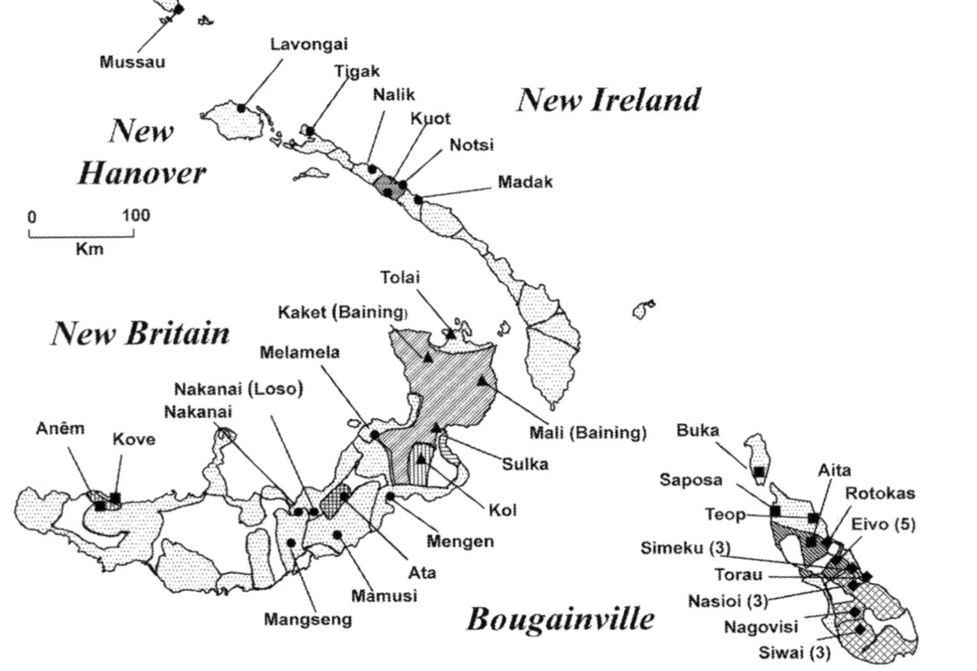

Location of additional field sites covered by JSF in Bougainville (in 1966-67: ♦ denotes covered language groups, with numbers of villages beyond 1 given in brackets), and in the Bismarks (in 1998: ▲; in 2000: ●; in 2003: ■). Sites of follow-ups to the Harvard Expeditions are given in Figure 3. Dotted areas denote Austronesian language areas, hatched areas denote different Papuan language group areas.

Father Nicholas Kutulas baptizing a newborn at Manetai Mission, September, 1966.

So, Father Kutulas said, "Friedlaender, I think you should start in Kopani village. I have a catechist from there named Hillary Arlaw, so Hillary can take you up there." I said, "Fine." Well, I was still unsure about my Tok Pisin, and I started doing some work with kids down at the mission school as a starter and practice, but after a day or two I was done with them.

Hillary Arlaw and I took the boxes of *kago* up to Kopani with help from 4 or 5 others. It was maybe an hour's walk, I can't remember exactly how far away, not too much further, in any case. That evening, I had to explain myself at a village meeting. I tried to lay things out with people in terms of what I wanted to do, and Hillary helped out a great deal. I think he was telling people what he had seen me doing down at the mission station with the children, some from their village. I explained that I couldn't pay them, but could give them a Polaroid photo as a thank-you. They started discussing where I should stay and work, and other issues around my plans. The conversation went on for what seemed like a long time to me, and I wasn't sure how it was going, since it was all being carried out in their Eivo language. That was a particularly anxious moment when I thought I might well be refused, not just because my Tok Pisin was rudimentary, but because the impressively large expedition group had gone and I had no cultural anthropologist mediator or accompanying physician to offer medical care as partial compensation.

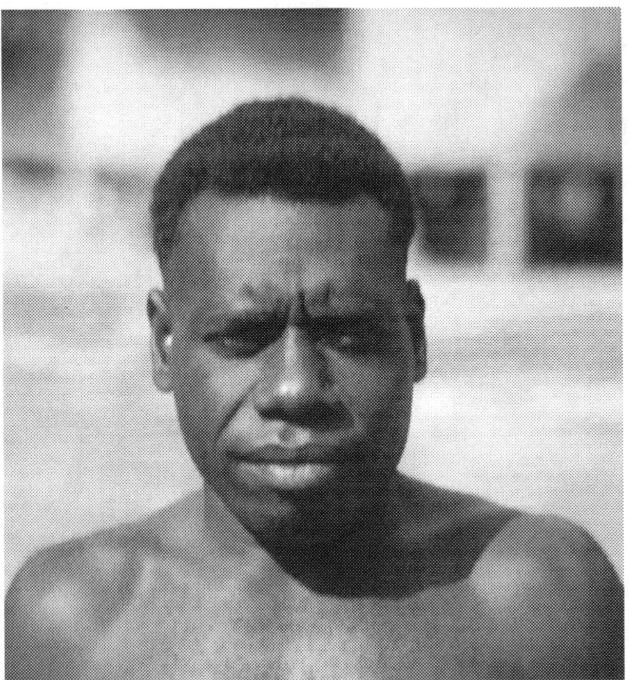

Hillary Arlaw. September, 1966.

Finally, Hillary said things seemed to be satisfactory, and so we set up our bedding, mosquito nets, and Tilley lamp in the *haus kiap* (the "captain's house," or guest house maintained for patrol officers and other visitors) and made dinner over the primus stove. To my great relief, people started showing up the next morning to the village meeting area where we'd set up the folding chairs and table we'd brought. It was best to get people early in the day, before they went to work their gardens or left the line village for other reasons. Things generally slowed down by about 10 a.m. and then would sometime speed up again after 3 pm. And so it began. We got a good sample from that village and that began to make me feel more encouraged to go on to the next village, and so on to the south. I suppose after I'd started, people down the line had a sense of what was coming. People from other villages would drop by to see what we were doing, since it was a novelty, and report back to their families and friends. It all became easier as time went on, especially as my Tok Pisin improved, and I no longer feared complete rejection by every village.

Atamo, a Bougainville "line village."

Developing a Weekly Routine

I wanted to develop a standard protocol that first week that I could stick with afterwards. I tried to be strict about using residence in particular villages as the requirement for inclusion. Before I entered a village, I would have already collected family data from the mission baptismal records – the *Status Animarum* books – establishing fairly well which were the families residing there, their birthplaces, information on their parents, and individual birth dates, or at least their baptismal dates (a close approximation for the Catholics). I could copy the records for a village in an evening on index cards, one per family, covering anywhere from 50 to 200 people. I used that information in establishing what are called marital migration distances (see my books on this, both the first 1975 monograph and the last one in 2007). I hoped to link patterns of isolation and migration from village to village to their genetic distinctions. My main conclusion was that the people who lived in these villages had mostly been born close by – they hadn't moved far at all from their birthplaces, and this explained a lot about their genetic isolation and diversity.

Then I would go to the village with Hillary or a subsequent assistant and discuss the proposed survey with the village adults. That was the kind of oral informed consent I obtained, talking to village groups on the first evening. With the adults, we'd go through the families we had records for, to check to see if they thought the records were accurate, and whom we were interested in ahead of time. People would know whether they were on the mission list. I would then begin on the first day by measuring the father of the family, and taking fingerprints of everybody, including the kids. I also took a hair sample, got saliva samples, did some color-vision testing, and checked the dental eruption status of the children, which Howard Bailit had convinced me would make for a nice paper (it did – our second paper together). I also started out testing people's eyesight, but I quickly gave that up – no one had poor eyesight unless they were old and going blind and the test took too long to administer. I could do my test battery on about 40 people a day. Then, on the last day, I would ask everybody previously covered to return, and I would take a 10 cc blood sample from everyone over the age of about 12 or 14, and then give people the Polaroid photograph as a gift. That evening, I would construct a village genealogy with the help of village elders, with all the assigned identification numbers represented (these could be long evenings in big villages of 100 people or more). These village genealogies I still have at home [they will be donated to the Melanesian Archive as well]. There's a picture of me making one of those in Nasiwoiwa Village in Eivo, early on.

Since I didn't have any means of refrigeration, the blood samples simply remained at ambient temperature over that night in a test tube rack, with a damp towel covering them (around 55 to 65 degrees Fahrenheit). There was never any major problem reported with spoilage.

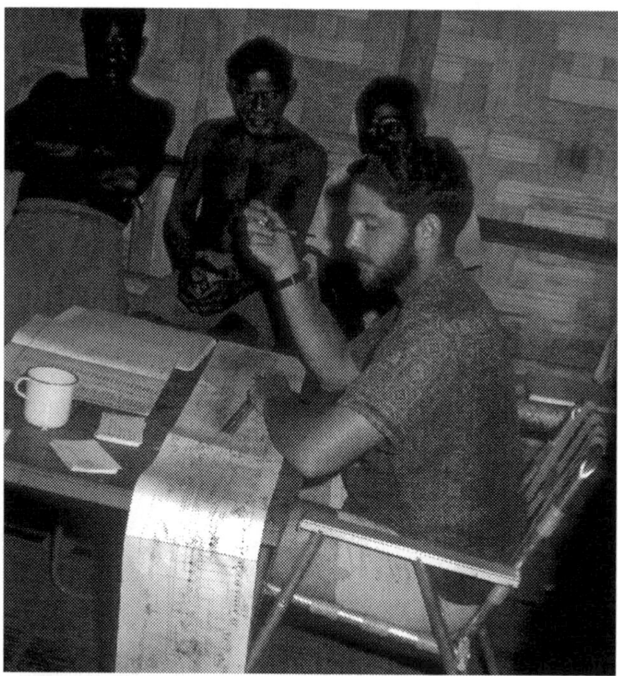

Constructing village genealogies after dinner with village elders. Nasiwoiwa, Eivo. 1966.

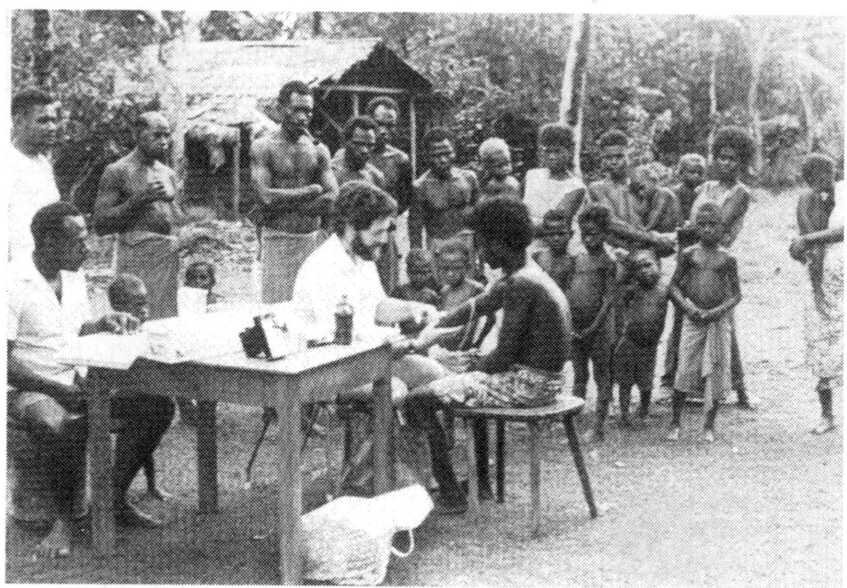

Taking blood samples. Gagan Village, Buka Island. 1973.

The next morning, I would travel down to Kieta. At first, this meant walking to Manetai and getting a motor canoe ride with Father Kutulas, and later, as I got closer to Kieta, it meant walking to the road being constructed to the mine and hitching a truck ride. I usually could get the samples refrigerated in the Kieta Hotel Bar walk-in refrigerator by 10 or 11 a.m. that day. I'd try to get them on the plane from the Aropa airstrip early the following morning. I would send the samples in their original 10 cc vacutainer tubes to Walsh in Sydney in big Chinese vacuum flasks with a bag of wet ice on top. These were large glass vacuum flasks intended for hot or cold drinks that I could buy at the local Chinese trading stores, about the size of the big coffee dispensers you see in convenience stores now. They would hold 50 or 60 tubes plus the ice bag on top. I had to buy at least one every week, and once I remember they ran out of them at the local trading store, to my horror (I'd probably bought most of them before). The airplanes flew out of Bougainville to Port Moresby two times a week. I usually aimed for a Saturday flight. Those flasks had to be transshipped at Port Moresby to Sydney, and someone from Walsh's lab picked them up at the airport (I would send a telegram ahead). He would do the red cell antigen and some plasma protein analyses, and he was also supposed to aliquot some plasma to be sent off to Arthur Steinberg's lab at Case Western Reserve in Cleveland, and also Baruch Blumberg at the Fox Chase Cancer Center in Philadelphia. Now I don't recall whether Walsh did one single shipment to Steinberg and Blumberg at the end of my collections, because I was flooding him with samples. I believe he sent one big shipment – that makes sense.

To fill out the picture of living in the villages a little, eating was simple unless people sold or gave me fresh fruit such as bananas or papaya, or (rarely) eggs or fish. Occasionally I could buy fresh bread, pineapples, sweet potatoes, and taro. I ordinarily had crackers with jam or butter, or cookies (*swit bisket*) and tea or instant coffee for breakfast, hot tea and sweet biscuits for lunch, and hot tea, rice, and some form of canned meat doctored up with spices and rice I'd brought along for dinner. I always had a wash or swim after work around 5 o'clock, which was refreshing, cutting through the humidity and heat of the afternoon. Villages were always situated near a river or stream. After the swim, I'd get the Tilley lamp going, change into pajamas, turn on the short wave radio for news and music from the Australian Broadcasting Commission or Voice of America, smoke my pipe, drink more hot tea, make dinner with Hillary or whoever succeeded him (lots of rice), and chat with passers-by until about 9 o'clock, when I'd go to sleep under my mosquito net, often in a sleeping bag. My health was not much of a problem. I never got malaria (chloroquine resistant strains developed later on). I had a bad infestation of bedbugs in one village, and had some other skin ailments, including some penicillin resistant staph infections. I also got occasional bad sunburns walking on the beach, and a fungus infection or two. I had one nasty flu or perhaps walking pneumonia episode where I lost 10 or 15 pounds and was quite weak for a period of 3 weeks or so. That was about it. There were some close calls concerning falls, hair raising seafaring escapades or small plane trips that could have ended up in a premature demise, but not much illness. Psychologically, the main problem was isolation and boredom, since I was moving from one place to the next in a survey mode and only made rather superficial contacts with people other than the assistants working with me. My daily routine of verifying family records, measuring, fingerprinting, and blood drawing quickly became tiresome. For occasional breaks on Sundays I'd arrange to go hiking or snorkeling. When I went into Kieta with the blood samples, I'd often stay at the hotel for a night, have dinner there, and maybe a beer or two at the bar – but I didn't hang out with many Aussies there – they were mostly miners, a pretty rough crew. I preferred the missionaries and often stayed at mission stations going back and forth. For Christmas, I flew to Rabaul, spent a few nights in an air-conditioned hotel room which helped my skin ailments, and ate lots of Chinese food. I always say that, after a year alone in the bush, sex fantasies gave way to food fantasies, and because of that, I planned my trip back through Thailand, Hong Kong, Taiwan, and Japan.

Obtaining Informed Consent

I should say a little more about my procedure of obtaining informed consent, since this subject has become contentious recently. It was an entirely different era in fieldwork in the 1960s. My approach certainly developed over the intervening decades, and I hope I kept up with what was acceptable behavior at different periods. I remember being questioned by a review panel considering possible funding for the Human Genome Diversity Project, in Washington around 1992 on how I continued to obtain informed consent in Bougainville and the Solomons, often from nonliterate people who were totally unfamiliar with such research. I said that, while the specifics of the consent process I used changed a great deal over time, I always intended to go back, so I tried to act in a way that would allow me to return in people's good graces. Certainly, I changed my procedures, but that attitude remained the same. I wrote this up more specifically in that ethics volume [on ethics in biological anthropology, edited by Trudy Turner]. In the early days, no one signed forms or listened to a formal presentation from me. It was just having the evening "council meeting" in a village, with questions and answers following my description and demonstration (often with anthropometer, scale, finger print paper, and blood taking tubes usually displayed and examined). It was clear that I couldn't require people to participate, that there was no coercion involved. In one instance in the 1980s, a local nurse who was acting as an assistant began berating certain families for not showing up, and I had to put an end to that.

There was one village, the first village I approached, where the whole village said, "We don't want to do that." I said, "Oh, well, O.K." I didn't have much choice. That was Vito near Manetai Mission, where I first landed with all my cargo. They were Austronesian-speakers who lived right on the beach, and I would have liked to include them. They had had contact with plantation owners for a long time, and had become especially skeptical of Europeans as a result. In many villages, some individuals just chose not to show up, a passive refusal. I do vividly recall one young man who angrily said he wouldn't come. His mother had just died of cancer at the Kieta hospital, and he said if the doctors there couldn't help her, what good would my survey be to him? I couldn't effectively answer that.

Expanding the Scope of the Research

The NSF Dissertation Improvement Award did come through, for the maximum, $9,000. When I read the telegram after about 3 weeks alone in Eivo, I was literally jumping up and down, and people must have thought I was crazy. They probably thought that anyway!

As a result of the grant, I was able to extend my survey down through 12 villages to the north Nasioi and an Austronesian beach group, and after a lot of hesitation, I decided to go to the west coast of Bougainville after Christmas and revisit the group that Oliver had studied in the 1930s – the Siwai. I thought if it didn't work out, I still had obtained a good sample from the east coast, so there was no downside risk. I had no contacts at all there, and it wasn't Catholic (no good mission records). It was also a much longer truck ride to an airstrip on a lousy road, and I had no idea if I could get blood samples refrigerated before shipment. I knew the samples would be shaken up on the bad road and risked becoming hemolized (the red cells would break open). I was apprehensive. I took my last two assistants from the east coast with me, Ignatius Bakamori and Michael Mandaku. The primary intent was to find and remeasure as many men as possible who had been measured by Oliver in the 1930s. Of course, I also took blood samples and the rest.

Ignatius Bakamori. Boira Village, Simeku, Bougainville. 1966.

That additional coverage turned out to be beneficial. Besides adding the southwestern Bougainville groups, it was fascinating to go to Oliver's old stomping grounds with his book and his old photos of people he'd measured. Even though there had been considerable disruption and displacement of people during World War II in that particular area (since they were between the American base just to the north in Torokina, and the Japanese base to the south in Buin), people tended to return to their former gardens and villages afterwards. Many had fled to the bush and then gone to the American base for food and medical treatment towards the end of the war. The older people remembered Oliver well and showed me where his old house had been – the house posts had taken root and become large trees. I read long sections of his book aloud and showed his illustrations. People were particularly interested in his accounts of their clan origin myths. They said it was important that he had recorded these in his book, as many of these accounts had been forgotten. People came from miles around to go through the old photos of the men he'd measured. I was able to locate and remeasure 26 men he'd covered in 1938 (he'd measured hundreds). Of course, there were many living relatives of those who had died, and they wanted copies. So getting all those photos copied and sent back to the right people after my return to Cambridge was a major endeavor.

Before I left Bougainville in March, I decided to push my luck again and try to extend the east coast sampling "line" further north from the Eivo, hoping to get some northern groups that had type B blood, to show the Eivo to be drifted from all the surrounding groups. I sampled two villages in the Aita/Rotokas region. My guess turned out to be both correct and incorrect – the northern groups did have some type B, but they also were more extreme in other gene frequencies than any of the more southerly groups, which made those gradients in allele frequencies down the island even more pronounced. They were also distinctive in their head and body measurements – big and broad mountaineers.

To sum up, my first field expedition had been a great success, and I had a large collection of fingerprints, anthropometric measurements, and blood samples. It took two years to do the analyses of the different datasets and write my doctoral thesis, with the help of 3 different labs. More would become involved later.

Peter Tumare looking at Oliver's picture of him as an adolescent in 1938. Turungum, Siwai. 1967.

Reunion of remeasured men from Oliver's time in 1938. Siwai, Bougainville, 1967.

Chapter 5.

Thoughts on the First Year of Fieldwork

Problems of the Privileged Outsider

No matter how short a time you stay in a fieldwork situation, you can get embroiled in difficult local political dynamics. Before I began my fieldwork in Bougainville, I had to check in with the District Officer, Max Denehy (this was the equivalent, under the Australian Administration, of getting a research permit – Bougainville was still part of the Territory of Papua New Guinea, administered by Australia under a UN mandate). He gave me only two explicit prohibitions. He expected me to be careful and not encourage anti-Australian sentiments, because people knew that independence was coming soon and the Australian officials were trying to prepare people for independence as best they could. He didn't want a young American rabble-rouser spouting off and making trouble. I tried to obey that caution. The second was that I was not allowed to pay people for their participation, or specifically their blood, because that could lead people to demand payment from the government malaria teams for their blood smears, testing for malaria parasites. Otherwise, he had no problem with my plans.

During my first week in Eivo, those young men who dropped by to chat often started complaining about their treatment by the Australian plantation managers and government officers. They said, "These people won't let us eat with them – if they come here, they sit down and eat by themselves – you are different from them." Then, they'd complain about being bossed around in different circumstances, or being cursed at or physically abused. I said, "I understand what you're saying and I don't know your situation well since I just arrived here. But you have to understand; I have to be careful what I say because the Aussies can kick me out if they hear I'm saying critical things about them, no matter how I feel." I was trying to be honest with them so they understood a little more about my own situation. The most important thing for them to understand was that I had no power to alter their circumstances. I always tried to be as open as I could about my motives and my situation when people began to discuss things like that, and that's also clear in the Introduction to that first monograph – naturally, they wanted to know what I was trying to accomplish for myself – was I going to make a lot of money, like the miners hoped to do from their land, or what? I said, "Well, you know, I'm trying to get my book done about the differences between people here, and that will help get me finally out of school and get a job." And they said, "Oh, so you're trying to become a teacher!" And I said, "That's right." That they could understand as a reasonable goal, and it was not too exploitative of them.

Other members of our teams in subsequent years had varied experiences. Some of them were extremely successful, becoming friends and confidants of local people, and others were not. John Rhoads, a part of our 1978-1980 team, who became assistant professor at Yale before he left academics, was excellent in the field. He was conscientious about trying to help people. They spoke extremely approvingly of him. Interestingly, he came from an old Quaker family in Wilmington, Delaware that had had a hard time, losing all their money just before the Civil War, because they were abolitionists involved in the Underground Railroad.

1978-1980 field team. Kevin Mohr, John Rhoads, and JSF. Wareham, Massachusetts.

The opposite was true for another member of our follow-up expedition in 1979, Kevin Mohr, who ended up hating being there, and was a failure. I heard stories when I went back of how he would keep to himself at night, not talk to anyone, and simply do exercises in his room (sit-ups, push-ups), which people found particularly odd. He also kept a long journal, as you know, that will go in the archive. Although I had it planned, he didn't get on-site training from either John or me about how to behave, or at least he didn't heed our suggestions. He insisted on going out without any overlap with either of us in the field, because he wanted to stay just a little longer at home with his girlfriend (she threw him over after he went to the field, much to his total dismay – a major reason he left early). Kevin became enmeshed in lousy bargaining situations, which you just can't do in Melanesia. His journal suggests at one point, because of a dispute over assistant wages, that things were stolen from him, and he had trouble getting people to carry baggage for him from a village down to the road.

People there may overcharge you for things in comparison with what they'd charge each other, but that was understandable. For example, in the Lau Lagoon area of Malaita, there's a weekly trading market between groups from the beach and bush. One day I said, "Let's go to the market and I can buy some fish." A local friend said, "Not you. I will go to the market and buy the fish and you can pay me back. If you go there they'll charge you twice or three times more than me." Everybody knew what the deal was. They also expected me to pay a higher wage to an assistant than a plantation worker would expect.

There were times when someone demanded considerably higher pay, for example Peter Tevu, who was a wonderful colleague, assistant, and informant in Nagovisi. Peter had been an informant and good friends with Don Mitchell and Jill Nash (cultural anthropologists in Nagovisi) and he knew a good bit about the mining company that was underway in central Bougainville. He knew what a European salary would be and how worthwhile he was to us. His son was working in the mine at that time, I believe, and their pay scale was "out of sight" in comparison to what had existed for local people. We were staying in Peter's house, or his neighbor's house, and he was our primary informant and assistant.

So he wanted a considerably higher salary, and I had to give it to him, particularly after he began to get especially agitated about it one day.

Of course, the cultural anthropologists, who lived in the same area for much longer periods of time, had similar issues, usually even more intense, as I mentioned in the case of Keesing and Maranda. The cultural anthropologists who worked in South Bougainville, Gene Ogan, Jill Nash and Don Mitchell, had excellent relations with people in those areas as far as I heard. If I had to generalize, the more modernized the group, the more individual and varied were the responses to the cultural anthropologists – the sort of group reactions that developed to Keesing and Maranda didn't usually apply in those instances. I would hear interesting stories in each area, sort of like checking up on how successful the cultural anthropologists had been in developing working relationships with people.

Perhaps the worst situation developed with the Aita in north Bougainville. John Rutherford was the cultural anthropology student there supported by the Harvard expedition. He was obviously a difficult character. I met him and his wife briefly in Hawaii, just before they went to the field in 1969. He had a lovely French wife whom everybody liked, including the Aita, but he was a bossy Brit, so that the gossip I heard from other expedition members was that when the expedition left the Aita, a major dispute erupted between Rutherford and the Aita. Of course there were refrigerators, generators, chairs, tables, and a lot of other equipment that the Harvard expedition couldn't keep for another two years – and this was way up in the mountains – a difficult five or six hour walk from the coast. Usually, they donated things to a local cooperating mission or government hospital. It was left up to Rutherford to take care of all this equipment, and my understanding was that he tried to sell at least some of it to the Aita for his own benefit, and they wouldn't buy it. They understood; what was he going to do? He wasn't going to carry all these things down the mountain himself. That was the situation he got into.

When I went up there in 1978 (obviously with no introduction from him), I asked, "*Dispela John Rutherford, emi gutpela or nogutpela?*" (Translation: "This guy John Rutherford, was he a good or bad person?"). The Aita answered, "*Em, emi gutpela liklik* (He was good, a little bit – he was O.K., I guess)," which was damning with faint praise, as they say, and of course the Aita were diffident and difficult people to work with in the first place.

The Aita were shy and, as they say in the Solomons, bushy in those days; they were the hillbillies of Bougainville. It was hard to understand them, even their names, so we had problems identifying people. They had strange accents and seemed to mumble or talk through their noses, and their language is famous for having only a few phonemes – less than 20. Peter Tevu, from Nagovisi, was working with me at the time, and he thought they were simply hilarious and tried to imitate them. Later on, I couldn't get them to cooperate in donating blood samples to make cell lines. Just as a final comment – Rutherford never finished his dissertation, and according to Oliver (saying this with appropriately raised eyebrows in obvious distaste and disapproval), Rutherford's final remark when he was leaving grad school was, "F--k anthropology."

Aita boys in traditional upe hats and bows and arrows. 1978.

In Malaita, there were three anthropologists studying groups that were not terribly far apart so that people could compare their experiences with anthropologists. For example, in Baegu, which was just inland from the Lau Lagoon people, a number of people complained to me. "Those anthropologists out in Lau, the Marandas, send them new fishing nets and all kinds of nice things, but our anthropologist hardly keeps in contact with us and he sends us nothing – one old typewriter was all. So, we're ashamed of our anthropologist."

There were all these kinds of unreal expectations that people often built up about anthropologists. I think this has been an important point that has been overlooked in anthropological field situations, including the unfortunate Yanomami situation.

JR: What do you mean, specifically – how the anthropologist negotiates how he is going to get by in the field? Or how the anthropologist negotiates with the government what is acceptable fieldwork practice?

JF: Well, both. When a cultural anthropologist comes and lives in a remote, marginal population for an extended period of time, he or she necessarily develops a role in that group, usually as a mediator and advisor in dealing with the outside world. This inevitably leads to complicated situations and high expectations, especially given the cargo cult environment in Island Melanesia. Because I never lived for an extended period in one place, I managed to avoid this situation for the most part, I think.

Nevertheless, you could always end up in a situation like Mohr or Rutherford did, where you're stuck with all this equipment in a bush village and nobody wants to talk to you. In the South Pacific, one common way of showing disrespect is stealing, which also reveals your total helplessness in their village. We did have some of that in Kwaio in the Harvard expedition, in spite of generally good relations. After the last work day and celebratory pig feast, a number of us woke up to find our shoes were missing, and Roger had to go and try and find them, or rather to convince his contacts to find out who had them and to return them. So, as Ogan said, it was critically important to establish yourself as a friendly guest and someone who could create a positive kind of interest. People had to feel that your presence there was not a hindrance or an annoyance at all, and could be beneficial.

Identity as a Fieldworker

JR: Do you want to talk about, because I don't think we got this on tape, your identity as a fieldworker?

JF: Well, after reading over some of my old letters home, it's clear that the year or 10 months I spent alone in the field, 1966-1967, was quite important to me. I found that I could operate as a fieldworker effectively. While it was true there were people and groups who said they didn't want to be part of the expedition or survey (and in retrospect, ethicists take that as a good thing – I didn't coerce people), in general I found I could go into a village with however small my team was, even just a local contact, effectively do a survey and come back years later, with good feelings. I became a known entity. In the South Pacific, the old adage is that the first time you enter to a village you're a stranger, the second time you're a guest, and the third time you're part of the family. I felt that I could operate in this situation well, and I had also found a situation that was going to be interesting scientifically and professionally.

The letters I wrote home make it clear that I realized I was having success by about January 1967, midway through my fieldwork period. That's when the first results came back from blood typing in Australia that the villages I'd already covered in Bougainville had considerable distinctions. I had found more than enough variability among groups to be interesting. I'd gotten a large enough sample, according to the design I'd worked out, and the geographical distribution was going to be interesting, even within this one island. I'm sure my success as a fieldworker was a major reason I liked to go back. In many instances, it was like visiting old friends.

A Fieldwork Failure

I never had a real failure in fieldwork until I went to west Timor, Indonesia, in 1973, which is a different area culturally and politically.

I didn't understand the Indonesian government protocol for issuing research visas, and I was not generally familiar or comfortable with the social environment in eastern Indonesia. I didn't like it there because it was a feudal, hierarchical society. There was a pasha who owned the water source, and he had one son in the local government, one in the military, and another in the clergy – still the feudal master. If you had the pasha's permission, he would literally line everybody up and you could do what you wanted with them in terms of taking blood or anything else. There was no real sense, as far as I was concerned, of a discussion or informed consent or anything with the subjects (I don't recall if I took the pasha's blood – probably not).

JR: You wrote a little about this in the chapter you contributed to Trudy Turner's volume.

JF: Yes, it developed into quite a scene. Jim Fox, another Harvard trained cultural anthropologist who graduated with me, now at ANU in Canberra, got me interested in the area because there are some Papuan languages spoken there. With his advice, I got my letters of approval in order from the Indonesian government scientific bureau (LIPI), and presented them to the Indonesian customs officer when I arrived in west Timor from Darwin, Australia. The customs officer said the letters were fine, but there was no research visa issued, and I should go see the governor. I went to the military governor of Timor, and he said I couldn't get a visa without going to the Immigration Office in Jakarta, which was about 1,000 miles to the west. I innocently thought I might be able to arrange it by telegram, and he said whatever I could arrange would be fine, but I couldn't begin work without a visa. So I sent telegrams for a couple of days with no answer, but meanwhile, while I was waiting for a response, I went up to the first village (with the pasha), and after explaining what I wanted to do with the pasha and giving him a nice shirt at Jim's suggestion, did decide, with his approval, to go ahead and begin collections while I was waiting for the permission. I collected about 30 samples and measured some people (a big mistake). That Sunday, I came down the mountain in an open jeep with the full cooler on my lap with a big red cross plastered on it, and we passed the governor on the road on the way into the hills (I waved).

The next morning, at the little hotel I was staying at (called a *losman* – one toilet room and one open well for all the guests), a large military policeman with rifle on his shoulder came to summon me to the military barracks. The manager of the *losman* was clearly terrified, and by the time I got to the military barracks I was apprehensive myself. There were a lot of cases of violence involving the Indonesian military then. I was taken to the Major's office. He was dressed in his white tennis outfit, just off the court. He said "Hi Sonny, sit down – you want a Coke?" (I accepted). "I spent two years in air force training in Texas. Now, the Governor is angry with you – what are you doing? Tell me what it's all about." I explained my situation with the visa, and he said, "You can't get the visa by telegram, you've got to go to Jakarta and present your permission letters to the different bureaucratic offices. That may take you a few days." I said it was difficult or impossible to get a plane reservation to Jakarta in that season (the start of the rainy season). He said "No problem, I'll get you on the plane *tomorrow morning*! Then you can come back with your visa." So I was basically sent out, and I didn't come back. I had already been away from my family a long time, about 6 weeks, and my baby daughter was only 1 year old. Returning with a visa would have made a long delay, and I also realized transshipping blood samples to Sydney via Bali would have been difficult without me accompanying each shipment to Bali from Timor – different from the situation in Papua New Guinea.

Fieldwork success

JR: And I wonder if you could speculate more – you said, "For whatever reasons, I felt comfortable." Could you talk about what it was about you, as a person, and your experiences that enabled you to get along so well in the field, or to want to stay there?

JF: O.K. Well, I think, first of all, being an American at that period was an asset. Because, I think—did I talk about the legacy of cargo cults?

JR: Yes.

JF: So, in many instances, I had to be careful not to promise too much. This was also true of the cultural anthropologists as well, the people who lived in these different villages – most of them were Americans. Now since I was moving rapidly through most of these areas (one week per village, more or less) I avoided that for the most part. I was seen as somebody, in most cases, who could offer something positive quickly, hopefully in terms of health. Following the Harvard example, in later expeditions I often tried to have a doctor along to hold a clinic, or give money to help train a local nurse. We were certainly a source of great curiosity, so that people would crowd around where I was doing my measuring or interviewing or blood sampling. I think my presence and my curiosity about them gave them a sense of self-importance as well.

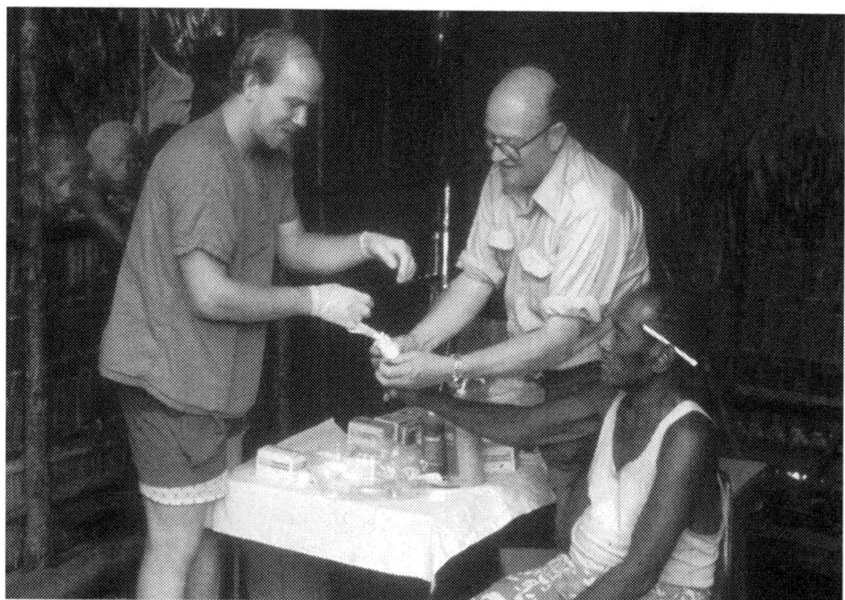

Lot and Jesse Page holding clinic. Foueda, Lau Lagoon. 1980.

People thought I worked hard (and I did). Just as a sidelight that illustrates this – when I was first in Bougainville, there was one Siwai man who was a microcephalic and obviously not smart, so that he couldn't speak Tok Pisin, which was a real sign of being dim – almost everybody spoke it in Bougainville. He did speak the Siwai language (Motuna), but of course I don't know how well. So I measured him (making him stand, sit down, turn around, raise his arms, and so on), and I took his fingerprints, and I asked about his genealogy, and I got that from his relatives. Then I said, "*Pinis nau* (I'm finished)." He got up, turned to the spectators, said something in Motuna I couldn't understand, and everybody around thought it was the funniest thing they'd ever heard. They started laughing, holding their sides, and rolling around on the ground and I said, "What did he say?" And one person said that the microcephalic had said, "Boy, I feel so tired. That was hard work!" They thought it was just terribly ironic, because I was the one who worked so hard. They'd never seen anybody doing this sort of, what they called "hard work" (*hatwok*), where I was sitting down in a chair and measuring and writing and fingerprinting for hours on end – not cutting down trees, gardening, or hard physical labor of the sort they were used to, but you know, a different kind of work. So, I was sort of the greatest show in the village for a while. So that was not bad, that was not bad at all. I did tell people that I hoped to be able to make a story about the diversity in Bougainville or the past migrations that might have come through. Now we do have a nice account that we've tried to get out, but I think I'm going to have to go back and tell them the final story, so...

JR: I'm going to keep pushing you a little bit more, just in terms of – we've talked a little bit about people whom it just didn't work out for in the field, on a personal level. As we've been talking you've definitely given a lot of signals about what it meant to you to be successful in the field, to deal with the loneliness and those day-to-day functions, so I guess what I'm wanting to get at is sort of that next layer –

JF: I'm sorry; I sort of got off track –

JR: No, no, it's all relevant – how to get by in the field and why did you feel – as you clearly did – that you were so good at that?

JF: Well, you know, I think people in these kinds of situations where you have Australians or Americans suddenly living among Melanesian populations, clearly at first you fall into neat preconceived dichotomies and categories. However, people are also ultimately quite sophisticated in the way they judge others and different kinds of personalities. In Bougainville, for example, from my perspective, I found a lot of interesting people to talk to, interesting characters, as well as alcoholics, megalomaniacs, and dull personalities. I didn't have to live there forever to find out these personality differences. They didn't have to be important people, but a lot of people had keen insights into their own society. On the other hand, some people were totally crazy – you could recognize the diversity in personalities, in spite of the cultural and linguistic barriers.

The obverse of this was that that they were certainly able to distinguish personality differences between individuals, the Europeans who were there. Nobody liked Rutherford whether they were Aita, whether they were Americans, or Brits.

I think I have an easy-going personality and that came through to people. I was not threatening. There are even a number of "Jonathans" named for me in some of the places I visited a few times (there are some "John Rhoads" and "Ogan" kids as well). If I have a personality aspect that has caused me a problem, it's that I have tended to shy away from conflict and not be forceful enough (my ex-wives would attest to that). It is easy to see where this came from in my background – "getting along" and ingratiating myself with others has always been my first impulse.

Political History of the Southwest Pacific

JR: Could you say a little bit about the Australians? And could you talk more about your sense of the significance of your being an American in the field? If you think it's appropriate, maybe you could also talk about the broader context of change, with the mine coming to Bougainville.

JF: Well, first of all, there's a history of Australian, German, and British influence in Papua New Guinea and the Solomon Islands as early colonial powers. The best thing about this area is that the colonial period was relatively short. It was only from the 1880s until the 1950s, 60s, 70s, and it was rather minor in its extent and impact. The Germans were early. They set up coconut plantations in the Gazelle Peninsula of New Britain (the Tolai area where George Koki is from), and along the north coast of New Guinea, and the German government followed.

Missions came in about the same period. The British had a smaller plantation presence in the South Solomons also before World War I, and the Australians, primarily out of fear of the Germans, demanded the British establish a colony on the south part of the New Guinea Island as Papua. European influence beyond the plantations, missions, and government offices was generally sharply circumscribed. After the First World War, the Germans were kicked out of New Guinea, and British and Australian influence expanded in these areas, now governed as mandated territories under the League of Nations (and later the United Nations).

World War II was a major event almost everywhere, first with the Japanese kicking out the Aussies and Brits, and then with the US Navy and Marines with Australians overpowering the Japanese. New roads and airstrips were built or expanded, the missions expanded, as did health care, schooling, and plantations as well. Mining developed in some areas, and independence came to both areas in the mid-1970s. Large areas of the best land on the east coast of Bougainville were turned into plantations ("alienated" is the term used for being bought by foreigners) where local people would go and work and earn enough wages to go home and pay for a bride. Bride price is a big element of most Melanesian societies. The same kind of thing happened in the British Solomons. The government was closely associated with the plantation owners and that sort of development or exploitation. Plantations are never a good thing, in terms of the developing dichotomies between the owners, overseers, and the cheap labor that's required, and that's one of the things that caused the infamous Bell incident with the Kwaio I mentioned.

In the Solomon Islands the government instituted a head tax on the local population at the instigation of the plantation owners. William Bell, who was a very sophisticated and smart government officer from Australia, who had succeeded in pacifying Malaita almost single-handedly, said, "Now, wait a minute, if you tax these people, they're going to want to know what they're getting in return. Roads? Boats? Schools? You're not offering them anything. The only people who are providing them anything in the way of healthcare or schooling are the missionaries." And the higher-ups in the government said, "We're going to do it anyway," because this was a way to coerce men to go work on the plantations, to earn money to pay the taxes, because the plantations always had problems in recruiting cheap labor. So that's how that situation developed. That's why Bell ultimately got killed. He had to go collect the head taxes and the Kwaio basically said, "No taxation without representation!"

You had the missions as one locus of European influence that was usually not so heavily Australian or British (early on, lots of Germans and French, and later Americans as well as Australians). In Bougainville, the Catholic mission became heavily American around WWII. So you had a bunch of rowdy Americans who thought they knew better than the Australian bureaucrats and missionaries. A lot of the Aussies were good people, but some were the sort who couldn't make it back home. The Australian patrol officers, called in Tok Pisin *kiaps*, or captains, were sometimes just 20 years old. They would make these walking tours through the bush and they were the face of the colonial government in the villages. Some, of course, were excellent. They would dictate policy – "You've got to build latrines, you've got to consolidate housing into 'line villages'" (closely situated houses that were easy to visit and control rather than dispersed hamlets). So there was a tension between the missionaries who were providing elementary schooling, by and large, and most of the healthcare, as ways of showing people the power of western religion and thereby recruiting converts, and the governments, who were working more closely with the plantations. It came to be a national distinction too, because of the difference in where the missionaries were coming from. It was a little bit different in the Solomon Islands, where the Anglican Church and the Seventh Day Adventists predominated (hence more Australian and British), but it was different in heavily Catholic Bougainville – not so many Australians, almost no British, a few Germans, and lots of Americans.

With the discovery of large scale copper and gold deposits in Bougainville in the early 1960s (this was the same time, as the Harvard expedition was conceived), the mine that developed became the basis for modernization on an entirely different scale, with the clear prospect of hundreds of millions of dollars coming into this region, this neglected part of Papua New Guinea. Bougainville was sometimes not even shown on maps of the Territory of Papua New Guinea in earlier periods. The reason it was considered a part of Papua New Guinea at all was just one of those curious happenstances of colonial history – because a woman who was famous in the area, nick-named "Queen" Emma by her jealous male competitors, ran a group of successful plantations in the Gazelle Peninsula of New Britain near modern Rabaul, and she used Bougainville as a recruiting source for workers. Because of the development of early plantations there, Rabaul was the capitol of German New Guinea, and when that became a colony or official territory, Bougainville was included, but not the rest of the Solomon Islands, which was sort of wild cannibal country with little prospect for economic exploitation. That became the British Solomon Islands Protectorate and ultimately the nation of Solomon Islands.

In the mid-1960s, the building of this large open pit mine at Panguna in Bougainville had begun, which was to provide the major income for the entire Territory of Papua New Guinea ($60 million or so per year in royalties early on). Douglas Oliver, among others, was asked to advise the mine on how to make the mine an acceptable development to the local people, because the mining officials were worried they might have something like the African Congo situation develop, with revolutions or government expropriation of the mine. They had some smart men who were in charge of the mine, and there was one, Frank Espie, who said, "I will judge this mine a success if it is not nationalized by the new national government, which we know is coming." And independence did come in the 1970s. He made the unprecedented offer to the new national government of a 20% share in the mining operation. Well, of course, in spite of their best efforts at trying to make an acceptable mine that pleased the local people as well as the developing national government, it did wind up with a kind of civil war or rebellion after 1986 (the last time I was there before 2003 was 1985), when the mine was shut down by violence. The Papua New Guinea military came in after dynamiting and other sabotage of the mine developed, and they call that "The Crisis" that lasted 10 years. The mine is still shut down and there is a new generation of young men with little or no education and a lot of guns.

The Panguna copper mine. Bougainville. 1985.

The mining officials saw themselves as having divergent interests from the Australian governing authority in the 1960s and '70s, and certainly divergent from the mission, so it was a tricky proposition politically. I don't know if they could have succeeded because of the inherent conflict between the local Bougainvilleans and the new national government that emerged. For one thing, their salary scale for all their employees was much higher than anything the plantation owners or the government thought was acceptable or could offer.

The missionaries didn't like the mines because they thought the miners were a rowdy bunch, and they were – hard-drinking guys from all over the place, from Ukraine, not just Australia, and there were always problems with them – with prostitution of local women as an obvious example. However, at another level, the missions resented the obvious attraction of the mine as a competing new power center. People who would have otherwise trained for the priesthood chose to take high paying jobs in the mine. The mine did make people much more aware of their own status and rights. The company did build a technical high school, and they wanted to train people to take on as high paying jobs in the hierarchy of the mine as they could. A modern hospital was built with company funds. People were encouraged to buy company shares (people who did were disappointed with the results, however). That was probably Oliver's and other people's advice, to try to get away from the sort of plantation duality. There certainly was no segregation in the mess halls or bunk arrangements. A lot of local people rose up through the mine hierarchy to rather high levels.

And people began to say, "This is our land, it's a Bougainville mine, our own resource, not a Papua New Guinea mine, and we want to be separate from Papua New Guinea – we have never felt part of that government or administration, and we don't like New Guinea men who have worked here, either on plantations or in the mine. We want the money not to support the government of Papua New Guinea, but to stay here in the province, like Katanga in the Congo."

It still remains a continuing controversy, but at this point there is a so-called peace. There's going to be a plebiscite for independence in the next few years, and there's no question that Bougainville will vote for independence, and there's also no question that the government of Papua New Guinea will resist and will fight the economic consequences, if the mine reopens. There's still a major tension there, especially concerning how the mining royalties should be divided, should the mine be reopened.

Conclusions on the Effect of Modernization in the Solomons

JR: I find this to be a compelling story, especially going back to some of the early writings surrounding the justifications for the Solomon Islands Project – that it was an effort to study societies undergoing transition and change and I know you did a follow up study around the mine. To give some perspective, I'll ask another hypothetical question: if Damon had remained involved, how do you think he might have interpreted these changes in terms of health and modernity, the health of the community, and things like that?

JF: Well, that was certainly the way he framed part of the goal of the expedition, without talking about a longitudinal study, because I don't think that aspect ever came into the original proposal (I never saw it, so I may be wrong).[12] With regard to things like blood pressure and weight and size changes, what he and Lot Page attempted to do was to rank societies in terms of their acculturation status at the time they were studied (that sort of ranking is difficult to do, controversial and a lot of cultural anthropologists didn't like it). However, groups also often tended to cluster together by island in things like blood pressure and weight, suggesting that other factors, hereditary, were involved. However, I did use that same scale of acculturation in the follow up studies in 1978-80, and we were able to talk about the important changes that occurred over a 10 or 15 year interval, during this 1960s-1970s period. It's quite logical to assume that, if Damon had lived and gotten the funding, he'd have also done follow-ups of some sort. I would guess it would have tried to replicate as much of the earlier data collection as possible, which would have been massive.

Permanent housing. Pomalate, Nagovisi.1985.

By 1980, the mine was going full blast and a lot of people were earning good salaries, primarily as truck drivers and machine

12 Note: The grant proposals for the project stored in the Harvard Solomon Islands Project files at the Peabody Museum Archive suggest that Damon did envision the Project in longitudinal terms. – JR, June 23, 2009.

operators, and then coming home and spending money, with new kind of diets – even new kinds of houses. This contrasted with the old traditional, what were called "*sak-sak*" houses, which were airy and nice, but that's a different story. We found some of the groups changed dramatically in obesity, especially, strangely enough, the Ontong-Javanese population, which was unaffected by the Bougainville mine (they'd developed trochus shell and bêche de mer collecting as cash crops). They became fat, especially the women. It seems also, from what Chuck Weitz did with exercise physiology tests in these modernizing groups, that the younger generation was much less fit than the older generation, especially the women. The older women would still just climb up and down the mountains in their bare feet, and they were used to doing much harder gardening labor than the young women, who were beginning to be involved with, or the beneficiaries of, the cash economy. So, yes, we could see real distinctions in fitness and obesity, as well as size, over that time period.

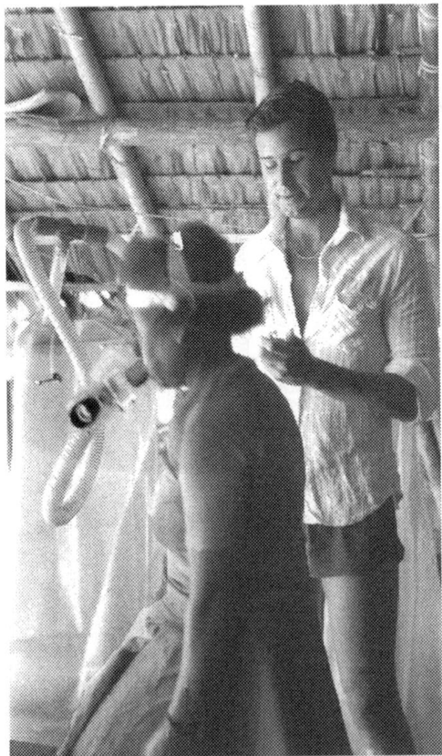

Exercise physiology. David Byerley exercising a Nagovisi woman on a riser. 1985.

I think that's one of the most interesting things that we published about the changes over time. However, some groups didn't change much at all. The Kwaio, who had not been affected dramatically at that point by modernization, continued to follow what we thought was an older bush pattern of weight gain during adulthood – or in their case, weight loss with increasing age, especially in adult women. After about age 30, they tended to get thinner, and thinner and thinner through the childbearing years, menopause and old age, rather than accumulating fat the way we do, and Solomon Islanders do, in the more acculturated populations. This was a major distinction.

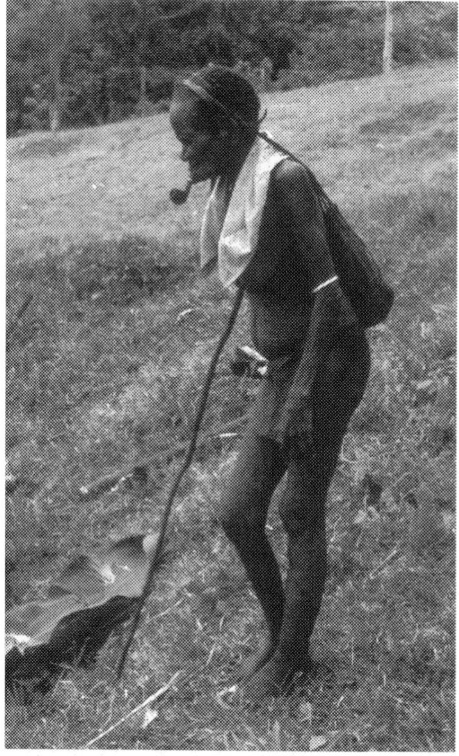

Elderly Kwaio woman. 1966.

The Developing Role of Genetics

JR: Looking at the Solomon Islands Project, there's every kind of measurement imaginable being taken. Your work winds up going in a direction focused on what can be determined by blood-based analysis.

How did the technology and your interests relate? Also, what is your understanding of how this fits within broader trends in biological anthropology?

JF: Well, from the beginning, that is from 1966 to1967 and even earlier, it was becoming apparent that there were some interesting distinctions to be made within Melanesian populations even with regard to some of the simple genetic markers people were taking then. In particular, there was Gene Giles' work.

A few years before I began, Gene Giles had done a straight blood-genetics study in the villages near Lae in the Markham Valley, New Guinea, emphasizing immunoglobulin (Gm and Inv) differences. He had found a neat distinction between Austronesian-speaking groups and Papuan-speaking groups (also known as non-Austronesian-speakers). Now, Gene was along on the first Harvard Solomons expedition and was then an assistant professor at Harvard while I was just contemplating my fieldwork. I was getting his advice, as well as Gene Ogan's, on fieldwork techniques and what to include in my survey regimen, and it was clear I had to take blood, if nothing else. I wanted to see if this distinction between Austronesian-speakers and non-Austronesian-speakers held up in Bougainville. Giles had published a paper with Gene Ogan and Arthur Steinberg on this distinction which had gotten a good deal of notice among physical anthropologists. He had included some Nasioi from Marai with Gene's help, but that was all that had been done on Bougainville before the Harvard Solomon Islands Expedition – his coverage was otherwise restricted to the Markham Valley of New Guinea.

I had three collaborating genetics contacts set up through Giles and Damon – Walsh, Steinberg, and Blumberg, as I mentioned. Gene had said, "Walsh will be excellent. He'll want to be senior author on the first publication, but after that he'll say, 'My role has been properly acknowledged.' He'll be prompt and conscientious. Don't send them to R.T. Simmons in Melbourne. Use Walsh." Walsh was a generous man and I developed a fine relationship with Steinberg, too. However, Steinberg said, "You've got to send me the genealogies along with the samples." I said, "Don't you want the genealogies *after* you type the sera?" And he said, "No, I want them *before*, so I can make sure our typing is consistent with the pedigrees." I was uneasy with this, since it might bias his results. But, in the end, I sent him copies of all my village genealogies. Anyway, it was clear that the blood genetic work had a real importance early on because of what it had already shown in other studies, and then by what Walsh found in the earliest results from Eivo [that there was no type B blood among them].

Now some other people subsequently said that the dichotomy in Gm that Giles found in the Markham Valley didn't hold in other parts of New Guinea. Sue Serjeantson said, "That distinction doesn't work in the area I studied (along the north coast of New Guinea near Madang – the Bogia area) and maybe the Markham is unusual – perhaps Austronesians just intruded there recently."

Well, the distinction didn't hold up the same way in my Bougainville results either. However, another immunoglobulin marker, Inv^1, showed a dramatic declining frequency distribution in my data. This was a distinction between north and south Bougainville, not between Austronesians and Papuans. When his lab results were done, Arthur Steinberg said, "You know, you ought to submit this to *Science.* This sharp change across such a small region is quite remarkable." So we did submit a short report, in about 1968, shortly after I got Steinberg's results. It was rejected by *Science*, and I was dejected. However, that was not the end of that story. At the next Physical Anthropology annual meetings, Moses Schanfield, who'd been at Harvard but transferred to Michigan, came up to me and said, "Hi Jon, I reviewed your paper for *Science* – I rejected it!" My jaw dropped, because I was surprised he would have been the reviewer for *Science* as a grad student, and also because he volunteered the information (his advisor Henry Gershowitz probably had given it to him to review). He was known as being quite brash.

JR: Did he offer any justification?

JF: I can't remember, but whatever he said didn't impress me. I was no longer crestfallen but just mad. It was because of that incident that I turned around and submitted it, unchanged, to *Nature* and they accepted it!

JR: Wow. What do you think his motivation for doing that was?

JF: Honestly, I can't remember. Moses has always been an outspoken fellow. He wrote a chapter in our recent 2007 Oxford University Press book. It was all on the gamma globulins, the Gm and Inv, revisited, worldwide. So we're on fine terms now, but, anyway, I'm getting off the track, I'm talking about . . .

JR: To continue, before we were talking about the developing role of the blood collection in terms of the genetic work.

JF: Yes, so that's why I had to have Steinberg's Gm and Inv analysis involved (because of Giles' work) and whatever else it was that Walsh could do, haptoglobins or transferrins, Kell, Duffy, the gamut of blood genetics available at that time – the more the better, as far as I was concerned, since I wanted to calculate overall genetic relationships among groups, and compare these with anthropometric similarities among groups, as well as fingerprint and linguistic similarities. That was the big plan, and that's what I followed for my thesis. There were analytic difficulties in using gene frequencies to calculate such relationships or genetic distances, especially since there were so few different markers then to use, but that was my objective. It turned out that the anthropometric measurements performed best and clearest in the thesis and subsequent book published in 1975 as *Patterns of Human Variation*.

Subsequently Walsh's lab worked on some plasma protein markers; haptoglobins, as many markers as we could get, red cell acid phosphatase, whatever the battery was that Walsh could handle. Laurie Lai was the person who did some of the subsequent lab work. I ended up being upset with him because he threw out the remainder of my samples much later on, without asking my permission, from Buka Island and west Timor (that were collected in that failed 1973 trip). These would have been extremely useful for later mtDNA work, for example. There is still almost nothing from Eastern Indonesia, 35 years later.

JR: So, I was going to ask, what was the protocol for sending these samples all over to places where you were not? How did you manage them and what was your sense of what you would do with the samples after the analysis? How did that figure into your thinking at the time?

JF: Well, I remember when we were watching Jerry Bloom taking the blood samples in the 1966 Solomon Islands Expedition, Howard Bailit said "The blood is gold, and it's going to be important down the line." I thought to myself, "Really? I suppose he's right." At that time I had no real comprehension that blood could be available as a long-lasting resource for future research. For example, no one conceived of being able to analyze the DNA directly from blood. Still, there was the sense from the outset that, even though the genetics results weren't terribly powerful in the 1960s, they inevitably would become increasingly important in the following decades as more and more genetic markers were identified. The main issue was which parts of the blood (red cells, plasma, or other tissues) to preserve. The prevalent notion was that protein structure, determined directly by gene variation, would be the most informative material. I was mostly concerned about the actual sampling regimen in that period, assuming the proper genetic analyses would become apparent as things progressed.

We also had no idea at the outset that I would collect 2,000 samples. Walsh became concerned early on. He said, "What's going on there? This is getting expensive! How about just doing every other village?" But then, when the results seemed to be variable and interesting (the type B variation I mentioned), he said, "Well, we'll test what you want." We suspected from that result that other variants would show distinctions, so he said then, "Well, we'll go on with your intensive sampling scheme." He wanted to keep some of the samples there, in Sydney. Steinberg was much more conscientious about retaining frozen plasma samples since he knew there would be new Gm allotypes being discovered in the future for certain, so he tried to keep as much as possible for retyping. Subsequently he had a lab fire that destroyed most of the plasmas, but not all of them. So we were able to reuse those samples from Steinberg's lab for the mitochondrial DNA analyses (mtDNA), from all of those 18 villages I had covered in the 1960s (that's the first paper of the new series, Merriwether *et al.* 1999).

JR: So – is it accurate to say that there was a general sense that these materials might be useful later on?

JF: Yes. The plasmas and then the red cells – remember, the general sense became during this period, "The red cells aren't going to be much use beyond the surface antigens (mature red cells have no nucleus, and therefore no DNA, and are mostly hemoglobin inside – it's the protein envelope that has the blood types and other antigens), but you want to save the plasmas because there are so many proteins there, and new ways will inevitably develop to analyze them. The white blood cells in the plasma were of course the real ultimate and unexpected payoff, since they did have DNA in their nuclei, and of course lots of mitochondrial DNA (in the 1960s, there was no prospect of directly analyzing the DNA). Anyway, the red cells would lyse and then they'd be more difficult to work with, and they'd often be discarded. The emphasis was on plasma protein analysis. One exception was the material that Andy Merriwether ultimately worked with from Neel's Yanomami study – this is the kind of thing you might want to ask Andy – he got mitochondria from the red cell samples that Neel had originally suspended in glycerol, because they had not been thoroughly purified. There were some residual white cells, containing mtDNA.

JR: So Walsh sent your samples to Steinberg. Did you bring them back to Temple at some point?

JF: Yes, much later. I kept them in a freezer in my office/lab, a simple -20 F temperature. Only more recently, 10 years ago, did the department get a -80 F freezer. I believe most of Andy's are also -20 F. He almost had a heart-attack in Michigan, where one freezer was unplugged by a construction worker there, undetected for months, and mould grew in all the tubes inside. Yet the mtDNA amplified beautifully. Talk about ancient DNA studies…

To sum up, we always expected the "blood genetics" to steadily improve in value over time, but not as dramatically as it did. In one of Lewontin's old papers, he graphed the rate of discovery of new blood genetic variants over time, so there was every indication that the rate of discovery would continue to increase, although no one had any idea how fast DNA typing (first with RFLPs, then with sequencing) would develop and transform things. Early on, the amount of information to analyze from the small number of testable gene loci was rather small. Things have certainly changed! If you've got 750 microsatellites[13] to characterize an individual or population, things like analyzing fingerprint patterns become totally irrelevant or passé.

Possible Other Research Directions

JR: Can I ask you a hypothetical or a counterfactual question? What if you had been able to go to Africa, instead of winding up in Melanesia? How do you think . . . just for fun . . . how might your thinking would have changed or would you have been able to do a similar kind of project, let's say, if it had even occurred to you?

JF: Well, I think that there's no question that once I was plopped down in the South Pacific, it was logical to find some interesting problem there to study that was salient in that area. When I started in the Pacific, I didn't know it well because I had prepared Africa as a region for my exams. What was obvious to me at the outset was that the interesting feature of the Pacific was the great linguistic diversity that might possibly be related to genetic distinctions, so that was the thing to study. That's what I latched onto after talking to Giles and Ogan in Bougainville. It was later that I began to think about island size having an effect on both language and genetic diversity.

Last year, when I was in touch with Jeff Long at the University of Michigan (he's an excellent human population geneticist there with an anthropological background and he's been to New Guinea in the past, a man of few but pithy words), he said, referring to our *PLoS Genetics* paper, "Jonathan, it's a great paper, it's wonderful to see how your career has come together around this. But you know it's not surprising the pattern of variability you found there, because the people live on islands!" That is the fact of the Pacific. People live on islands, and so that's got to affect the pattern of genetic and language diversity.

13 Microsatellites are highly variable, repetitive segments of DNA, 2 to 5 base pairs in length, scattered throughout the genome in non-coding regions between genes or within genes.

I can't be sure what I would have done in Africa if I'd gone to study the San. It probably would have been a genetic comparison of San and neighboring populations speaking different languages, seeing how related they were to Bantu speakers there – how much intermixture we could detect, and so forth, and the Gm system would have been most important, probably in collaboration with Arthur Steinberg and Trevor Jenkins. However, I could well have gone in a different direction, since Lee's controversial work on San subsistence and survival strategies could well have influenced me to do something less strictly genetic, dealing with their comparative health, fertility, and so forth (his work suggested their hunter-gathering life style wasn't very stressful at all, a very controversial position). Remember, I only decided on the genetic and linguistic emphasis of my work after I arrived in Bougainville.

I don't recall what the early genetic studies of the San showed in terms of internal diversity – I think not much internal diversity. The people who did comparable work to mine on the Kalahari project were Henry Harpending and Trevor Jenkins. Henry was a year behind me in biological anthropology at Harvard, and is good in theoretical issues. Henry is now interested in looking for evidence of natural selection. He's not been involved in African genetics for some time. He's bright and also controversial – politically conservative. Sarah Tishkoff's recent African work is, at least in conception, something I always thought needed doing, and perhaps I might have ultimately done something along those lines. She will soon be publishing a fine paper on over 120 African population relationships, with my wife's analytic help.

Chapter 6.

Wisconsin: 1969-1971

JF: My first position after graduate school was at the University of Wisconsin. I call it my "Men's Room" post doc, which needs some explaining. A couple of years after I came back from the field, in 1968 I think, I presented the Bougainville material results for the first time at the annual meeting of physical anthropologists in Chapel Hill. I had been analyzing my collected materials for my thesis, still as a graduate student in Cambridge. This meant my first introduction to computer software programs and multivariate statistics.

The anthropometry, which we haven't talked about much, gave the most striking results, much more interesting than the rudimentary genetics. As I said before, I had taken just 12 different measurements on the adult males in the Bougainville villages, and the multivariate analysis of them showed not only a dramatic north-south distinction in Bougainville, but also showed that village multivariate averages (or centroids) clustered neatly by language group, even within that north-south distinction. Of course, I was following Howells' use of multivariate analysis in this instance. The northerners were bigger and broader than the southerners, both in the body and face.

I'd made a nice model of the results in the first three dimensions, and my talk was well received. After I gave it, I went to the men's room and Dick Osborne, who was a professor at Wisconsin, was standing next to me at the urinals, and he said, "Jonathan, I liked your paper a lot. Why don't you come to Wisconsin on a Population Council Post Doc?" And I said, "That sounds pretty good!" Osborne had a connection to the Population Council in New York, and I'm not sure how he made the case for supporting my work, because I think of the Population Council being primarily concerned with understanding the dynamics of population growth and population control. But I got the post doc and went out to Madison for a year – 1969 to 1970. Did you see pictures of the model?

JR: I didn't see it, but Muriel [Kirkpatrick, Director of the Temple Anthropology Lab] was telling me about it.

JF: I wish I could remake it. It was a plexiglass rectangular box with numbered balls suspended inside, representing the 18 Bougainville village scores in the multivariate analysis of anthropometric measurements. The colors of the balls represented the different languages spoken by the different villages, so in a sense it was four-dimentional. I bought the colored balls (big plastic beads with holes through for stringing) from Woolworth's. The same-colored balls, representing villages from a particular language group, clustered neatly together in the model. It was attractive as well as informative.

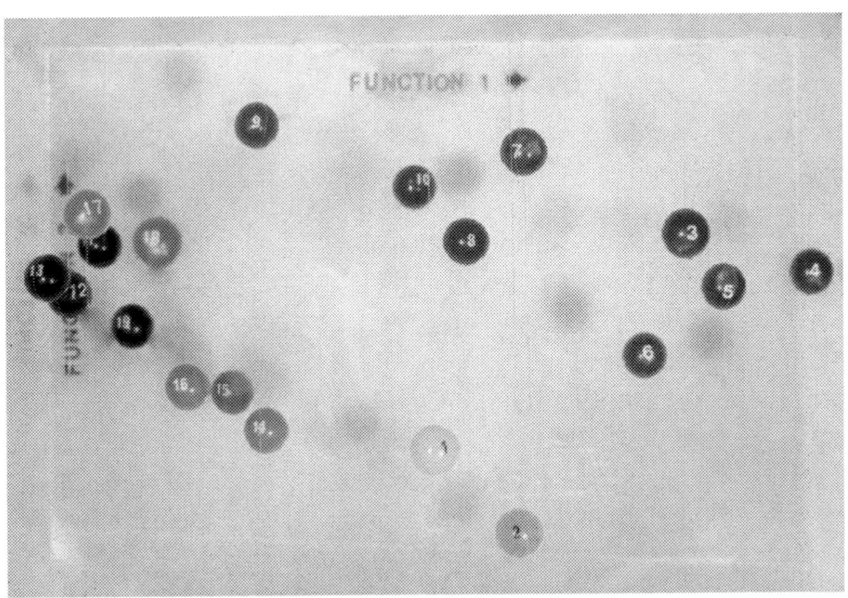

Model of the discriminant function analysis of measurements on men in Bougainville villages.

To make the model, I plotted the village scores on the first two dimensions from the analysis on two facing 8 ½ x 11-inch sheets of the plexiglass, and drilled holes through the plexiglass sheets at those 18 points. Then I constructed the box by gluing the panels together with acetone (there were five sides, with one side left open to manipulate the balls and string). I then strung a single transparent fishing line through the holes on the two opposing sides, looping the line through the appropriate ball as the line crossed to the other corresponding hole for that ball's 2 dimensional location. Looping the line through the ball held the ball in place, and having the loop pass over the glued number made the number always face up (by simple gravity). I could then slide the ball on the string to the correct position to represent the third dimension, and so on for all 18 balls, all strung on one continuous fishing line. The positions of the balls would remain fixed by the tension. The only glitch was that the plastic fishing line tended to sag after a while under the tension, so it had to be periodically tightened, and after a few years it finally it broke. I repaired and restrung it any number of times, but after a while, the plexiglass became heavily scratched, and it finally came apart.

I took this around with me when I got to Madison, to the Genetics Department. I wasn't associated with the Genetics Department – I was in Anthropology – but Osborne had suggested I ought to go over to Genetics and introduce myself to James Crow, which I did with some trepidation. Crow was a famous population geneticist there. Sewell Wright was also there, but he was a very old man at that point, perhaps in his late eighties or nineties. I went into Crow's office and said, "Dr. Crow I wanted to introduce myself – I'm here on a post doc and I want to tell you briefly about my work in the Pacific." He turned out to be a lovely man. The model intrigued him, and after asking me about my research, he informed me that, for my genetics, I'd performed "quasi-complete population sampling," a phrase I used thereafter (it meant I'd sampled essentially everyone I could get hold of in each village).

Toward the end of our chat, he said, "You need to talk to Ken Kidd." Ken was studying the genetics of Icelandic cattle and their relation to cattle in Europe. I went straight down to his lab in the basement, showed him the model, and Ken got excited about the genetic aspect of my work, because he was making tree diagrams out of the cow genetic distance relationships – which populations were related to which. He said, "We can do that with your Bougainville genetics data." So, he did what is still considered a statistically appropriate way of constructing tree representations of these population distances, and we published it as a joint paper in the *American Journal of Human Genetics* in 1971, one of my early publications. He used the maximum likelihood estimation procedure for finding the best tree representation (with so many populations that becomes a major problem). It took a long time to run on the mainframe computers in those days, however. Laura Sgaramella-Zonta was also involved in that paper. Along with Blumberg, she and I also worked together a little later on the familial clustering of the Australia antigen in Bougainville, which is the hepatitis B virus. Blumberg subsequently got the Nobel Prize for his discovery of that virus.

Ken left Madison to do a post doc with Cavalli in Pavia, Italy, and later moved with him to Stanford. So he was first a student of Cavalli's and then a junior collaborator with him. We didn't collaborate again for over a decade, but when he and Cavalli started collecting transformed cell lines in the 1980s, he and Judy Kidd contacted me about the possibility of gathering samples for cell line transformation from Bougainville (which I did in 1985, from the Nasioi). Then when the Human Genome Diversity Project became a possibility in the late 1980s and early 1990s, we began to meet again – Cavalli, Ken and Judy Kidd, Ken Weiss, and Mary-Claire King and other people trying to get it launched. Mark Weiss was the NSF Physical Anthropology Program Director who initially tried to get it considered for major funding. The idea was to collect cell lines from a representative set of populations around the globe that could be used for any future genetic testing. I was brought to NSF to try to continue its development after Mark. I continued my relationship with the Kidds when I served on a board overseeing a major ongoing project of theirs – ALFRED (the Allele Frequency Database). You may want to check that out on their website.

Going back to my Wisconsin years, those were the height of the Vietnam War protests, when the U.S. was invading Cambodia, the draft deferment had ended for students, and tensions were extremely high. When I was a post doc, Osborne asked me to give a lecture in his introductory course to about 200 or 300 students, who were very restive and disruptive. I showed my slides of Bougainville and talked about my work, showing pictures of the model and so on, and afterwards, when I asked for questions, one guy standing in the back said, with some hostility, "What was it you were really doing there?" Perhaps he thought I was working for the Central Intelligence Agency or something similar – it was certainly an accusatory tone. I said, "Well, I was trying to get my thesis material for my degree so I could get a job!" – the same sort of thing I had told people in Bougainville. It made everyone laugh and diffused the tension. Of course, I went on to talk about the findings, but the hostility was gone.

It was a bad time then, people forget. After the 1-year post doc, the anthropology department there offered me an assistant professorship, which I accepted (beginning 1970-1971). The National Guard was called out to control the demonstrations on campus, and I recall beginning to weep in the middle of a lecture – that's when I realized they were using tear gas outside. So, like other professors, I cancelled classes, but I tried to continue to distribute class notes to make it easy to finish the course if the entire semester wasn't cancelled. I also held my small seminar at my apartment. While I was very much against the war and the Cambodian invasion, I was troubled by the extent of the demonstrations and the potential for violence and even civil war. I did do some anti-war political work (later on I worked a little in New Hampshire for Eugene McCarthy's presidential primary bid). In fact, that was the year when someone set off an explosion in Madison with a truck filled with fertilizer at the Math Research Sciences Building, killing someone there.

Chapter 7.

Harvard: 1971-78

Accepting the Harvard Offer

JF: In the middle of that second year at Madison I got a phone call from Bill Howells, Dr. Howells, saying "Jonathan, I'm not going to do you any favor by this, but we would like to have you become an assistant professor here in the department. You know that tenure is difficult for junior professors to get here, it almost never happens, but we'd still love to have you. You may want to think about it." I immediately said, "Yes!"

Again, I have to say, a lot of it had to do with non-professional, personal reasons. I hadn't been able to figure out how to date anybody successfully in Madison. It was a strange department (I was the only unmarried person, and by far the youngest and most junior) and Dick Osborne who was my sort of mentor, said, "Don't go out with graduate students in the department. That's like shooting fish in a barrel." I'd never heard that expression and didn't understand it at first – It means doing something that's too easy, as well as inappropriate, I think. So I didn't know whom to go out with. I dated a few grad students in other departments, but I was lonely. It was also ferociously cold in the winter. I wanted to run back to Cambridge. I was married within eight months of my return.

I also thought, "Well maybe, just maybe, I can just possibly get tenure at Harvard. Who knows what will happen, things are so uncertain." Gene Giles suggested that it might be possible even though he didn't get it – Irv DeVore and Lamberg-Karlovsky had recently managed to be promoted with tenure, and the times were unsettled. At that moment Harvard's pay scale wasn't compelling. Certainly at the junior level, it was the same as Wisconsin's. In fact, I recall I took a $1,000 pay cut when I moved. I may have realized Howells was due to retire fairly soon. I thought, "I'll just make myself indispensable." Well, I was indispensable alright. I taught all kinds of classes, everything under the sun, from osteology to human genetics, a seminar on the Solomon Islands, plus introductory courses. I even taught primate anatomy (I'd had one class in that before), all kinds of things that I had no business teaching, and the good students knew it. Of course, they ultimately got rid of me!

The First Book and Relevant Controversies, 1975

JF: When I went back to Harvard, I wanted to make my dissertation into a monograph. In 1971, I published my first major papers on the Bougainville work (almost all genetics), but I wanted to do the book as well. My revised dissertation, with Howard's dental materials added, ended up being published in 1975 as *Patterns of Human Variation* with Harvard University Press.

JR: And will you say if it was common or not for a dissertation to be turned into a book in your field at that time?

JF: You know, I hadn't thought about that. I don't think it is – usually it's a string of articles. I was pleased with the whole prospect I guess. That was something I wanted to do. It was also delayed because the manuscript got lost for a while in Korea for about a year, where it was being typeset.

Edward O. Wilson was the syndic for biological books at Harvard University Press, which meant that he was the authoritative faculty reader/reviewer and advisor. I had an old friend who was the editor of medical and biological books at Harvard University Press then named Bill Bennett. I had known him during undergraduate days. An extraordinarily bright guy – he was elected to Phi Beta Kappa in his junior year (so-called "Junior Eight", meaning one of the top eight students in his class). Bill was handling the book submission and gave it to E.O. Wilson to read, and Wilson said, "This is excellent and has importance beyond anthropology. It's a fine monograph and Harvard University Press ought to publish it." The editors responded, basically, if this specialized monograph has wider importance, it needs a forward by a well-known figure in evolutionary biology or human genetics to point out its greater relevance than only to Melanesian diversity and Pacific anthropology – somebody like Luca Cavalli-Sforza.

So the question was whom should I ask to write the Foreword? I don't recall exactly what was going into my mind. I thought Luca was perhaps too obvious a choice? Perhaps I was afraid of asking him? I didn't know him at all at that point, and I didn't know how he'd respond – I think that was probably my main concern. Richard Lewontin had just come on the Harvard faculty and, of course, he subsequently became a great enemy of Wilson's. I thought Lewontin would be maybe a more unexpected choice, but still excellent. You know, he had done important work that was relevant – Lewontin and Hubby's work in the 1960s on fruit fly polymorphism, and then I'm not sure when his famous paper on human polymorphisms and racial variation was. I think it had just come out before I decided to ask him. Do you know the thing I'm talking about?

JR: I do, it was 1972.

JF: "The Apportionment of Human Variation" is the title . . . Anyway, he was the new boy on the block and I thought he was extremely smart. Mayr had cited his work many times in his major book, *Animal Species and Evolution*, and obviously had been lobbying for hiring him at Harvard (he was a Harvard undergrad before doing his PhD with Theodosius Dobzhansky at Columbia). I don't remember exactly whether I knew that he was going to be such a contentious figure, but I must have suspected it – he was known as an outspoken Marxist. Also Irv DeVore became an enemy of Lewontin's, besides E.O. Wilson, who wrote *Sociobiology* just a bit later – in 1975 – and I thought Lewontin's arguments early on against sociobiology were pretty telling. There was a lot of naïve material that Wilson wrote early on, for example about the inheritance of South American Indian face painting patterns being hard wired in the brain, or whatever (I'm not making that up). It was just breathtakingly naïve, and he later dropped it, and people have forgotten it. I wonder if Chagnon had anything to do with that. I'd bet he did – otherwise, why would Wilson have picked the Yanomami for an example?

Anyway, if I thought Lewontin would be an ally in any upcoming tenure decisions, it was a poor political calculation, given that DeVore was in my department. You probably don't know Lewontin at all except from the sociobiology controversy—

JR: Well, I've read his work, but I don't know him.

JF: Personally, his students all loved him. They said "His politics are one thing, but he looks after his students" – even people who didn't agree with his politics. He became a committed Marxist during the Vietnam War when his son, I think, was drafted, or subject to the draft – a major activist. So, I met him, I don't remember the exact circumstances. Soon afterwards, I said, "You know, I'd love it if you'd read my book because it's been accepted by Harvard University Press, but I've been told I need somebody to write a foreword to broaden the appeal. I'm hoping you could do it." So he looked at it and after about a couple of weeks, he said, "Yes, Jonathan, I'd be happy to do it. I'd be honored." Well, I thought that was just wonderful, I was tickled pink. It was a very nice piece he wrote, comparing my Bougainville work with Neel's among the Yanomami, saying those were the only two comparable studies of human population genetics in groups with simple social structures.

As a note on the Harvard political controversies in the early 1970s, I was aware of my ambivalence between the two warring intellectual camps and their origins. Lewontin came from a sophisticated New York Jewish intellectual background, was a connoisseur of classical music and literature, and sprinkled his lectures with quotes from French philosophers and Latin phrases, impeccably pronounced, while DeVore and Wilson came from much simpler and probably conservative southern backgrounds, even though their politics as adults were liberal, I'm sure. Steve Gould, who became an ally of Lewontin's, came from a similar New York Jewish background as well. He liked to sing arias in class (that turned me off, I have to say). Of course, as I said, I came from a southern Jewish intellectual background and had interests in both animal behavior and also genetics. Wilson's and DeVore's arguments were fascinating and new to me, but I tended to agree with Lewontin's criticisms on sociobiology, and felt he was misrepresented and vilified in various debates. In many cases, he was absolutely correct. However, I was turned off by some of his grand-standing tendencies. Just as a gratuitous gesture, for example, he resigned from the National Academy of Sciences because he felt it represented the intellectual elitist status quo. Afterwards, he regretted it, and wanted to get back in, to "change from within," as he said. I was perfectly aware that most other faculty, certainly within Anthropology, thought of him as a trouble-maker. So, within Harvard Anthropology, having Lewontin write a foreword was not the smartest thing to do politically. It was almost like thumbing my nose at all of them.

Also, Bill Bennett, my editor, had arranged (and I don't know how) that my book was going to get a major review in *Science,* with photos, and that Gene Giles, my old connection from the Solomon Islands Project, was going to be asked to do the review. That would have been wonderful. But Gene never turned in the review. That's something that I don't understand to this day. I never asked him about it too directly. At that point, he was head of the department at Illinois and busy, but he developed the reputation of not doing things promptly at all, being almost irresponsible that way. It might also have been competition or jealousy, but I honestly don't know. I thought of him as a friend and almost an advisor. I can't believe he would have simply passed up the chance to do a major book review for *Science*, so there must have been some motivation or reason he didn't – I never figured that out.

Science waited for months, and they finally asked Mike Crawford to do the review. It was a negative review and it was not well done. I never forgave Mike for it. He was disparaging. I remember his comment on the remarkable diversity I'd found within Bougainville went something like this – "Intermixture could explain the distinctions Friedlaender found among Bougainville villages – American soldiers must have been involved in causing that variation during World War II." That's simply not true, and I knew it at the time (with my genealogies, which went back before the war). If anybody needed to have that validated, the microsatellites in our recent *PLoS Genetics* paper certainly show there wasn't any admixture. There is no African or European hereditary signal at all in Bougainville. It was a competitive, snotty review, and showed he hadn't read the book carefully.

JR: Well, he's been active in trying to establish himself as a leader in the field now.

JF: Yes, like right now? What's he doing now? I haven't kept up with his publications – I don't think he hasn't done much new research in a while.

JR: He has a book that came out . . . He had in 2007 a pretty fat volume on *Anthropological Genetics.*

JF: I don't know anything about that. He was an editor for a long time at *Human Biology,* and a good one. He had a decent group of students. A particularly good one is Dennis O'Rourke, whom Mark Weiss and I recommended to take over the slot at NSF after me.

Mike and I go way back – lots of friction, competition, and I'm hardly the only one he antagonized unnecessarily. Early on, I recall he attacked Mary-Claire King (who subsequently played a very important role in the discovery of the breast cancer genes) fairly nastily (and erroneously) at a symposium at the physical anthro meetings, for her statistical treatment of qualitative data. She was trying to show a relationship between breast cancer susceptibility and different types of earwax. He said she couldn't include qualitative data, especially present-absent data, in a multivariate analysis.[14] I stood up and basically said, "Mike, you're wrong." I went into some detail, since that was something I had done myself in my dissertation, specifically with individual blood types, and I'd checked this approach out carefully. Mary-Claire said, "Yes, that's what my husband said was O.K. to do, and he's a statistician." So Mike probably took that as a put-down and personal embarrassment, nurturing a wounded ego for years thereafter.

What else was I going to say about him? Oh, yes, early on, he published two volumes of anthropological genetics. It was also called

14 His argument was that, since present-absent data do not have normal distributions, they cannot be used in multivariate statistics that require an assumption of normality for proper classification. However, it is the transformed multivariate factor or vector scores that must be normally distributed, not the underlying distributions of the individual variables.

Anthropological Genetics. The first volume was supposed to be theory. The second volume was supposed to be applications. This was in the late 1970s, I'd say, perhaps 1980s. You could check my vita. I got a sort of back-handed invitation from him to contribute something on Bougainville and the Solomon Islands to the second one. He made it clear that it was somehow after-the-fact, sort of a substitution for someone else. It was just typical Mike. But when I got to NSF, administering grants as the program director, he took me out to lunch. Not over $20, though (the acceptable limit).

JR: Noted.

JF: He's a strange fellow. That review in *Science*, though, I thought was a nasty blow. It came right when I hoped I might be considered for tenure. I remember Irv DeVore's wife sort of rubbed it in, telling me that the photos were also just terrible (they were poorly converted from color slides to black and whites). I'm sure the review didn't make a critical difference, though.

JR: So back to the Bougainville book itself, in the acknowledgements section, you thank a number of people for their feedback on various chapters. Cavalli-Sforza was one, Stephen Gould was another.

JF: O.K.

JR: Could talk a little bit about what that connection was, if you remember?

JF: O.K., I'd totally forgotten about Cavalli. I must have showed him part of it – I don't recall showing anything to him. I hadn't met him. I must have sent it to him without any introduction.

JR: I think it was Chapter Two.

JF: Gould suggested some alteration in the Introduction.

JR: It said "various."

JF: Various . . . I think he looked at the whole thing and said it was just fine. I remember he suggested only one clarification. I made this dichotomy in the Introduction. If I pulled the book out I could tell. It involved the argument between the neutralists versus selectionists, following an argument of Lewontin's that evolved from Mayr's contrast of population thinking vs. typological thinking, that I liked. Hold on one second, I'm going to get a copy. Checking the Introduction, I had originally said there was a controversy between geneticists and fieldworkers in biology in the early 20th century on the importance of natural selection, and Gould reminded me it was not all geneticists, just the experimental (lab) geneticists who were terribly impressed with mutation, and who suggested selection wasn't important.

JR: So now you are looking at the Introduction to your book on Bougainville.

JF: [looking through book]. I'm having some trouble finding it . . . ah, yes. I think this is it. I was talking a little bit about the history of evolutionary theory. [reading from text] "It was during this period that the division between *experimental* geneticists," that would be Hermann Muller and others, "particularly Hugo DeVries, became so impressed with what appeared to be variation caused by spontaneous mutation that they discounted the ordering role of natural selection in evolution" . . . so that the contrast was not between all geneticists and naturalists, but between experimental geneticists and naturalists – I think he wanted me to make that absolutely clear – that that was the distinction. That was it.

JR: Do you remember what he felt the significance of that was, or why that was?

JF: Saying "experimental geneticists" or lab geneticists was more accurate than just saying "geneticists," since there were important geneticists working with natural populations with contrary ideas. It was the lab men who were known as the "Mutationists" then. It was the fruit fly lab folks, in particular, who were so impressed with mutations they could cause with x-rays that they even talked about new species being created by macro-mutations, without any reference to natural selection. Muller had this sense of a population or species being relatively genetically homogeneous, except for rare deleterious mutations, so that the process of developing a new species by a group of small genetic shifts or frequency changes seemed unlikely from this perspective. The worst was probably Richard Goldschmidt. He had this ridiculous notion of "Hopeful Monsters," or novel creatures created by macro-mutations, that had to find, during their lifetimes, other "monsters" of the same sort in order to "perpetuate" their new species (they were "hopeful" that they'd find a similarly mutated individual to mate with before they died without offspring). Mayr attacked him decisively, and apparently this led to Mayr's formulation of his biological species concept.

On the other side were the naturalists. They saw variability leading to different adaptations in different ecologies as the result of differential selection (and perhaps even direct environmental influences, something we don't believe in now). Later on, population geneticists like R.A. Fisher, Sewall Wright, and J.B.S. Haldane talked about possibly beneficial variability coming from small mutations, which opened the possibility for the existence and maintenance of substantial variability within a population and species. Dobzhansky's book on *Genetics and the Origin of Species* in the 1930s was absolutely critical because it incorporated the idea of extensive genetic variation in natural populations, plus natural selection, as the two major elements of evolution and speciation. Shortly thereafter came Mayr's work on systematics and the biological species concept, Simpson's on paleontology and slow rates of evolution, and other contributions that together constituted the "Modern Evolutionary Synthesis." At its core, the primary guiding force of evolution was seen as natural selection, acting on mutations of small effect. Mayr endlessly repeated the formulation that the evolutionary process had two steps – first, the random production and reassortment of heritable or genetic variation, and then the editing process of natural selection.

A lot of concepts have changed in the last 70 years in evolutionary theory, but these two essential parts have not. That was all in Dobzhansky's book.

JR: And who would have been among the naturalists?

JF: Well a lot of early Germans, Mayr talked a lot about the German naturalists – even people like Christian Bergmann and those other biogeographers, like Allen and Constantin Gloger, talking about population variability that was adaptively related to their environments. However, they were inclined to a rather Lamarkian[15], non-Mendelian, notion of how adaptation came about, suggesting that the environment could directly shape hereditary change during an individual's lifetime. The naturalist group should also include Dobzhansky's intellectual forebears in Russia (Chetverikoff, Timofeef-Ressovsky, and others, since they began this tradition of experimental genetics within a naturalist framework, not at all like Muller's). So, that was the kind of thing that I got from some of the exposure to Mayr and Simpson at Harvard. Steve Gould, whose primary contribution was in the history of evolutionary theory, along with promoting the idea of varying rates of evolution, was interested in that as well. Also, Lewontin, probably Dobzhansky's major student, discusses this in his papers (it's especially nicely covered in the first chapter in his book, *The Genetic Basis of Evolutionary Change).* He talked about this early conflict between the lab geneticists and the naturalists, as did Mayr. This controversy in the early part of the 20th century led to the remarkable synthesis of evolutionary ideas right around the Second World War, or about 15 years before I began graduate school. So it was a common topic of discussion even then and had come to be the accepted orthodoxy.

More Theoretical Controversies: Neutralism, Panselection, and Sociobiology

Now, the controversy in evolutionary theory that was hottest when I was doing my dissertation research and shortly thereafter involved the new "neutral" theory of mutation-driven evolution, by Motoo Kimura about 1968. He'd worked with James Crow in

15 The mechanism of inheritance was not properly understood at all prior to the 20th century. Jean Baptiste de Lamarck, a French natural philosopher of the 19th century, believed that changes caused by the environment could be passed on to offspring. For example, under Lamarck's notion, if humans are heavily tanned by sun exposure, their children will be genetically darker. Gregor Mendel's hypothesis that the hereditary materials (later called genes) were discrete particles, uninfluenced by the environment, finally clarified this important issue, but this was not realized until the 20th century.

Wisconsin. The new idea was that the accumulation of mutations over time in populations was not strongly affected by natural selection. Selection was not ubiquitous, all-powerful. This was supported strikingly in an important paper by Jack King and Tom Jukes that appeared in *Science* in 1969. It showed that the relative amounts of different amino acids in a group of known proteins were strongly correlated with the number of codons for them. Codons are the different triplet combinations of the 4 DNA bases (A, G, C, and T) that determine which amino acid occurs at a particular place in a chain making up a protein. For example, King found that if five different codons specified a particular amino acid, the amino acid occurred five times as frequently in proteins as an amino acid that had only one codon, for example. This implied that the relative occurrences of different amino acids had little or nothing to do with natural selection. They called this selective neutralism or "Non-Darwinian evolution." These and other papers and Kimura's book opened the door for considering a great deal of existing genetic variability to be hidden from natural selection, and therefore had to be determined primarily by the other forces of evolution – mutation and also drift/migration.

This was important to me, as it was a counter-weight to the pan-selectionist position of Mayr and others – the variability in Bougainville might be totally non-selectively determined. In my 1975 monograph Introduction, you'll see I frame the predictions of diversity in that way, in an understated way, saying selective explanations can't be effectively proposed in such a small region, or at least that I didn't know how to do that. You can imagine Mayr was opposed to "neutralism," and on the other hand, Lewontin was open to it. In a real way, this represented something of a revolt from the new orthodoxy of the Modern Synthesis by the next generation of evolutionary theorists, which coincided with the Vietnam War protests. They were upsetting the apple cart of the intellectual establishment represented by Mayr, and loving it.

The sociobiologists, then just getting underway at Harvard and led by E.O. Wilson with DeVore in support, were also predisposed not to like neutralism, since they assumed selection acted even on features with low heritabilities[16] (they were of course mainly concerned about the extremely low heritabilities of behavioral features or strategies, and wanted to think that, somehow, every aspect of the phenotype was subject to selection). Of course, politically, sociobiology represents a conservative justification of the social status quo – we have male dominance because it's biologically predisposed, and so forth (even if many of sociobiology's adherents are politically generally rather liberal).

In any case, I remember being impressed with a talk Lewontin gave during this period (at a Boston meeting of the AAAS, I think) where he used a simple linguistic analogy. He listed four words – it was "father" and three earlier English forms, and said, "these all have the same meaning, but have been modified by chance phenomena over time – it is reasonable to think that this sort of change could occur in the biological world as well, so that many alterations could occur without changing the selective 'meaning' of a DNA sequence or amino acid chain." Of course, now we accept, among other things, the distinction between synonymous and non-synonymous mutations (those that make an alteration in amino acid sequence, and those that have no effect), the existence of very large sections of non-coding DNA, and so forth. But that was a contentious idea at the time.

These neutralist papers established the importance of mutation rates, but in a way they also made the acceptance of other non-selective, demographic events (drift and migration) more acceptable as determining distinctions between human populations, rather than selection differentials. That's what all the subsequent modern genetic and genomic studies have underlined, beginning with the "Out of Africa" mtDNA studies in the early 1980s. Differential selection, or selection of any sort, is largely irrelevant in these papers, in all the

16 Heritability is best thought of as the proportion of the variation of a trait that has a genetic basis, contrasted with the proportion of variation that is not, or is attributable to environmental effects. Characteristics that are affected much more by genetic variation than environmental effects will have high heritabilities, approaching 100%, and vice versa for characters with low heritabilities. There are different sorts of heritabilities and ways to calculate this proportional statement.

microsatellite papers, and in the mega-SNP[17] genome scan papers as well. Things have been totally turned on their heads in this regard, and people don't talk about this remarkable intellectual shift much at all. Searches for the evidence for selection from a genetics perspective now start from the assumption that mutation/drift effects determine the great majority of frequencies of variants/polymorphisms, and the "candidates for selection" are assumed to be those variants or combinations that are the rare outliers to predominant profiles, which are determined by mutation/drift effects. Geneticists now like to talk about how selection is very "subtle" in its signature, very slight and hard to detect in its effects, as opposed to drift, migration, and mutation.

I feel this has also affected the presumption of adaptationist arguments in an important, but not generally acknowledged, way – the burden of proof on them is much higher than it used to be. Just because a biological distinction or genetic polymorphism is shown to exist hardly means that differential selection is likely to be responsible, even if there's an associated functional distinction.

There was also an important paper by Dick Lewontin and Steve Gould about 30 years ago with an off-putting erudite title Gould must have been responsible for, the "Spandrels of San Marco and the Panglossian Paradigm," that was controversial at the time. Its point was that even proving a feature may have a functional effect (like a mutation that causes an amino acid change) does not mean that selection is, or has been, at work. Proving that selection has been at work requires a different, rigorous statistical proof. This is still an extremely important point to keep in mind in today's searches of selection effects in genome studies – Andy Clark, Carlos Bustamante, and R. Nielson recently [2008] wrote a nice review on this issue in *PLoS Genetics*. Also, the Kidds have given a nice recent example of how one should attempt to show the effects of positive selection, having to do with alcohol metabolism. It's not easy.

17 Each human egg or sperm cell contains a linear sequence of 3 billion DNA building blocks (the sequence is divided into 23 segments for the different chromosomes). While there is very little variation in the sequence among people, there still remain millions of positions where more than one kind of building block, or nucleotide, may have been found thus far in humans. Such a varying position is called a single nucleotide polymorphism, or SNP, and it has become possible to scan for variation at very large numbers of SNP sites, currently over 1,000,000.

I think the importance of my early work was that it showed the extent of biological variation (both genetic and anthropometric) that could be attributed to drift/isolation effects without any appeal to natural selection. Since I hardly mentioned selection, a lot of biologists probably thought of my work as essentially unimportant or simply a curiosity, along with other non-selectionist arguments such as the molecular clock, which are now also accepted, with modifications, by the mainstream.

On a rather different issue, trying to find convincing genetic and environmental associations often leads to oversimplification of complex situations. For example, when I finally did study health aspects of biological diversity in the Solomons, I was careful to stress not only the effects of modernization, but the preexisting diversity in ecologies among the traditional cultures there. I think this was an important distinction between my approach and that of both Neel and Damon. As I mentioned, they both saw the organization of biological diversity in something of a simple dichotomy between "moderns" and "primitives." Neel's avowed purpose in studying the Yanomami was to see if he could detect differences in the mutation rates between "us" and "them." He thought that both human-induced radiation and new environmental mutagens might be acting on us in a much more extreme way than on the Yanomami and other primitives. That's how he got funding from the Atomic Energy Commission (a line item in the AEC budget, in fact), although he never could identify any obvious differences in mutation incidence or rates. My point is that he assumed that things were pretty much the same in all non-western groups – that he could generalize from the Yanomami to all non-modern groups. Damon's model of the effects of modernization also, at least at the beginning, was overly simple in this way – that there were simply two opposite extremes – "primitive" and "modern," so groups would be expected to be arranged along that single vector.

However, it was obvious that in the Solomons there were a lot of existing distinctions in health effects between the different groups prior to any modernizing trends. For example, the mountaineers were much more muscular than the beach people and carried heavy loads up and down mountains (especially clear in the women), but the mountaineer diets lacked protein, which the beach-dwellers got in good amounts from fish. There were other possibly important differences among traditional groups in exposure to carcinogens (like wood smoke in fires, betel nut chewing, and many others).

Following this line, I argued that modern groups are exposed to a new set of environmental agents that are likely to be homogenizing in their effects. So I tried to develop a model of blood pressure change with homogenizing effects of modernization in the articles with Charles Sing's group. Our hypothesis was that with modernization, blood pressure and their heritabilities would rise and also become homogeneous across groups. However, we couldn't prove this. The results were unstable. The model was complex and the samples were too small. That was a major effort that was largely unsuccessful, and after that, my research career stalled for a few years before I turned entirely to molecular genetics.

Further Exposure to Genetics

I should mention that twice during my years on the Harvard faculty, I spent two weeks at a summer short course in human genetics at the Jackson Labs in Bar Harbor, Maine, run by Victor McKusick and his group from Johns Hopkins Medical School. While I didn't take full advantage of it (I had my family along, and it was part vacation, so I skipped the afternoon labs), this provided continuing exposure to the rapidly developing field. It at least made me aware of what was happening in areas such as biochemical genetics and clinical genetics. There were even a few presentations in genetic linkage studies and evolutionary genetics, and there was a good bit of talk about the neutralist-selectionist controversy (everyone there was basically against the neutralist arguments). I incorporated a lot of these materials into my own course lectures.

Also during this period, I was invited to participate in a small conference of about 20 people at a luxurious Austrian medieval fortress run by the Wenner-Gren Foundation (The Burg Wartenstein Conference Center). I was the most junior participant, and a great many of the leading figures in human population genetics were there – James Neel, Arno Motulsky, Walter Fitch, Newton Morton, Harry Harris, Pat Jacobs, Friedrich Vogel, Francisco Ayala, and others of that sort – extremely prominent figures. The conference was organized by Francisco Salzano, and an edited volume was produced as a result, called *Natural Selection in Human Populations*. I was intimidated, but I think the exposure was good for me. However, my paper, on Bougainville diversity, had nothing to do with the conference topic, natural selection!

Burg Wartenstein Conference Center, Wenner-Gren Foundation, 1972. Mentioned attendees, from left: 2nd – Newton Morton; 3rd – Francisco Ayala; 4th – Walter Fitch; 6th – JSF; 7th Pat Jacobs; 11th – Harry Harris; 12th – James Neel; 13th – Francisco Salzano; 14th – Friedrich Vogel; 17th – Arno Motulsky.

Chapter 8.

Temple and the Follow-up Pacific Fieldtrips: 1978-1986

Outline of the Following Field Expeditions and Their Objectives

While I continued to go back to the Southwest Pacific over the years, the objectives of those expeditions changed from season to season. I didn't plan for genetics to become gradually more important. But in the end, as I became less enamored of tracking environmental or modernizing effects, and as the power of molecular genetics dramatically increased, that is what I chose to emphasize, finally almost to the exclusion of other data collection (e.g., blood pressure and lipid levels, fingerprints, anthropometry, and dental casts). However, I had always wanted to have a genetic characterization of all groups that were covered, almost as a baseline for any other comparisons.

I should try to recap and detail briefly the objectives of each expedition after 1966-1967 to show how this "strategy" survived the other research forays. Some of this will repeat earlier remarks, but the sequence is confusing if I don't outline it this way.

1970. That objective was straight-forward – to get dental casts from the same villages on the Bougainville east coast I'd done for my doctoral thesis, with Howard Bailit (and a grad student of his – Glen Rappaport) doing the casting. The dental materials were included as a chapter in my 1975 monograph. Once they were successfully underway, I went to the western side of Bougainville (the Siwai again) and collected more detailed, deeper genealogies and other demographic data, building on Oliver's old genealogies, to try to calculate long-term inbreeding estimates. No blood-based genetics was done.

1973. This was a solo blood collection trip to Buka Island and west Timor, Indonesia. The objective was to extend the blood group genetic coverage to other groups in north Bougainville and Papuan-speaking groups at the western extremity of their distribution, in Indonesia.

1978-1980. This was my first follow-up study building on the Harvard Solomons Project, funded by a National Science Foundation grant. The objective was to study changing adolescent growth profiles in the six different groups in Bougainville and Malaita (no genetics or blood taking was involved). This meant traveling around 6 groups, measuring adolescents approximately four times a year for two years. I also measured adults who had been covered a decade earlier by the Harvard Expeditions. John Rhoads and Kevin Mohr were the other members of the field collection team – we formed a sort of relay team – I went first for about 8 months, John second for about a year, Kevin for about 6 months, and then I returned for the finish in 1980. Some of these data were published in the 1987 Oxford monograph. I also visited Ontong Java for the first time, at the end of the field stay in 1980, with Lot Page and his son Jesse.

1985-1986. This was a second follow-up of the Harvard Solomons study. The focus of this NSF funded research was on changing blood pressure and lipid levels with modernization. I headed a team of 5 or 6 people. In 1985 we surveyed the three groups on Bougainville, and in 1986, we surveyed 2 on Malaita as well as Ontong Java. The objective was to develop a model of changing blood pressure heritabilities with the continued modernization of many of the groups, assuming that the heritabilities would rise and homogenize with modernization, as I mentioned before. We did take blood samples to study changing cholesterol and other blood chemistries (triglycerides, apolipoproteins, etc.) associated with cardiovascular problems. Other collected variables included anthropometry, fitness assessments, and electrocardiograms. The results of these studies were published in the *American Journal of Physical Anthropology* in one issue. The blood samples were later analyzed for mtDNA variation, but this was not the primary objective of the original study. We collected the Nasioi samples for transformation into cell lines in 1985, as well.

1998, 2000, 2003. These field seasons were not follow-ups to the Harvard expeditions and represented a new research direction. They greatly enlarged the genetic coverage in Island Melanesia. These surveys in the Bismarck Archipelago focused on the pattern of genetic variation in this region, to link it to the established patterns in Bougainville, Malaita, and Ontong Java from the earlier work. George Koki from the Papua New Guinea Institute for Medical Research, Andy Merriwether, Heather Norton, and I collected demographic data and skin and hair reflectance measurements along with the blood samples. The collected samples were analyzed for a large battery of genetic markers – mtDNA, Y chromosome, candidate genes for pigmentation, and later 750 microsatellites. The results have been published in a series of papers up to the present, and in an edited volume with Oxford University Press in 2007.

1978. Measuring children in Funafou, Lau Lagoon. 1978.

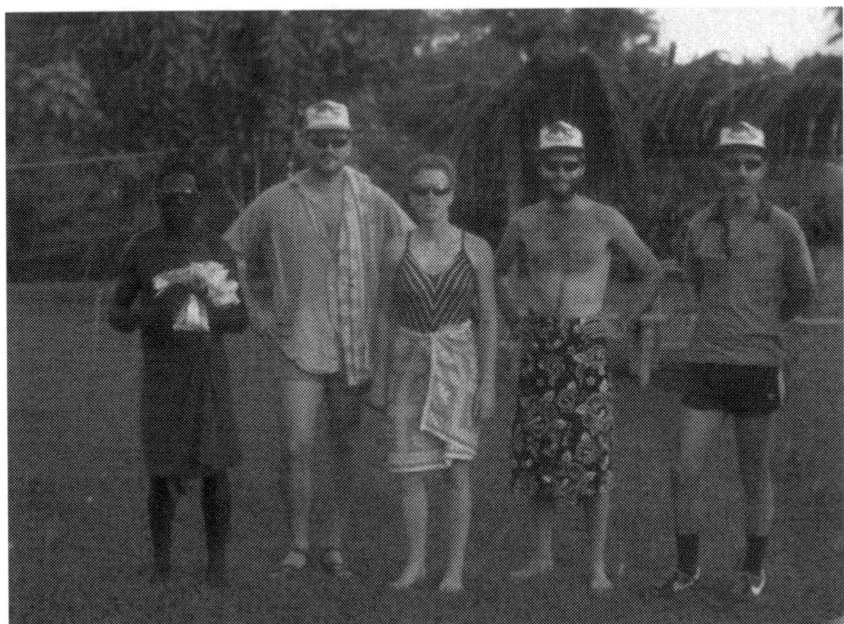

1985 expedition members going for a swim after work, with "Phantom" sunglasses and souvenir hats of the Pope's visit to PNG , "our country" (*kantri bilong yumi*). From left: Peter Tevu, Dan Hrdy, Tina Lesser, Jay Pearson, and Chuck Weitz.

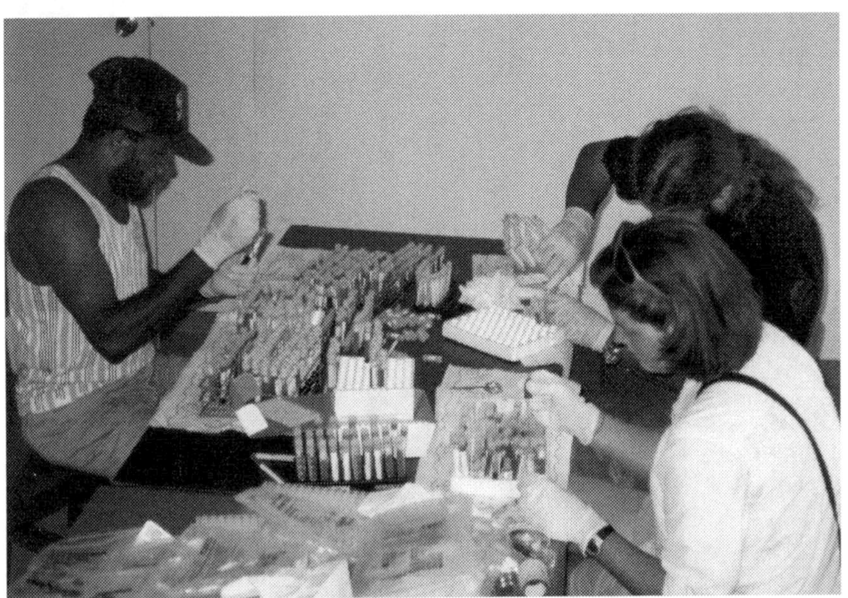

2000. Laboratory work in New Ireland. George Koki, Andy Merriewether, and Heather Norton.

The Harvard Project Follow-ups

After my Bougainville thesis study, after Al Damon died in 1973, and after I had been brought back as an assistant professor to Harvard in 1971, it was clear to me that there was a real possibility of doing a useful restudy on the Solomons materials collected under Damon's direction. By 1976, that was roughly about 10 years after the expeditions started, it made sense to look at the effects of modernization on these groups again.

My first grant application for a follow-up proposed, "We're going to do a follow up on a variety of aspects of the Harvard expedition dataset," and the NSF reviewers said, "No, that's not focused enough – too much of a fishing expedition." I got upset (it was the first time I'd had a grant proposal declined) and I tripled the budget request to $300,000 and said "We're going to do a focused study on adolescent growth and its relationship to modernization and acculturation, so we will have to do a series of visits to the groups every four months for two years to remeasure the adolescents." They then said, "That sounds much better, we'll fund it." So of course, we proceeded to do the adolescent study plus what we originally planned.

I got the grant right after I'd been denied tenure at Harvard (almost inevitable) and accepted the Temple position (the only offer I had – I was an associate professor by then). Incidentally, a great attraction of the Temple offer was that Baruch Blumberg had indicated that he'd support me half time in research at the Institute for Cancer Research in the Philadelphia suburbs (Elmer Miller, the chair at Temple, had agreed to this arrangement in principle as well), but when I got to Temple, he said he didn't have the necessary grant funds.

It took a year to get all the research permissions in both Papua New Guinea and the Solomons lined up. So, that's how those expeditions developed in the late 1970s and it was on that basis that the book in 1987 came out, which did pull together a lot of the Harvard Solomons data, as well . . .

JR: This is the synthesis volume?

JF: Right, with Clarendon Press of Oxford University Press. The data we collected in 1978-1980 established the restudy aspect and pulled a lot of diverse material together.

Introduction Issues

Now, entering new areas was always cause for anxiety, and going to six new places, when we were following up the Harvard Solomons study, was a daunting prospect. So, I contacted the cultural anthropologists ahead for introductions where it made sense. Jill Nash and Don Mitchell I knew and had corresponded with, as well as Gene Ogan. I stopped at Pierre and Elli Maranda's house in Quebec on my way to the field, and they wrote letters of introduction for me to the Lau (of course, I brought along copies). I also wrote to Roger Keesing and he gave me advice, and he also wrote his Kwaio friends and got them to build a house for us (they made it theft proof, with thick walls of whole bamboo and only one entrance – of course, I was expected to pay a guard to sleep at the entrance). So, those entry points were easier for me because of those contacts. In some groups, I wasn't in touch with the original ethnologists, ordinarily because they'd dropped out, John Rutherford being a prime example I mentioned earlier.

Identifying the Same People

I had to find and verify the correct ID numbers for people from the original Harvard Solomons study. This meant using the old photographs from the Harvard Solomons study and their family information that I had Xeroxed at Temple and brought along – a time consuming preparation (this was mostly done by Tina Lesser and Muriel Kirkpatrick). These records were absolutely invaluable in the longitudinal work. We're still working with those, and we have over a 50% recovery rate of people over a 16-20 year period (from 1966-1972 to 1985-1986). That's almost unique.

A Cargo Cult Incident

JR: You have spoken about some of the unique challenges cultural anthropologists face in the field. As a biological anthropologist, you face your own challenges in the field. What do you think those have been?

JF: Well, part of it was the cargo cult hangover. There were a few times when this surfaced. For example, in 1985, we were going up to the Aita area of Bougainville. We sent word ahead that we wanted to go there and to send along the information. Chuck Weitz was along, Dan Hrdy, Tina Lesser, and there was another graduate student (Jay Pearson). It was about a five hour walk, the most difficult walk in Bougainville, up into the mountains. We got up there in the late afternoon. It had been raining and we'd been walking through rivers and up slippery hillsides, so we were tired, wet, and muddy. As we were entering Kusi village, the people came out and they started dancing and singing around us in welcome. Now, this was unusual. It went on for a long time. I remember Tina said, "Oh, Jonathan, this is special!" and I said, "I never have seen anything like it." It didn't stop. It went on for perhaps 20 minutes? A half an hour? I thought, "What is going on here?" And finally, one man abruptly stepped up and said "Stop!" Everybody immediately stopped. He came and shook my hand formally and said, "My name is John God. (*Nem bilong mi, emi Jon Got*)!" And then he continued, in Tok Pisin, "We're honored to have you here. We expected you, you're doctors from America." Then we were led into the village. He said, "We expect you will build a hospital for us and, in fact, we expect to secede from the government of Papua New Guinea and North Solomon Province (the province Bougainville belonged to then), and we expect to become citizens of America. You will all live here as our doctors at the hospital you build." So, I said, "You know, we'd like to be of some service, but we simply can't do that." It became clear that he was a cargo cult leader in this area. It was like a paramilitary organization where he would line everybody up at attention, not in uniforms, but they would all salute him and march around the village doing his bidding. I remember them using old gasoline powered lawnmowers to cut the odd patch of grass in the village, something you never see and quite unnecessary. It was a strange scene that made my skin crawl.

Cargo cult welcoming dancers, including John God. Aita, 1985.

That was a Saturday afternoon. He wanted me to come on Sunday morning to the religious services and give the sermon. I've done that a number of times in fieldwork situations, so that in itself was not unusual. That night, I said to our group, "Look, we're going to get out of here, this is just not a good situation, and there's no way anything good can come out of this. I'm going to give the sermon tomorrow, thank them for their hospitality, and then we're going to leave promptly. So have all your bags packed and ready to go before there's a chance for John God to think how to stop us. I'm going to tell him it's not going to work; no hospital is going to be built." We were apprehensive about what was going to happen, mostly because of the commanding manner of "John God." I thought he could be psychotic and easily turn angry and possibly violent if we refused his wishes. It was also unpleasant because there were a lot of rats in the place where we were staying; they were crawling all over our feet that night, and it particularly spooked Tina – no one slept.

The next morning I gave my sermon about how, in spite of our different appearances and life-styles, all of us were children of one god ("*Olgeta yumipela emi pikinini bilong wanpela Got*"). We were there to study how people were different from one another, but we were sorry, we were going to leave because we were not able to make people American citizens and build a hospital. We didn't have that much money, and we were not U.S. government representatives.[18]

JR: Do you have written versions of that which would give more of the full sense of this sermon?

JF: No, I don't have anything written down. I talked about what I and other biological anthropologists do, studying how people in different parts of the world had come to look different, and why that might be (for example, the skin color story and malaria story) and then turn to Bougainville and the differences we found even there, between northerners and southerners, that northerners had broad faces and chests, while southerners were thinner and had narrower faces – some of them said they thought that was correct from what they'd seen themselves.

That was the kind of tense situation that did happen occasionally, although this was extreme. There was another occasion in my first year when I was on my own in Bougainville. I was told that there was a man making cargo cult interpretations of my work. A man from Bairima village in Nasioi was apparently telling people that I was signing people up for American citizenship so that when the American invasion came to drive out the wicked Australians, those who had been made U.S. citizens would be in charge. It seemed possibly believable because I was taking Polaroid photographs of people (according to him, while I was giving people the Polaroid prints, the alleged "negatives," that they were familiar with from the available film cameras there, were hidden inside the camera, and I was sending these to the U.S. government). I was also taking blood samples and fingerprints, both also suspicious. After I was told about this, I made sure to address that idea in village meeings. "I've heard people who have said that's what I'm doing [signing people up for U.S. citizenship] but I'm not. I'm just a graduate student – a school boy [*skulboi*]." But you never know how people are thinking about

18 Dan Hrdy recalls that JSF told Jon Got he would arrange a meeting between President Reagan and Jon Got (JSF has no remembrance of this at all).

things. That was something that was often underneath the surface. But this was also true with all these American expeditions, the Harvard Solomon Islands Project, too. My letters discuss this problem a bit.

Increasing Lawlessness (the Raskals)

In later years, when the mine was having a major impact, we were aware that some groups of young men were becoming increasingly rowdy, drunken, and lawless. They were referred to as the "*raskals*." They would wander around drunk and could be an unpredictable hazard that we had to be aware of. One morning we set up our tables and equipment on the major east coast road in the lowland Aita area, and 4 or 5 drunken young men staggered into the area and disrupted our work. They were carrying machetes (very common), and one started banging his machete on Chuck Weitz's expensive pieces of exercise physiology equipment. Chuck got upset (unusual) and started yelling at him to stop (I just wanted Chuck not to get hurt). Finally, an old lady who was the *raskal*'s putative grandmother grabbed his arm with the machete and started yelling at him, telling him he was no good and so on. The drunken *raskal* suddenly became meek in the face of her harangue and the tension immediately dissolved. Later on after they'd sobered up a little, he and his friends came back and asked if they could be included in the survey. Chuck took great delight in exhausting them, exercising them to their maximum capacity . . . But they or their *raskal* friends were also accused of raping a teacher nearby, so they were not harmless, by any means.

The Adolescent Growth Study

Another problem developed with the adolescent study aspect in 1978. Experts in adolescent growth I consulted told me I must include determinations on the timing of the onset of male and female hormonal changes at adolescence, to detect if this was coming earlier with increasing modernization. This meant, in simplest form, recording early stages of breast development or breast budding in girls, and in boys, the enlargement of the testes or penis, as well as the onset of pubic and underarm hair growth in both sexes.

My first day in the field in 1978, my first subject was a 10 or 11 year old boy. After taking a few measurements on him, I took him by the hand and we went around the back of the houses to some bushes, I turned on my flashlight, and I asked him to undo the top of his trousers. I looked down his pants with my flashlight, and in a flash, he immediately ran away, never to return. All the village spectators nearby doubled over laughing. So that attempt in boys was immediately abandoned.

For the girls, we thought grading breast development on the recommended scale of 0 to 5 would be simple enough, whether they had blouses on or not. However, when we looked at our records after a few rounds, some girls declined from a 3 to a 2 (!) in successive measurement cycles. So that became questionable information.

The adolescent growth material with the multiple measurements has basically never seen the light of day, even now. But it may yet, on account of Chuck Weitz' interest. You're probably not familiar with this, but longitudinal studies generate horrendous databases to work with. First off, we ended up with different time intervals between measurements (the intervals were never perfectly 3 or 4 months, for example, and few kids were measured in all eight cycles – lots of missing data). Making sure you've got the same individual every time is also an issue; there are also differences between measurers in technique; and also ideas change over time as to what should be included in the measurement battery. So in the end, we do have multiple measurements on a number of adolescents over this period, but there were a lot of inconsistencies. Nevertheless, Chuck is interested in tying these longitudinal adolescent results to subsequent adult finesses, blood pressures, and lipid levels. It's a unique dataset. There's nothing comparable from non-urbanized societies anywhere.

The Blood Pressure Study: an Impasse

I already mentioned that the blood pressure and lipid work, while interesting, didn't lead to the end result we'd hoped for. It was just too complex and difficult, even working with some excellent quantitative geneticists at Michigan (Charles Sing, Kim Zerba, and Craig Hannis). At that point after 1986 I didn't know what direction to take in future research, and I felt somewhat stymied. It was clear, even in this line of work, that searching for specific genetic effects on the phenotype (such as blood pressure or skin pigmentation) was going to be a future direction of research and funding, and calculating heritabilities was no longer of much interest. Charlie Sing acknowledged as much. This was when simple DNA analysis with RFLPs[19] was catching people's interest, before actual DNA sequencing was feasible.

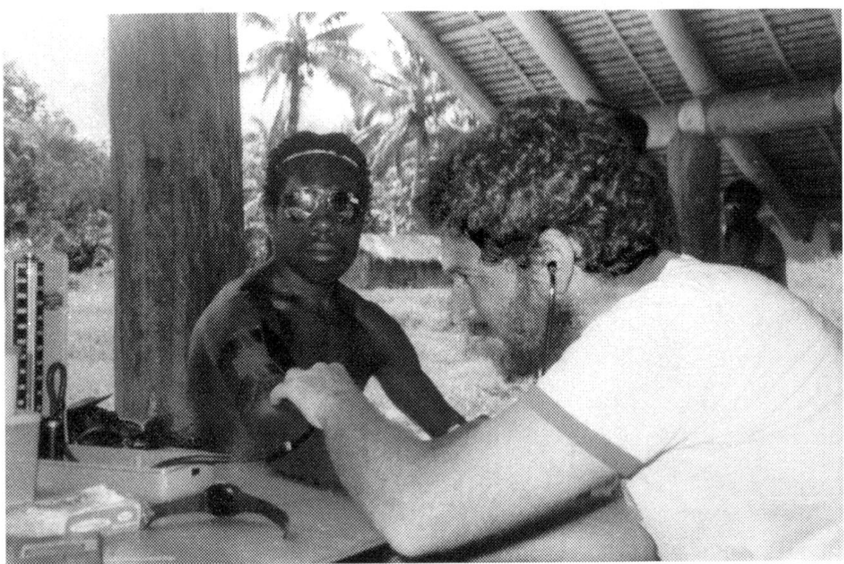

Taking blood pressure of a subject wearing "Phantom Glasses." 1985

Collecting Cell Lines

One bright spot during our restudies involved getting back in touch with Ken and Judy Kidd around 1985. Ken and Judy knew that I was going back to the field in the mid-1980s, when cell line transformation had matured as a technique, and Ken said, "Jonathan, it would great if

19 RFLP stands for restriction fragment length polymorphism. Restriction digestion involves treating DNA with an enzyme that recognizes a specific short sequence (for example, GATATC) and cleaves the DNA there. This will result in a particular array of DNA fragments of differing lengths, depending on where GATATC occurs. If that particular sequence is no longer present in one location because of some earlier mutation, there will be one larger fragment in the array rather than two smaller ones. This was the most popular way to analyze limited sorts of DNA variation in the 1980s before actual sequencing of the DNA was developed and automated.

you got some blood samples that we could transform into cell lines. We think this is going to be a great resource." I said, "What do I have to do?" He said, "You've got to get the samples back here unfrozen, kept at 4 degrees centigrade, within 50 hours of their drawing." I said, "It takes just about that long to fly from Bougainville via Australia to the USA with connections – I'll see what I can do. How many?" And he said, "As many as you can get, but probably 20 to 25 per group would be enough."

We collected the samples for the cell line transformations successfully for the Nasioi in 1985. A night shortly before the end of the expedition, I talked to a group of people in the village we were staying in (Sirompa). I said, "There's something extra I want to do. This will be for future research. I don't know exactly what the samples will be used for, but hopefully there will be some benefit, either in terms of population history or medical science. We can't predict how they will be used. I hope you will help us, and we will not be making money from them. Your names won't be made public, either." About 30 people said "O.K." So we had a going-away dinner party for them, and at the end of the party we took those people's blood late in the evening. Tina Lesser took some on the plane with her early the next morning, back to San Francisco, where Cavalli's assistant met her at the airport. Chuck Weitz took a set back to New York a few days later, and the Kidds at Yale had somebody come and pick them up at Kennedy Airport. So those were transformed, at both Stanford and Yale. That's how they got the Nasioi cell line count of about 27. In those days, there was still a high rate of failure in the transformation of cell lines, so both labs "lost" about 30% of the ones we drew, but they were not always the same failures, so the overall result was satisfactory.

The Nasioi cell lines were almost immediately used in world-wide comparisons by Cavalli, Kidd, and their colleagues. Anne Bowcock was the lead author on the first of these. It examined a large group of microsatellites (for then) in a handful of populations from different areas of the world. Quickly, the power of this approach was made clear, because even with a small set of microsatellites, different populations were easily distinguishable. However, the open-ended nature of the cell lines ultimately meant that they were difficult to control, so the Kidds laid down strict rules on who could get the DNA harvested from their cell lines – basically, no profit-making research ventures. The cell lines themselves remained under their (and Cavalli's) control.

We also tried unsuccessfully to get cell lines from the Aita, those shy northern Bougainville mountain people. They didn't show up at the appointed time. I tried hard to convince them, or at least some of them who were at Asitavi Mission Station, to give us samples for cell line transformation. I made something of a fool of myself at Asitavi, trying to be friendly and open myself up and everything. I chewed some betel nut in public and got quite dizzy and pretty sick. I was sweating profusely and had to lie down on the lawn. It didn't work.

Here's a related story. When I went back to the Aita area in 2003, there were young men there walking along the road who knew about me from before (they must have been kids then or heard about me from their parents). They didn't believe it was me from the Olden Days of 1978 or 1985 – perhaps my ghost. They said, in Tok Pisin, "*Tru, igat wanpela man, nem bilong em Jonatan, emi man bilong Merika, ibin istap hia long taim bipo. Tasol, dispela Jonatan, emi longpela, na tu ino gat planti gris.* (Yes, there was a man named Jonathan who was an American, who came here a long time ago. However, that Jonathan was tall and wasn't fat.)" I answered, "*Em mi tasol!* (That was me!)." Unconvinced, they went on, "*Tasol, dispela Jonatan bilong bipo, emi save wokabaut long mauntan na bik bus. Ino save sindaun insait long ka long rot olgeta taim.* (This Jonathan from the past went walking into the mountains and big forests. He didn't just sit in a car on the road all the time)." I answered again, "*Em mi tasol!*" Finally, they said, "*Dispela Jonatan, emi bin go long misin stesin na kaikai buai, na ai bilong em, emi bin go raun, na tu emi gat wara long sikin, na sampela sik, na emi paun daun long graun* (This Jonathan went to the mission plantation and chewed betel nut, and then his eyes went around in circles, he sweated a lot, he felt sick, and he had to lie down on the ground)." Again I said *"Em mi tasol!!!"* So that story was well remembered.

Going to the Bismarck Archipelago

After the various follow-ups had run their course, I had to consider extending the genetic coverage to the northwest, to the Bismarcks (New Britain, New Ireland, New Hanover, and other smaller islands). Gradually, one might suggest imperceptibly, like the movement of a glacier, I had begun to think more regionally, more broadly, which I had not seriously done before. I had focused at first on Bougainville diversity and subsequently the South Solomon Islands in the context of the Harvard follow-ups, and only paid begrudging attention to what was being reported in New Guinea, for example. Things seemed more complicated there, and the populations were much bigger.

It became clear to me, from just the materials that we began to collect, including materials from Blumberg's collection of sera where we did mitochondrial work, that the variability to the southeast of Bougainville declined considerably in amount, down the Solomon Islands chain, through eastern Melanesia, and beyond into the central Pacific (Andy Merriwether did mtDNA analysis that was reported in our 1999 *AJPA* paper, plus our Santa Cruz paper in *Human Biology*). Bougainville had exceptional internal genetic variability, and I began to realize that the amount of variability probably had to do with island size, that the larger the island, the larger the population differentiation. Language diversity appeared to be a good surrogate for genetic diversity, since the same is true linguistically – the language diversity gets less and less as one moves out from New Guinea into the central Pacific.

It was a good bet that New Britain, which was three times the size of Bougainville, and maybe New Ireland as well, also would have high internal genetic variability. So that's why ultimately it made sense to me to extend the coverage in that direction, to the northwest of Bougainville, and not to the southeast, where I assumed it would be all comparatively uniform. It's turned out that's true. Looking back, it was a pretty obvious conclusion.

Biogeography and Politics

JR: And why did you make that assumption?

JF: Because the islands to the southeast were smaller and linguistically they were almost all Austronesian languages. Also, if you look at the linguistic map of even a relatively big island in the south Solomons like Malaita, the languages extend from one coast to the other. They go across the island like stripes and the languages are all related.

In Bougainville, the languages are diverse. Besides the Austronesian languages scattered along the coastline, there are northern and southern clusters of old Papuan languages. Also, the language areas don't generally cross the central mountain chain. This pattern is even stronger in New Britain. Parts of New Britain are still highly volcanic, so some interior sections are uninhabited. When I started thinking about going to New Britain, I expected to find something similar to Bougainville in patterns of variation, but I wasn't sure about New Ireland, which is a thin long island with only one Papuan language in the middle section. The languages were distributed stripe-wise across the island as in Malaita. It turned out there's rather little genetic variability in New Ireland.

This all made me think back to island biogeographical models from Robert MacArthur and E.O. Wilson's book from 1967, *Island Biogeography*. Also, years ago, I participated in a Smithsonian conference where Jared Diamond talked about his analogy of human and bird dispersal abilities, that perhaps the Polynesians were like widespread "super-tramp" bird species and the Melanesians were like localized over-exploiter birds. So I thought, "Perhaps Diamond was correct, maybe it has to do with modes of migration or modes of travel, that the Polynesians or the pre-Polynesians who were in this area were able to travel the seacoast and live in different areas – offshore islands – successfully and pass through quickly with their revolutionary seagoing sailing outrigger canoes, as opposed to the early Papuan-speaking settlers who ultimately penetrated the island interiors." And that's worked out nicely. In our more recent surveys of the Bismarcks, it does appear that the Polynesian ancestors (the "Lapita People") passed through rather quickly and didn't have a lot of genetic exchange that we can detect now in those regions.

Now when I mention these island biogeographical model explanations to some archaeologists and geographers, they say, "Well, that's a little simple and passé . . ." Diamond and MacArthur's models, and Wilson's from the 1960s don't fit so well." David Stedman, in particular, who recently studied the ancient fauna of Pacific islands, in a book called *Extinction and Biogeography of Tropical Birds*, is hyper-critical of Diamond and Mayr's book on *Birds of Northern Island Melanesia*, published in 2000 (Diamond and Mayr argued that there's a close correspondence with the distribution of birds with different dispersal abilities). Steadman argues that current bird species distributions in the Pacific generally are different from what he thinks may have existed 1,000 years ago, before humans arrived, because of the marked extinction or depopulation of bird species by humans and their conspecifics like rats and snakes. However, after reading Stedman's book, I would say that's undoubtedly true for Polynesia and the smaller islands in the central Pacific, but even he somewhat qualifies his remarks for the big Melanesian islands close in to New Guinea, where I think the large island sizes made it less likely that birds would go extinct so quickly or completely with human invasion. The biggest birds and other mega-fauna certainly were driven quickly to extinction, but I'm talking about the rest.

So I still think MacArthur and Wilson provided an insightful and important model, and Diamond as well, concerning the distribution of genetic variability. It's important to think about the underlying dynamic across these Pacific islands in both the bird and human cases, of isolation and migration among islands. There were different kinds of technologies or migration capabilities that different cultures had. The Polynesians and their ancestors began to develop remarkable seafaring skills in the region of eastern Indonesia and Near Oceania (what has been called a seafaring nursery by Geoff Irwin). They were constantly going back and forth between the islands in that archipelago. That had to have a dramatic effect on genetic diversity in those groups, no matter how small they were. It would not have allowed a great deal of isolation and differentiation among these seafaring groups to develop, compared with the groups in the island interiors.

I have to say that we still don't know too much about New Guinea genetically. One would assume, by extrapolation from our work and the linguistic situation there, that New Guinea would be the most genetically diverse internally of all these Pacific islands. We don't have any indications of whether that is true with regard to mtDNA, Y chromosome, or microsatellite variation. What is clear from our work is that the overall variability within a typical New Guinea population is larger than the typical New Britain or Bougainville population, but the differences among groups may not be any more substantial (perhaps even less). This would be similar to the African situation. Perhaps there have been relatively recent population expansions in the New Guinea highlands, for example, that have homogenized things across populations. So that's still an unresolved issue. As you go farther west to Indonesia things may be different because of the closeness to mainland Asia. I would assume more recent intermixture and movement from the mainland, and the overlays may have created a lack of diversity between populations. That would be my guess from a biogeographical sort of perspective.

I also had practical reasons for going to the Bismarcks. We'd covered large sections of the Solomons at least for mtDNA, Bougainville was closed because of The Crisis, and I didn't want to go to New Guinea. I was afraid of the New Guinea highlanders. It is outlaw country. People would set ambushes by rolling down boulders on a passing truck, smash the front window, and then steal whatever they could from the passengers at gunpoint. I'm not the only one who feels that way. I was talking to about this to Glenn Summerhayes (he wrote the archaeology chapter in the 2007 Oxford University Press book), and he said, "I won't go there either. They're crazy, it's the Wild West!" And it is – just to go to the grocery store in Goroka, people take a shotgun or have an armed guard stay with their pickup truck. This is different from groups that I studied, by and large, although you have to be alert to volatile situations in any locale.

The Solomons were also closed to researchers oftentimes. For much of the last few decades, no new researchers were allowed in, but if you had been there before, you could go back, so I was grandfathered in a few times. In the last few years, however, Malaitamen who moved to the capital town Honiara became the focus of a great deal of resentment, and the Solomons entered a period of civil strife that had to be ended with New Zealand and Australian troops. So there were few places that were continuously open or reasonably safe places to go.

JR: And what time period would this have been?

JF: This was in the 1990s. Here's where you see, beginning in 1990, things get thin in my publication list.

Chapter 9.

The National Science Foundation: 1991-1995

National Science Foundation Program Director

That's when I became department chair at Temple and then a few years later got the position at NSF – getting involved in bureaucratic things, since I didn't have a clear or compelling research path. I'd followed a number of different research threads that for the moment seemed to lead nowhere. I was also trying to get out of Temple. There was a faculty strike here when I was the department chair, and it was quite unpleasant. My wife encouraged me to get out of academics altogether, and I even interviewed with a job placement person in Philadelphia who suggested I might make a good mid-level tour guide or some such. It made me realize my identity was firmly set as a biological anthropologist, no matter the problems.

So, I called up an old friend of mine at NSF, John Yellen, another former Harvard grad student in my cohort who was the NSF archaeology program director. I said, "John, is there a position open down there?" I knew that people often went there for a two-year term, and it made them more visible for other upper level jobs in the profession. Also, I was in an extremely difficult marriage and this would have offered a trial separation (this is also a common situation at NSF – a lot of the people who go there for a two year term are either single or trying to get out of difficult marital situations). He said, "Not this year Jonathan, but next year there will be an opening." And I said, "Please keep me in mind." So he called me up the following year because Mark Weiss, who was there as physical anthropology director, and who was excellent, was rotating off. He said "We'd like you to interview for the program directorship, especially with regard to developing the Human Genome Diversity Project. Mark thinks you'd be good for moving that along." I said to myself, "I know about that. It's Cavalli's baby and controversial." So, I went down to NSF and they kept me there for three years because they were trying to get the Human Genome Diversity Project off the ground even though it ultimately didn't work out, at least in the form we envisioned.

I should mention that, as a result of my NSF stint, I thought I'd become appointed the chair of the anthro department at Northwestern in 1995 (I had the recommendation of their search committee, the department, and the dean). At the last minute, their provost vetoed it. He said, "It looks like his publications are kind of thin recently, and it seems he's done with his research and has become a bureaucrat." Well, they *were* rather thin for that three-year period during the early 1990s. So I went back to Temple and Philadelphia in 1995.

The Human Genome Diversity Project

JF: Since the Human Genome Diversity Project was something I was brought to NSF to help promote, I should give more detail on its rationale and failure to gain federal funding.

With the development of transformed or immortalized cell lines beginning in the 1970s, it became a real possibility to think about a world-wide sampling of human diversity that would provide an essentially limitless DNA resource for future genetic work.

Immediately, there were two conflicting notions of how to sample the world's human genetic diversity. One was Cavalli's, and the other one was Allan Wilson's – two of the most influential human population geneticists of their generation. Cavalli's was more appealing to me. He said, "We want to look for variation across populations. Different languages would be a starting surrogate for the definition of populations – we don't have a better definition for a human population than a language group."

He then asked, "How many people, how many samples, do we require to represent each linguistically defined population?" Well, they did some largely irrelevant calculations and came up with a magic number of twenty-five "unrelated" people per group, meaning 50 chromosome sets per group. That seemed to be enough and satisfactory as a manageable number. Of course, it was primarily driven by budgetary considerations. More samples certainly would have been better, especially if they wanted to address issues concerning, for instance, linkage disequilibrium. Ken Kidd would have liked 100 people per group for that sort of analysis.

How many populations? Well, again, that depended on how much money they were going to get. Since it was going to be based on linguistic diversity, the areas of greatest language diversity would get the most intensive sampling (like sections of West Africa and Melanesia).

But Allan Wilson said, "You don't know that language patterns have anything to do with genetic diversity, and you're therefore injecting a strong starting bias into the sampling plan. We should just throw a grid on the world and have one person sampled per 10 miles on the grid intersections or something equivalent, since we can't know ahead of time the pattern of genetic diversity, or proper population limits. After that, we can talk about genetic diversity patterns and their correlates." Well, this argument still continues . . .

JR: I'm well aware . . .

JF: . . . Yes – with Svante Pääbö, who was Wilson's student, and on the other side, people who followed the linguistic theme of Cavalli-Sforza's. Those arguments have a history and their own continuing life. Of course Wilson died shortly thereafter, which considerably weakened his argument (!), and Cavalli was instrumental in trying to push a Human Genome Diversity Project for his own research agenda. While Pääbö continues to publish criticisms of Cavalli's approach, implying it was somehow racist because there was an implication that language groups have analogs to discrete populations, I think it's now clear that Cavalli's approach has been fruitful (and far more practical than having fieldworkers go to thousands of specified points on the map and take single blood samples from someone who happens to be there! How well would that work in New York or Bombay, for example?).

Also, there is no question that the distribution of human genetic diversity is uneven across the globe (I've called it "lumpy"), with many areas of genetic uniformity over large regions (like most of Asia, for example). Other regions, like Island Melanesia and parts of West Africa, are extraordinarily differentiated, so Wilson's grid approach would have glossed over a great deal of important information in those regions and would have been unnecessarily intensive in others.

So while I was at the NSF, I did what I could to promote the Human Genome Diversity Project. A lot of anthropologists, archaeologists, and physical anthropologists, maybe 40 or 50, came to Sardinia in 1991 to discuss the possibility of developing a Human Genome Diversity Project (this was just a month before I took over from Mark Weiss at NSF). There was another big organizational meeting at Penn State a year or so afterwards. Cavalli was very much behind the effort, of course.

Cavalli also came to NSF and gave a talk to the other program directors in population biology and the two sections of NSF possibly involved (Biology and Social Sciences), and we went to NIH for a presentation as well (he was not impressive – that's another story, but his talks always sounded too simple-minded; I think he talked down to audiences too much – I even heard one cultural anthropologist NAS member say, after a presentation, that he thought Cavalli was a charlatan, which was just a stupid ill-informed remark. A more telling criticism was that he was getting old, that his language betrayed an earlier generation's colonial attitude towards indigenous groups, and that he didn't appear dynamic enough to lead such an effort).

The most supportive person at NIH of the Human Genome Diversity Project was Irene Eckstrand, but unfortunately, she didn't have much clout. Judith Greenberg was her superior, I believe, and was a program officer in General Medical Sciences at NIH and involved in the Human Genome Project, or what became the National Human Genome Research Institute. James Watson was a major early proponent and head of the Human Genome Project, and was succeeded by Francis Collins after Watson's resignation. Greenberg's support was essential to get if the follow-on Diversity Project was to succeed, both for financial and political considerations. When the political winds started blowing

Human Genome Diversity Program organizational meeting in Penn State. Mentioned individuals, from left: 1st row; 2nd – Trevor Jenkins, 5th – Judith Kidd, 6th – Mike Crawford, Irene Eckstrand. 2nd row: 2nd – Marc Feldman; 6th – Mark Weiss; 8th – Luca Cavalli-Sforza. 3rd row: 1st – Henry Harpending; 3rd – Francisco Salzano; 7th – JSF; 10th – Mary Claire King; 13th – Kuldeep Bhatia. 5th row: 1st – Ken Weiss; 4th – Ryk Ward; 10th – John Yellen; 17th – Napoleon Chagnon; 20th Mark Stoneking.

against the Diversity Project, especially from Native Americans, North and South America, Greenberg got scared off. I also think she was not convinced that she wanted to devote NIH monies of any kind to this project, so it pretty much died that way. It wasn't clear, at least at that point, what the medical or clinical health benefits of the Diversity Project were going to be in the future, so NIH's involvement would have been problematic even if there hadn't been the political uproar, I believe. Bureaucrats who succeed are often quite timid or don't have particularly great vision, only following in the assured paths blazed by scientific leaders, and I would include Greenberg in that group. The other major problem was that the Human Genome Project itself was so expensive that it was vacuuming up all the available funds. A diversity project couldn't compete.

We even tried to get money from the Department of Energy (former Atomic Energy Commission) because of the history of Neel's Yanomami project being supported by them, but that was a total dead-end. So I was unsuccessful in this whole thing. I don't think anyone blamed me, though – it became an impossible sell.

The political opposition got to be discouraging. I received a letter when I was at NSF from a Native American chief (I don't know if he was a *bona fide* chief or not) of a Seneca group in New York State, essentially saying, "We are worried about the use of our sacred blood, we don't want this project done, and you must respect our rights" and so on. Others at NSF and especially NIH were concerned about this and other protests from indigenous rights groups. I don't know if I have a copy of that letter or not. I bet it's in that *Cultural Survival* issue I guest-edited on the whole uproar. Did you see that?

JR: Yes.

JF: It might be in there.

Carol Jenkins and the RAFI Controversy

JF: Also, it was during this period when Carol Jenkins was being attacked by RAFI.[20] Carol was a wonderful researcher, a medical anthropologist at the Institute for Medical Research in Papua New Guinea. She also had become involved in the gene patenting controversy.

During the first Bush administration, Bernadine Healy, the head of NIH, made it a policy that NIH scientists should commercialize scientific discoveries as they made them. So gene patenting was encouraged and became a common practice at NIH. Accordingly, a researcher in Panama, I believe it was Rick Yanagihara, filed a patent application on the cell line within which the HTLV-1 virus was isolated – following Healy's directive. That's what was picked up by RAFI, which was originally concerned with patenting of plants in rural areas where a great many indigenous groups lived.

Carol, in Papua New Guinea, was involved in HTLV-1 research with Rick. She was surveying an isolated group in the fringe highlands called the Hagahai. She explained carefully to them what was involved. "If any money ever is to be made from your blood that might come to me, I hereby sign that money over to you" – I saw this on tape as documentation. This is discussed in that *Cultural Survival* issue, as well. I had her teach at Temple for a semester and the students were hanging out the windows, she was popular as a lecturer – great stories, and a compelling personality doing good work. I think Muriel Kirkpatrick [head of the Temple Anthropology Laboratory] had said you had looked at the health education cartoons she developed. She also wrote or edited a book on abuse of women in New Guinea, with a lot of interviews and personal stories, which caused a great deal of controversy there. The Powers That Be didn't like it one bit, or her subsequent work on the spread of HIV-AIDS in Papua New Guinea. She was heavily involved in women's rights and health and a real dynamo. It was extraordinarily unfair that she was so ferociously attacked by RAFI. They were a 2-bit outfit of about 4 people with a computer in Ottowa who thought they were doing "good things" in a totally unsophisticated, rabble-rousing,

20 RAFI stands for the Rural Advancement Foundation International. It is now located in Pittsboro, NC and focuses on agricultural issues in North Carolina and the Southeast.

way. I have printed out a long history of my angry internet exchanges with them over Native-L, if you want to see those – interesting, I think. Those will go into the archive, as well [The Melanesian Archive at the University of California, San Diego]. They got especially irritated when I accused them of using Jesse Helms-like tactics of guilt by association.

My alleged role in any gene patenting was easy to refute even if it meant I had months of sleepless nights. RAFI just put 2 and 2 together, and got 6. They saw I was government-supported, that I was working at NSF and had also done research and took blood samples in Papua New Guinea and the Solomon Islands, so therefore I was probably patenting peoples' genes as well. This was simply not true. But I couldn't be involved in further collection of blood for transformation into cell lines – it was clear when I went back to the Solomons and PNG that cell lines were "out" in the 1990s and being involved in the Human Genome Diversity Project was also out. Those things became totally taboo. So world-wide, the prospect of collecting cell lines for the prospective Human Genome Diversity Project (or any other sort of study) became a *cause célèbre*. The Nasioi cell lines we had helped establish in the mid-1980s remained acceptable in terms of informed consent regulations at that time (grandfathered in, one might say), as do others collected in that early period.

Those from the 1980s form the basis of the "Human Genome Diversity Panel" now with CEPH[21]. This is what became of the attempt to develop the human genome diversity project, with a small number of transformed samples from a variety of populations around the globe. As I understand it from the Kidds, this was, again, Cavalli's suggestion to Jean Dausset at CEPH, and Dausset had the money and interest to support it. The Noah Rosenberg *et al.* paper from 2002 on the analysis by Marshfield of 300 microsatellites in those samples was the obvious first product. Cell lines have enormous advantages over any other repository, since they offer essentially unlimited amounts of DNA – and with whole genome scans, large amounts of DNA are now required. The other advantage of cell lines will be that, since they're

21 *Centre d'Étude du Polymorphisme Humain* – originally founded to support work in the HLA genetic polymorphism, which is an extremely variable gene that is involved in the immune response

actual cells rather than just the DNA, it's possible to study what's called gene expression – which gene variants produce specific protein or amino acid products in functioning cells.

So, in the end, Cavalli got a diversity collection, considerably smaller than originally envisioned, essentially because of convincing one critical man (Dausset), rather than the U.S. funding agencies, to support the effort.

Andy Merriwether's Role

JR: Maybe now is just a good time for you to explain who Andy Merriwether is and how you came to work with him.

JF: Sure. While I was in Washington at the NSF, I went to a genetics meeting sponsored by the Air Force in Alexandria, Virginia, and I heard Andy give a talk there. The meeting was on how genetic diversity could inform ideas on ancient population relationships. Of course, the military was beginning to use more powerful genetic identification methods in identifying MIA remains from Vietnam and elsewhere.

Andy's paper was on his thesis, on mtDNA diversity in the Americas. He started as a student of Doug Wallace who was an early American mtDNA worker, and then afterwards with Bob Ferrell at the University of Pittsburgh. I'd been aware of the mtDNA advances, especially because of the grant proposals I read at NSF and other meetings in Washington. MtDNA analysis had taken off in the 1980s, primarily in Allan Wilson's lab, before the development of PCR (polymerase chain reaction[22]), so it required whole placentas for analysis (these are particularly rich in mtDNA copies). I remember approaching Wilson early on about the possibility of a collaboration, but I had no way of obtaining placentas, so that fell flat at the time – instead, he got some New Guinea placentas from a hospital in Goroka, with Kuldeep Bhatia's cooperation (Kuldeep was then at the PNG Institute for Medical Research).

22 The polymerase chain reaction (PCR), revolutionary in its time, is now a widely used technique in genetics laboratories of making thousands or millions of copies of short stretches of DNA. This enables many different analyses of DNA from a single individual.

Andy's was the first mtDNA paper I'd heard that comprehensively sampled a lot of populations across a large geographical region. He was using the PCR reaction to get decent amounts of DNA from each sample. It wasn't just what I called "stamp collection" sampling – a one from here, one from there sort of thing. He was able to describe frequency variation from Alaska to Chile in different mtDNA haplotypes. This was much better than Wallace's early work in the Americas. Wallace had identified four distinctive genetic combinations, which are called haplogroups, that he named A, B, C & D. He rather naïvely said, "One migration carried Haplogroup A, another carried B, another C, and a last one carried D, and they were distributed almost discontinuously in the Americas." That was a little silly, because it was obvious that one initial founding population of the Americas could have had all four haplogroups that underwent subsequent genetic drift and differential loss of certain haplotypes. Andy showed a lot of haplotype variability across the Americas. So after I heard the talk, I went up to him and I said –

JR: Where had he gotten his data from?

JF: I think a number of different freezer collections. I can't recall, but the numbers were much larger for each population than what I'd seen before, especially from the early studies 5-10 years before, that relied on placentas and had perhaps only 100-150 samples in total. You could find that out just from looking at his old publications, probably.

JR: Andy Merriwether had an article called, "Freezer Anthropology." It's a survey saying, "We've got this new technology, we've also got these frozen sera; what would happen if we put the two together?" He added some speculations about that. He does say, "These are the people that I know of that have these sera," so he names you, he names Baruch Blumberg . . .

JF: We obtained a number of samples from southern Island Melanesia (primarily Santa Cruz, New Caledonia, and Vanuatu) from Baruch Blumberg that were analyzed and published in some of our early mtDNA papers, including the Santa Cruz one, which was just on Blumberg's samples. Andy has them . . .

JR: He has Blumberg's samples? But doesn't Blumberg have a lot of samples still as well . . .

JF: He has tons. He was known as a "Have syringe, will travel" kind of collector.

JF: So, I went up to Andy after hearing his paper at the conference, and said "I like your population approach," since I had always believed in intensive sampling of populations. I said, "I have these old plasmas from Bougainville. Do you think you could work with these from the 1960s and 1980s?" He said, "Yes!" He was familiar with my work I guess, but I learned later that Andy always said "yes." There was never a new project offer he could refuse! That's how that collaboration began. He did find a lot of interesting variation in Bougainville, this sharp distributional cline related to this marker, this mtDNA 9-base pair deletion – do you know about this?

JR: I've read about it in the publications.

JF: It was early associated with the spread of Austronesians and Polynesians through the Pacific. Polynesians had a marker in high frequency, a 9-base pair deletion in one part of the mtDNA associated with some other mutations (making it a variant of the B haplotype), which was missing in the highlands of New Guinea. It appeared this could be traced back to Taiwan, and its precursors were in East Asia. This appeared to have been closely associated with the spread of the ancestors of the Polynesians. It was the basis of a lot of what Jared Diamond talked about with the "fast train from Taiwan" model of Polynesian origins. We found in Bougainville that the distribution of this marker closely mirrored that old north-south Inv distribution Steinberg and I had found. It didn't delineate Austronesians from non-Austronesians in Bougainville. Yes, the Papuan-speaking Aita, up in the northern mountains totally lacked it, but as you moved south it became extremely common, even in the southern Papuan speakers. So, that's what we wrote our 1999 paper about. At first, I said to Andy, "Are you sure about this result? Those Papuan-speakers in the south, you sure the 9-base pair deletion is almost 100% there? Go back and redo those." He did, and the first test results were confirmed.

It was on the basis of that mtDNA variability within Bougainville that we put in a new grant proposal together to NSF when I went back to Temple in 1996 or thereabouts.

Chapter 10.

Fieldwork in the Bismarck Archipelago: 1998-2003

The Field Teams and the Fieldwork Progression

Our first application for NSF funding for a survey in the Bismarcks was unsuccessful, but on reapplication (or re-reapplication), Andy received a medium-sized NSF lab-based grant, and I got other grants from the Wenner-Gren Foundation and National Geographic for the fieldwork aspect, beginning in 1998. That was also the first time I was affiliated with the Institute for Medical Research in Papua New Guinea. They had insisted on it. The director, Michael Alpers, said, "You can't come independently any more. You've been doing this long enough by yourself, Jonathan. You've got to have a training aspect of your grant for Papua New Guineans as well."

1998. George Koki, Dan Hrdy, and JSF

So I took along their house geneticist, George Koki, who had been trained locally by a couple of good laboratory workers, especially Kuldeep Bhatia from Australia, who specialized in HLA analysis. George is a Tolai, who live on the Gazelle Peninsula, where Queen Emma had her plantations. It was an easy thing for him to go back there in 1998, even though he worked at the Institute of Medical Research, which was in the New Guinea highlands. He was an excellent blood taker as well as a laboratory geneticist. The officials at the Institute (Alpers and Charles Mgone) insisted, "George is your man." And of course, I said "O.K." I had no choice! So I met George in Goroka, we went off to the Gazelle Peninsula, and we started out sampling Tolai villages that he knew well. I said, "George, we also want to do this neighboring inland group, the Baining," but it was clear that he wasn't as comfortable there. It was a slow fieldwork season because we would first talk to people one day in a village, and then we would decide on a later day when we would come back for sampling. Sometimes that would be three or four days afterwards. Also, a lot of the villages were Seventh Day Adventist (*Seven Dei*), so you couldn't go on a Saturday. Others, you couldn't work on Sundays, and since George was a *Seven Dei*, that would often mean the entire weekend was out. It meant a lot of delays. As time wore on and we came to be more comfortable with each other, he understood that I wanted to get more samples. So we covered the Tolai and the Baining during that season with a total of about 450 samples, which was O.K., especially since the Baining have turned out to be the most distinctive group genetically in New Britain or the entire region.

Because George had a long history as a nurse in Papua New Guinea, he knew a lot of people in the health service all over the country. This came to be a standing joke in our 2000 expedition, which included Andy and Heather Norton as well as George. We'd go into a town for supplies and we wouldn't want George to get out of the truck (he had the driver's insurance coverage and had to drive), because if he got out of the truck, he would be recognized by all kinds of old friends on the street and have to stop and talk to them. It was, "Here comes the 'Knows George' routine again." He was a friendly and well-known character. So, he was absolutely critical to our success as things developed in New Britain.

Dan Hrdy, old Harvard Solomon Island Expedition alum with a Harvard MD/PhD, also was along for about half of the 1998 field season, and helped greatly with the blood taking and processing, as he'd done in the 1980s as well. Dan is an excellent fieldworker, reliable and even-tempered. His training is primarily as a virologist, and he's been involved in publications from the Pacific in HTLV-1 variation.

He and then George left towards the end of that 1998 season, and then I went off by myself to a remote group in the mountains called the Kol, who were supposed to be ferocious head-hunters. George didn't want to go there because he was scared of them! The supposedly ferocious sub-group was called the Makolkol. I was running out of blood collecting tubes and also experimenting with cheek swabs, so not too many of their samples were included in the microsatellite battery analysis by Marshfield, which required more DNA. But that's another story.

JR: Would you say that it's more common now to use saliva than blood? Do you think there are any implications there (i.e., does the actual swab get saved as the blood did or is it just the DNA inscription?).

JF: What you get with a cheek swab are cells scraped from the inside cheek – from the endothelium. Cheek swabs are certainly easier to use and less intrusive or painful than a blood sample, but the DNA yield is many times smaller than for blood. No matter how hard you scrape, unless you start to get blood, you're not going to have many cells with DNA. Cheek swabs are totally inadequate for most contemporary genomic studies that include many hundreds of microsatellite markers or hundreds of thousands of SNPs. For mtDNA and a few Y markers, they're acceptable. Often, even 10 cc. of blood isn't sufficient. We even had to amplify our buffy coats taken from the blood that contains the white cells (with what is called whole genome amplification, or WGA) to get enough DNA copy yield for analysis, and any process of copying can lead to errors in typing. It would have been far worse with cheek swabs, if it were even possible (and the Kol cheek swabs were not adequate – Andy's lab tried). You never know all the important variables, however. In Island Melanesia, there is a great deal of betel nut chewing, so you can't effectively get a decent cheek-swab from someone who has a mouthful of betel nut juice or other detritus in his mouth. Seventh Day Adventists, however, don't chew betel nut, so cheek swabs were a possibility in those groups (that meant the Aita in Bougainville and the Kol in New Britain, especially).

2000. Koki, Norton, Merriwether, and JSF

Our 1998 expedition set the stage for George's continuing involvement. In 2000, Andy got NSF money for George to be trained at his Michigan lab in mtDNA sequencing and alignment. So George came to Ann Arbor just before Christmas of 1999, and in June of 2000 we all went out for a field season in the summer together, with Heather Norton – the four of us.

Heather's is an interesting story as well. She was an undergraduate at Penn State in biological anthropology and got her own traveling fellowship from there. She had never been out of the country. She didn't have a passport, much less a research visa from PNG (those take forever to get – about a year, ordinarily – I spent hundreds of dollars on long distance phone calls to the Papua New Guinea Immigration Office trying to get our visas processed in the months before we left).

It began when Mark Shriver, her advisor, wanted to bring down two or three of his grad students to Temple to talk about possible collaborations on my collections and data, and I showed them around. Before they left, he basically volunteered Heather as a team member, much to her surprise (this was about April, and we were leaving in June). The idea was to add skin and hair color reflectance measurements to our battery with a sensitive new instrument they were using, a DermaSpectrometer. I thought that would be interesting (the Harvard Solomons study had done reflectance with an insensitive reflectance instrument called a PhotoVolt – one of my jobs in the first expedition I forgot to mention – but since it was so primitive, everyone came out with the same dark readings – I could make far better distinctions with my eye). She got her passport and we managed to get her research visa just in time for her to join us. She was great in the field, and she's done well since then. Her doctoral thesis was on the materials she collected and analyzed in 2000, supplemented by the skin and hair reflectance data I took in 2003, and a fine published paper resulted. Among other things, it shows that Bougainville people are as heavily pigmented as the darkest West Africans (while New Britain and New Ireland populations are considerably less so), and that a series of gene variants that influence skin color in Africans are apparently not the ones responsible for the dark pigmentation in Bougainville – it appears there are other variants that are responsible.

George was the key field person. George took the blood samples, Andy was doing the interviewing for demographic data because he was unfamiliar with the actual blood-taking, and Heather was doing skin color reflectance and hair color reflectance. I was left to do the "consenting" of everybody and taking pictures and glad-handing and so on. I had worked myself out of a job in the survey line, which felt quite strange to me. I was used to doing something more in the way of data collection, whether it was measuring people, taking blood, or doing the demographic interviews. One day, I remember, we sampled over 100 people. It was just overwhelming. People liked the idea that George, a local man from New Britain, was taking the samples and being part of this scientific investigative group. That was a positive thing. While initially I had not been particularly keen on collaboration with someone from the Institute for Medical Research, once it was imposed on me, it was obviously beneficial. George turned out to be essential. As I said, besides being our phlebotomist and general ambassador, he was our driver. So later, when I organized the symposium for the American Association of Physical Anthropologists in Tampa, in 2004, I paid for George to come over and present one of the papers. He did well, and we had a great time.

2003. Koki and JSF

George and I went back in 2003 for a last season together. It was just the two of us, to finish up some of the other groups, in West New Britain and north Bougainville and Buka. That was an interesting trip, a lot of it on video. George gave educational chats to interested villagers, explaining basic medical genetics. I have a video of him using bananas, oranges, and papayas to illustrate how malaria parasites invade red blood cells, make them sickle in some people (not in PNG), and how ovalocytosis protects people from malaria as well (a common condition along the PNG north coast). He ended up getting malaria himself in Bougainville, and we had to abort the field season a few weeks early as a result.

JR: Is he O.K.?

JF: Oh yes, he's fine, although he did have one relapse subsequently. He hadn't brought a mosquito net in 2003 and claimed he didn't need it, since he was from Rabaul and had developed an acquired immunity. What he didn't realize was that he'd spent so much time in the malaria-free highlands that he'd lost his acquired immunity. I'd offered to have him sleep under my net with me, but he'd refused. Fortunately, I had enough malaria prophylaxis pills to get him through the attack until we got him back to Goroka Hospital. I'd never cared for anyone with a severe malaria attack, and it was frightening. He had a high fever (I had no thermometer, so I'm not sure if it got to 105, which is critical).

He was shaking uncontrollably, and was getting disoriented. I wasn't sure what to do – my prescription was for a prophylactic dosage of malarone, and I didn't know how much more to give him, and so I tripled my dosage and held him next to me (probably a mistake – a bath in a cold stream would have been better). His condition improved overnight, to some degree, so we just left Bougainville and went back to Goroka as fast as we could.

That was the last time I've been in the field – 2003.

Chapter 11.

Analysis of the New Genetic Data

Initial Problems

I was relying on Andy to do the mtDNA lab work and also the subsequent data analysis. But Andy had so many irons in the fire in the late 1990s, plus moving to Binghamton from Ann Arbor, that he couldn't handle that expeditiously, and I was always complaining.

JR: Was he at Binghamton already at this time?

JF: He was. Part of the problem was he was in transition from Michigan to Binghamton, so that was an interval when he was delayed in terms of laboratory analysis. Andy's an excellent, conscientious laboratory worker, but because of various interruptions and other reasons his publication list isn't as long as it should be. As a result, he hasn't been able to compete successfully over the long haul for the small amounts of money that come out of NSF for Anthropology. I think that is one reason he has increasingly turned to alpaca genetics work.

JR: Can you say a bit about what you know about the alpaca work or at least how do you think his training in working with human materials and human genetics prepared him? Or, how hard of a transition do you think that is to make, to go from working on humans to working on animals?

JF: DNA sequencing is the same universal technique. Comparing the sequences with known variants from a particular species is where the specificity comes in. You need to know the key mutations that define the major haplogroups for the species you're dealing with. He is working on an alpaca genome project. He and his wife began to raise alpacas in Michigan. So that's where it started. When he was denied tenure there and was looking for places to move, he wanted to make sure he had the ability to have an alpaca farm. So that's what they did. He'll take you there – or he should.

JR: That would be wonderful. I would love that.

Françoise's Role

JF: This is where my wife Françoise's involvement in the data analysis became critical, and was a big surprise. Sometime in 2002 (we met in 2000), I was working on the adolescent growth material from the 1980s, and she looked over my shoulder and said, "You know, I think I might be able to help you with this." And I said, "Really? Please give it a try." So she began to be able to identify outliers and pull it together efficiently and effectively. We spent months going through those old data sets together, putting them in good shape.

Then, a short time later, while I was becoming increasingly worried we were going to be scooped on the mtDNA findings because of the slow pace at Andy's lab, she came to the rescue again on the analysis of the mtDNA data. There was a series of network software programs developed by a German mathematician named Hans-Jurgen Bandelt that created networks of haplogroup relationships separated by their stepwise mutational differences (these are known as Bandelt networks). That had become the standard analytical tool for mtDNA papers. Françoise said, "Maybe I can run that Bandelt program on the data." I said, "Well, sure, give it a try." In a day or so, she quickly learned how to run the Bandelt networks on the mtDNA data Andy had generated in his lab, and then went on from there to essentially take over the data analysis of the mtDNA work. I was flabbergasted.

While I was in the field in 2003 with George, I called her up at one point, and she said, "I found a woman on the web (from Alberta) and we've been working on the mtDNA materials from the Pacific that we've compiled from 1998, and from everyone else's publications before. She, Gisele Horvat, was clarifying unassigned published mtDNA materials as a hobby, and our samples fit in nicely. We think we've been able to solve the puzzle of how some of these distinctive haplogroups in the Pacific fit with those from other parts of the world." I said, "That's great!" She said, "Some are clearly entirely new branches of haplogroup P and haplogroup Q." P and Q were the only ones that had been tied into the world-wide mtDNA relationship tree at that point – Pacific mtDNA was a mess then. I said, "Hmm, that doesn't sound so exciting..." I was hoping that some of our unusual mtDNA haplogroups were entirely distinctive or perhaps distantly related to Africans. In fact, it turned out that the new side branches of the Ps and Qs that she and her Internet friend Gisele found were the basis of one of our most cited papers. Tad Schurr also contributed to this analysis. It's called "Expanding haplogroups P and Q in the Southwest Pacific." What she wanted to call it was "Mining the P's and Q's" (as in data-mining, and also minding the P's and Q's – a double pun).

JR: That's cute.

JF: I said, "No, no, the geneticists aren't going to like that. It will be rejected as too cute. The serious geneticists like Bandelt will just snicker!" So we called it something less eye-catching, but certainly it should have been "Mining . . . ." I've subsequently heard it referred to as the 'Mining the P's and Q's paper'. It's such an obvious unstated title, it's become known that way.

JR: That's a great story.

JF: The P and Q paper was our first big mtDNA tree paper published in a higher profile biological sciences journal – in *Molecular Biology and Evolution* – than the *American Journal of Physical Anthropology*, for example (it has a much higher impact value). It was put online in an early edition, pre-publication format a week or so prior to general release. Within a couple of days, I got an email – with a very superior tone – from Hans-Jurgen Bandelt himself (whom we'd never met) saying, "Dr. Friedlaender, we all make mistakes, but we think this part of your tree has had an error, and this part of your tree has about five or six big errors" – that Françoise had made in her first big mtDNA tree construction. He said, "You're going to have to publish an erratum" (an embarrassing prospect, but it happens fairly frequently). He had become well known for pointing out, in print, all the errors that were cropping up in the published mtDNA trees of others. He and a colleague named Yao in Bethesda became known among us as the "mtDNA police."

Françoise looked at his email details and said, "My god, he's right!" Fortunately, we had about a week before final publication. So she corrected the tree and we wrote him an email that said, "Thank you very much Dr. Bandelt, we appreciate your corrections, and fortunately we had a chance to change the manuscript because it was just in a preliminary form online before the final publication data." I added, "Can we put you on in the Acknowledgements?" And he said, "Sure." So it was a putdown for our first big attempt in this area, but we recovered in time.

A couple of years later, Françoise and I gave our first big paper on the mtDNA, Y, plus the new microsatellite materials to a small select group of 25 participants in Uppsala, Sweden in December, 2006. Yao was one of the other participants. He turned out to be young, about 26. We said "Oh, we thought you were 60, since you are part of the mtDNA police." And he said, "I'm just a small policeman!" He's a charming guy, and he loved our paper we gave there.

Going back to the P and Q paper, which was our first joint one, Françoise was not where she should have been in the author list. She was buried somewhere in the middle.

JR: Is this kind of issue compounded in any way by the unique collaborative nature of genomic-based anthropology work? For example, does the person who procured the samples get listed as an author? In other words, is the fieldworker considered an author? What about the person who runs the lab analysis versus the person who analyzed the data versus the person who developed the hypothesis/research question, etc?

JF: Author placement in papers is a contentious and unclear proposition, and the conventions vary from discipline to discipline. In typical lab science articles, the two most important places are first and last (the first and senior author positions). A post doc often does the major analysis in a major professor's lab and drafts the paper, so he/she will be the first author, and successive authors down the list are supposed to be of decreasing importance or involvement until you get to the final, senior author, position, who is the person in charge of the lab and makes sure everything is up to snuff. All this is important when 10, 15, or even 20 people contribute. However, other considerations and negotiations enter in. If someone is up for tenure or promotion, they might press for a higher ranking than others think appropriate. Or someone might have been "promised" a prominent author position early on, even if they didn't finally deserve it. I did most of the writing in all our collaborative papers on mtDNA, but since, for example, Andy was responsible for all the lab analysis, and he wanted to be first author on the first mtDNA paper in 1999, as well as the *PNAS* paper[23], I thought that was acceptable. This is why many journals now require an "author footnote" that specifies the nature of the contribution of each author. In anthropology, this convention is not followed so precisely. Some people in anthropology tend to feel that there should be only one author (the one who wrote it, with perhaps some acknowledgement to helpers in the field and lab). Others feel that lab work should be acknowledged only in the first report, and not thereafter (as R.J.Walsh believed, as I mentioned earlier).

Returning to Françoise, she and Andy's group, who performed complete mtDNA sequencing on a number of samples (that was Jason Hodgson, Sal Cerchio, and Robin Allaby), with some assistance from Tad Schurr, established that the remaining odd unclassified mtDNA haplogroups were remotely related to the large M family of haplogroups, and hadn't been seen anywhere before and must have had a separate 40,000 or 50,000 year history. That was another important paper, in the *PNAS*, where we named these three old Melanesian mtDNA haplogroups (M27, with three deep branches, M28, and M29).

This was before Françoise got involved with all the analysis of the microsatellite data analysis, of course. She learned the necessary analytic techniques for that from the third author, Floyd Reed, who was a post doc with Sarah Tishkoff (Floyd is an exceptionally bright young geneticist that you'll hear more about as time goes on). The main program she used for that is called STRUCTURE, which has become the standard for this sort of genomic analysis – and now she's using that for Sarah, for her

23 *The Proceedings of the National Academy of Sciences* – a prestigious scientific journal.

paper that's not out yet on African populations. She's just remarkably good with this kind of data manipulation and analysis.

JR: There are at least two other parts to this story. One is the rise of sophistication in computational power and statistics that enables you to do these kinds of analyses. The other is the personal dimension of work. In the history of science there are numerous stories of collaborations with spouses. However, it has not always been the case that a wife would be included or acknowledged at all—

JF: You mean, as an author.

JR: Yes, as an author.

JF: The unacknowledged power behind the throne . . . You know, I think that we can talk about it now; I have to look at that paper. I think that she was down the line in the author list in the first mtDNA paper, the P's and Q's, where she was cutting her teeth, but had been responsible for most of the analytic work. She was third or fourth. She shouldn't have been. She should have been second author. She never did any writing, that's not her *forte*. That generally disqualifies her from being first author. Now she's sort of my little secret that's no longer a secret. She's the best (free) help around. For example, Sarah is just amazed at what she's doing on that African paper. I think it's fair to say she's saved Sarah's paper, since Floyd left Sarah's lab and took a new position in Germany. Everything had to be redone because of program bugs that spoiled the first set of runs. I mean everything. That includes runs that take days and even weeks to convert and run. Sarah wasn't going to do it. Nobody else was going to be able or willing to do it.

And now, the Kidds are just waiting to have her as a collaborator, so Françoise can get involved there. So, she's a hot ticket right now.

JR: It is an interesting story though, how your relationship has made a difference to the science.

JF: Oh yes, it's been wonderful. Especially between 2002 and now, it has made a big difference, and I retired in 2004. That's what we did to occupy ourselves. We'd sit around with our laptops all day and I would go over what she was running, and she would read what I had written, and we'd go back and forth with different suggestions and criticisms. It became a great collaboration.

We got married when I had a recurrence of my melanoma in early 2004. When I discovered that, she said, "You have to retire," and I said "And we have to get married! Because, there's no reason not to do it, and I want you to be able to be around at the hospital and so on." The Oxford book came out after a couple of years' more work, and all these fine journal publications appeared, all in an apparent flurry of activity. So my illness has been a large goad or slap in the face, to do what I was going to do while I could. It's been a wonderfully productive period and it's been wonderful in terms of our relationship as well.

One last story—a few years ago, just when we were writing up the papers on mtDNA trees that were subsequently published in *PNAS* and elsewhere, I was asked by Sarah Tishkoff to give a seminar at Maryland. I accepted, but the next year she asked again, and I made it plain I wanted Françoise to come as well. Sarah said "Oh, how cute!" What she didn't realize until the seminar was that I wanted Françoise there to answer any questions on methodology. Subsequently, I've made it clear that we both had to be invited to different seminars, since she's been primarily responsible for the increasingly complex data analysis.

JR: Can you go back and say a little bit about Françoise's background?

JF: Yes, her maiden name was Rubinstejn (we've both been married three times). She came to this country from France when she was 20 to escape a terrible family situation. Her parents were Polish survivors of World War II who'd come to Paris in the 1930's and escaped first Polish anti-Semitism and then the Nazis and French collaborators there – they were both damaged emotionally, and she had extremely poor parenting as a result (she was born shortly after the war). Her mother died when she was 8 and her father expected her to be a seamstress in their tailoring business. But she was always smart, always good in math, and necessarily independent, and so she lined herself up a job at University of Washington in St. Louis as a med tech in 1967.

She discovered that people in the lab at Wash U, even just with undergraduate degrees, were being paid more for the same work that she was doing, so she decided she was going to get an advanced degree, even though she didn't even have a bachelor's degree in France. She said, "I have a French technical school degree, the equivalent of an American undergraduate degree. I should be entering a PhD program." It was late August and they needed a Teaching Assistant, so they put her on a probationary period and entered her into the theoretical chemistry program, which she chose because it was the shortest way to get a PhD among the math, physics, and chemistry programs. She finished in four years, at age 24. Now she says she can't understand what she wrote for her dissertation!

Then she married. Her husband got a job at DuPont in Wilmington, and she went there as well after finishing her doctorate at Wash U, and then did a post-doc at Penn in quantum mechanics. She stayed at DuPont for 30 years (she was an early woman professional there). She ended up in financial modeling of business performance incorporating a lot of, "what ifs?" as she says [interaction options]. She is comfortable and facile with a large variety of software programs and large complicated data sets. Her colleagues called her the "Excel Ninja."

We met on the Internet, in 2000, a few months after we had both divorced our previous spouses. So we fell in love, but none of her mathematical skills and applications to our data entered into the personal calculations at all, as the work collaboration didn't begin until two years later.

Y Chromosome Analysis

It is also important to talk about the Y chromosome analysis of our Island Melanesian samples. This turned into another successful collaborative project, with Michael Hammer and Tanya Karafet at Arizona, and Joe Lorenz at The Coriell Institute in Camden. A graduate student of mine, Laura Scheinfeldt, had been trained by Joe Lorenz in a number of molecular genetics techniques, and she, with Joe's help, performed the Y chromosome analysis. I also had her get in touch with Hammer and Karafet, who were the earliest and perhaps most authoritative Y chromosome workers for advice. A fine paper came out of that collaboration (along with Laura's thesis), which showed an analogous pattern to the mtDNA of hyper-diversity in New Britain and Island Melanesia, with some interesting distinctions, showing gender differences in patterns of migration and intermarriage. They also identified some new, or previously unknown, Y chromosome haplogroups.

I don't know why, but this paper hasn't yet received as much attention as our mtDNA papers, but I think ultimately it will. Again, Françoise was involved in the analysis, as she had become involved in training our graduate students in learning the fine points of Bandelt networking, sequence analysis, and so forth. Two other grad students, Danielle James and Krista Latham, are completing their dissertations on Pacific mtDNA and Y chromosome work, as well, and Françoise has also been a major help to them, too. Because of all her involvement in graduate training, I wanted to have her given a title in the Temple Anthropology Department as a Research Associate or some equivalent, but Chuck (then the chair) said since she didn't have a degree in anthropology, that wasn't possible. I thought that was a short-sighted mistake, but Françoise didn't care about it, so I didn't contest it. So in the publications, she's listed simply as an "Independent Researcher," as is Gisele Horvat – this is unheard of in scientific journals.

Sarah Tishkoff and the Marshfield Clinic

Another important development occurred at the meeting of the American Association of Physical Anthropologists in Milwaukee in 2004. Françoise and I went there just for a day because there were a couple of symposia we wanted to see and some people we wanted to talk to. One morning symposium had almost all the human population genetics papers. Lisa Matisoo-Smith was in the audience, and I also wanted to talk with Keith Hunley about a possible collaboration and a chapter for our Oxford book. In the symposium, Sarah Tishkoff was giving a paper along with her post doc Floyd Reed, and so were Jeff Long, Keith Hunley, Joanna Mountain, Mike Hammer, their post docs, and so on. Sarah came up to me afterwards in the hall and said, "Jonathan, there's a chance of a lifetime for you. You have to apply to have your materials analyzed by Jim Weber's Marshfield Clinic

Group for their large microsatellite battery. They're closing up shop soon, and it's now or never. You have to apply to have your samples analyzed there immediately!"

And I thought, "James Weber? I remember an application from him when I was at NSF. Wasn't he involved in that big microsatellite paper in *Science*? Can we get our data analyzed for lots of microsatellites for free by his group?" I hadn't dealt with that. I looked on their website and thought, "Oh, my god, he's now got over 700 genetic markers in his test battery (he'd had only 300 in the first big Rosenberg paper on the CEPH panel)," So I told Andy about my conversation with Sarah, and he said, "They don't do normal populations. They're only interested in clinical genetics." And I said, "That's not what Sarah says, she's having her African data done there." He said, "Well, I didn't know that, let's apply." It turned out that when they started with their 10 year NIH grant, their emphasis was on clinical genetics, mapping disease genes and so forth. But, as they were winding down, they were convinced by somebody, I'd guess Cavalli or someone in his group, to do normal population variation in selected regions of the world, using the CEPH human diversity panel. That's the background of the Rosenberg *et al.* paper in *Science* that I've talked about. It won the best scientific paper of the year award.

Sarah is extremely well connected and always has her ear to the ground anyway. She's a real go-getter, competitive, but she can be generous. She was having her African samples done by him, and she said we should try ours.

As a result, Andy and I put in a proposal to Marshfield stressing the mtDNA and Y variability we'd already established, and the proposal was approved, and that's made a major advance in our research because, yes we had important mtDNA results, yes we had interesting Y chromosome results, but I think the nuclear markers, the microsatellite analysis has become the capstone of our work. That was on account of that short conversation with Sarah. Getting her excellent post doc Floyd Reed involved was also critical.

Chapter 12.

Some Final Opinions

The Interplay Between Linguistics and Genetics

JR: Could you maybe say some more about the linguistic dimension of your work? How much did you need to know about linguistics to do it? This might be a naïve question, but I think it warrants explicit (even if brief) attention. Also, do you know anything about linguistic "salvage" projects (i.e., the effort to collect and preserve disappearing languages)? If so, do you see any connection between that kind of effort and your own attention to genetics of "remote" populations?

JF: I'm not a linguist, and I'm not competent to do more than accept the classifications and distinctions they provide. But I certainly have used and rely on their data, beginning with my first work in Bougainville. I assumed that patterns of linguistic variation should at least provide some indication of genetic variation, even if it wasn't always a strong relationship. Exploring the correspondence of language and genetic patterns of diversity resurfaced again in our most recent paper on language and genetic coevolution this year (with Keith Hunley as first author, again in *PLoS Genetics*). Our latest findings clearly suggest that, when people of different language groups begin to interact, they tend to intermix genetically rather quickly, while their languages generally come to influence one another much more slowly. This was not clear to me before, I have to admit. The implication is that languages may often provide better information on relatively recent historical population relationships than do genetic distinctions (which tend to get blurred relatively fast because of intermarriage). As an example, English is the native language in many countries that were heavily settled by English-speaking people many centuries ago, but which subsequently have had extensive genetic migrations from other areas (as in the U.S., Australia, and elsewhere). The fact that English is the major spoken language in the U.S. is revealing about a part of our settlement history. The same is true of Spanish and Portuguese in Latin America.

JR: This example makes sense to me, but I'm hoping you can clarify something. If linguistic data are potentially more informative that genetic data, what is the implication for the seemingly continued intense interest in using genomics to trace migratory history? Can you help explain it because I think this is a point that confuses people in my field?

JF: The short answer is that they should both be used, and they can be informative at different time scales. This is something Keith Hunley and I, at least, want to write more about in the coming year. Let me use the Pacific example. The linguistic signal of Austronesian settlement and migration over the last 3,000 years is strong and clear, while the genetic signal for this recent population intrusion is much weaker in Island Melanesia. That is consistent with the idea that the older Papuan-speaking populations were larger at the time of contact. The new arrivals had a lot of influence culturally and linguistically, but their impact genetically was rather small in those big islands.

The problem with language is that change is so rapid that relationships older than about 6,000-10,000 years are all but impossible to reconstruct. That is where genetic signals of relationship are most helpful. The genetic signals may be diluted and are hard to localize to specific islands or regions since they spread over time, but they're what we're left with, and for certain genetic segments, like the mtDNA and Y chromosome, one can construct gene trees to get at ancient age estimates (these have large estimate ranges, however).

Here are some more specific conclusions on this relationship from our Melanesian work that has come out of our collaboration with a group of European and Australian linguists.

1. Genetic exchange occurs faster than language borrowing in contact situations because biological populations have no special cohesion, while languages occur in a social context and in many respects are constrained not to change too much too

rapidly. For example, fast language change could compromise the ability to communicate among individuals.

2. Some aspects of language will tend be more conserved than others in contact situations. We think this is likely to be true for many other aspects of culture, including parts of material culture that tend to function together (like seafaring technology, or religious rituals).

3. For genes, the dispersal rates between adjacent groups should be directly affected by a) the different population sizes of the groups (the larger groups seem to have more of an effect on the neighboring smaller ones than vice-versa), and b) different sex-biases in migration (Y vs. mtDNA signatures). There are lots of established cases where one sex moves around more than another, and I think our data also show the effects of different group sizes.

4. As I mentioned, over much longer periods, gene phylogenies are certainly going to be more informative than linguistic ones because the rates of language change are so fast. Our mtDNA work is a case in point. Those mtDNA trees show that for Island Melanesia; a) there is a set of old mtDNA haplogroups that are in the 30,000-50,000 year age range that originated in Near Oceania, and b) there is a second, much younger set, that developed in East Asia and Taiwan, and was brought to Near Oceania in the last 10,000 years or so (remarkably, there is no evidence of anything being introduced between 30,000 and 10,000 years ago –an unbelievably long isolation period –20,000 years. Ancient homelands for certain of the old haplogroups can be roughly established, but linkage with specific language groups isn't possible. We can suggest that certain gene variants, because of their distributions, likely arose in particular sub regions or perhaps particular islands of Melanesia. However, that's the best we can do, because new gene variants can spread relatively rapidly.

In a sense, there is a rough correspondence in our work and current linguistic "salvage" work on dying languages. The extreme patterns of genetic variation in Island Melanesia soon also will be a thing of the past. People are moving from their remote bush villages to roadside gardens and plantations, or to towns. Inevitably, this means more genetic intermixture and less patterned differentiation. The same is true worldwide.

The Relation of Fieldwork and Contemporary Genetics Lab Work

JR: So one of the things that's interesting is the collaborative nature of this work and the ways that you rely upon other kinds of scientific experts to help you interpret your materials – blood, in particular. How has this particular aspect of your fieldwork, collecting blood, reoriented the relationship between the lab and the field in anthropology? Because, it would seem that currently studies are being done by people, drawing upon materials collected years or even decades ago, who never worked in the field.

JF: Early on, a number of people who were strictly laboratory workers never did go to the field. Moses Schanfield is a good example. He made it his business, beginning in the 1960s, to collect other people's plasma samples that they had used for other purposes. Exactly how this works out with informed consent and those issues is problematic, I believe. At one point, I learned that he had a lot of old samples from Australian Aborigines as well as some of Carleton Gajdusek's materials from New Guinea and other places. He'd been a major plasma pack rat. I asked him if I could get some plasma samples from the Pacific, for Andy to do some mtDNA analysis. He said, "Sure. But you've got to come do the aliquoting, and of course list me as a co-author." That was reasonable enough. So I went out to his place in Denver for four days and after looking over the bags of samples in his freezers, I'd say, "Can I use these and these?" And he'd say, "OK." So I'd aliquot those and send them to Andy for the mtDNA analysis. We finally included those results in the P and Q paper in 2005. Moses did a good deal of his publications based on the analysis of other people's samples.

Andy was another person who was trained as a lab worker with limited field experience. He wanted to go to the field with me in 2000 because he felt that was a gap in his experience as an anthropologist. He played an important role that year. We were efficient in large measure because of him. He was busy collecting the demographic information on everyone, and then took the major role in the aliquoting and the preparation of the samples for shipping. We had an excellent sample season on account of that pushing. He wouldn't put up with a lot of sitting around waiting for more discussion with village leaders in advance that had happened in 1998.

You also question whether lab researchers need to do any collecting now, relying on other people or already collected samples for that. While it's true to an extent, and depends a great deal on the questions to be addressed, most of the best research is still done with well-designed sampling, which often means new collections. Comparisons that might not require strict population definitions avoid these sorts of problems (for example, for Chinese, Cavalli simply used a collection of Chinese college students studying at Stanford).

Disposition of the Blood Samples and Databases

JR: What happened to the samples you collected?

JF: Most are in Andy's freezers. The 2003 samples are primarily at Temple. The Kidds have some because they want to do some large SNP scans.

JR: How many samples would you estimate that you have, in general?

JF: From the 1998, 2000, 2003, there's close to 2,000. There are a lot of samples that have never been touched, frankly, that are related people or females. Males are preferable because they include the Y. For doing the microsatellites, the laboratory at Marshfield, Wisconsin was specific that they only wanted around 20 to 25 samples of "unrelated" people from each village. In some villages we had a sample of 100, so there still are a lot available.

Then there are all the other plasma samples from before 1998 that are in poorer shape. I can't tell you exactly, it must be another couple thousand, it's a large number. They'd be more than adequate for mtDNA work, but most of the interesting work there has been done and is now published.

JR: I guess a related question that we sort of discussed but that I want to make sure I'm clear on is that there isn't any kind of central database or guide to who has what samples from where/when, right? It seems that people know who has what via their personal networks.

JF: Those public databases are important, and many journals require DNA sequence information be deposited in such a database before a paper can be published. Our whole mtDNA sequence data were deposited in GenBank, meeting such a requirement. One of the conditions of getting the microsatellite analyses done was that, after a year, the results had to be made public and available to other researchers (since it was done by a NIH-funded lab). It has been posted on the Marshfield website, but the names and other identifiers by group are only available through us. In our papers, we said that the materials were accessible on request from us. This is because certain groups told us, after the fact, that they wanted some control over who analyzed their samples, and for what purpose. Of course, we acceded, and the requestors have honored this situation, even though technically they don't have to by U.S. regulations.

The Social Context of Fieldwork and Science

JR: Could you reflect about the ways in which the various social contexts in which you found yourself working influenced the production of your scientific work?

JF: I talked earlier about the fortunate social circumstances of my fieldwork situation in Papua New Guinea and the Solomons, and before that, the opportunities that were presented to me as a Harvard graduate student. Beyond that, the collaborations that subsequently developed with other researchers were a product of two things. First, I collected an unusual dataset in an interesting area with a most intensive sampling regimen that was particularly attractive to potential collaborators – they wanted to work on my sample set. Second, I was often just in the right place at the right time. Harvard as a major research institution was a terrific place to become acquainted with current intellectual controversies, and to develop research collaborations. It was a real luxury and a wonderful thing – also in terms of excellent students to work with. It is far more difficult to remain current in a peripheral institution. However, the internet is modifying this to a considerable degree.

Subject Remuneration

Paying subjects, or reimbursing them appropriately for participation, was always a tricky issue. I mentioned how I handled that in the first year, after being told not to pay money to people for their blood.

On the Harvard Solomon Islands Expedition, there were remunerations or gifts of one sort or another; in the Kwaio, everybody who participated was given a machete, which was a prized and useful item. Keesing said that people who arrived the night before their exam called that evening "The night preparing for the knife." With the Nasioi, I think they were given cloth. It wasn't money, in any case. But in some groups later on, like the Lau, I was told they simply wanted money. Since it was in the Solomon Islands, without the same concerns as Papua New Guinea I mentioned, I think the expedition did pay cash on sort of a compensation for time loss argument. This was also true in Ontong Java.

In the 1978-1980 seasons, we tried different things, trying to respond to what people wanted. I had a fairly large grant to go back and restudy these groups, and, as part of my initial entry, I would meet with different groups from a village and we would discuss not only what I wanted to do for the project, but what I or John Rhoads might be able to do for the community in return. I would say, "I have some money to compensate you for your cooperation (compensation is a well-understood term in Melanesia), but not a lot, a few hundred dollars, and there are different ways we can help people." In one area I said, "We can help fund the training of somebody from this group to go become a medical orderly here for your area, and we can buy medical supplies for him. Or, if you want – I don't like to – we can pay people by the head for their collaboration or whatever else you can think of."

People would discuss the issue and decide what most of them wanted. One group surprised me because they said they wanted to buy a movie projector with the money. I said, "Why do you want to buy a movie projector?" They said, "The Parent Teacher Association wants to be able to show movies and raise money for the school." That was one solution I would never have thought of. For the grand premier, I rented a film from Honiara with a title that sounded to me like a Western (*Blood in the Saddle*, I believe the name was). It turned out to be an old Polish film about a medieval struggle between the evil Teutonic knights and the heroic Polish people. I had to stop the movie multiple times to give a rough account to the audience of what was going on (it was in Polish with English subtitles, so I roughly translated it into Tok Pisin). They must have thought it was crazy, but they loved the costumes, the horses, and the knights lancing and killing each other.

JR: Oh my! Did you want to show a Western because that was what people thought about America?

JF: No, there was a list of available film rentals in Honiara, and of those, I thought an action Western would be the most entertaining. It would also rely less on verbal exchanges, which I'd have to interpret in Tok Pisin. People were aware of a number of media action characters, like Rambo and the Phantom (a particularly popular figure in Papua New Guinea – at one point, we gave subjects in Bougainville sunglasses that everyone called "Phantom glass").

In any case, I preferred to make it a gift that everyone would agree to at one time, that would be purchased or paid for more or less while I was there, and not subject to future debate (like development fund accounts in Kwaio I mentioned). But those things change over time as I said, and some groups decided they preferred simply to be paid or compensated by the head.

During the last few field seasons, we did different things. George Koki, who had taken a lot of blood samples around Papua New Guinea for years before I met him in 1998 said, "Just give people a tin (can) of fish – good for their diet." Sometimes we did give cans of fish and Polaroid pictures as well. Other times I took videos that I sent back to people of their singing groups and custom houses. We tried to avoid cash payment.

Genomics and Politics

JR: I had a question about a conversation you and I previously had. You were talking about how biological anthropological fieldwork experiences vary dramatically in different regions of the world, depending upon the postcolonial dynamics in a particular place. I think this would be something interesting to discuss.

JF: O.K., as an example, there's a good paper on microsatellite variation in the Americas by Wang and others. Do you know that paper?

JR: No.

JF: Well, it's another paper in *PLoS Genetics*. The analysis was similar to the original Rosenberg *et al.* microsatellite paper. It came out of the Stanford group as well – Marcus Feldman is a co-author. It appeared about a month or two before ours, and had comparable genetic analyses as ours, since the data were also generated by the Marshfield Clinic.

The Wang paper purportedly covers the Americas with an enlarged sample from the Rosenberg paper, but the new samples are almost entirely from South America. There's nothing from the U.S., for political reasons I'm sure, since almost none of the Native American groups in the U.S. were willing to participate. That's my point. There's a big political split between northern plains Native Americans and southwestern groups as well. The Lakota and those other groups in the north are vehemently opposed to any collaborations with European Americans in terms of any research, whether it's health related or not. They're not so strident in the Southwest. Now, I'm not sure why that is, but I know there's got to be a long history. Jeff Long would know better because he was caught up in the Jemez Pueblo sample controversy (those had to be returned and destroyed). There have been lots of controversies about genetic studies of Native Americans in the U.S. Another one, that Michael Hammer got caught up in, was in Arizona.

Terry Markow, who is basically a fruit fly geneticist, was allegedly the main culprit there (she was at NSF as a rotator when I was there, as the Program Director for Population Biology, too). She had collected samples from a group in the Grand Canyon, the Havasupai Apaches. Apparently the samples were collected for diabetes research and then she ultimately gave them to Mike Hammer for doing Y-chromosome analysis, I think that was it, or the accusation.

JR: It wasn't the Pima, was it?

JF: No, not the Pima. That was another well-known diabetes study. The Havasupai Apache sued the University of Arizona for $60 million or something like that. I don't recall the specifics, but it was all over the papers in Arizona. So, as a result, when you look at the Sija Wang paper on Native Americans and it shows you the kind of problems in cooperation – politically based – the same thing is true in Australia. It's difficult to get collaboration with Australian Aboriginal groups. Other similar microsatellite analyses have been published successfully on South Asians (Indians), and Tishkoff will be publishing a large series on Africans.

JR: Can you specify what you mean by "political?"

JF: I think it's fair to say that we were lucky in Papua New Guinea and the Solomons because of the local political situation and history. The villagers we studied had political power, both locally and with regard to the national government. In both countries, the national government was elected by them, as opposed to them being peripheralized like Native Americans or Australian Aborigines, who had been almost eradicated by European invaders and who'd always felt – or who developed – an acute sense of being exploited. In those cases, any proposal for genetic research was an easy way for them to say, "No. What's in it for us? We're not getting anything. This is just another attempt at eradication or exploitation so you Whites can get richer at our expense. You're going to use our blood to experiment on or to make money."

We had to talk about this all the time, since people wanted to know what we were going to do, especially with their blood. We were able to avoid being viewed as part of a dominant-subservient relationship, first as Americans, and later especially because George Koki became a major figure in our group.

We also pointed out that our research in population relationships could help them develop their own sense of their own national history – where their ancestors came from – their own origin account. In our consent form we developed in 2000, we talked about how in U.S. history books, Christopher Columbus came and discovered the Americas, and more people came after that, but there were Native Americans before that time. As a result, our nation has a well-developed sense of its history (certainly back to Columbus). But in Papua New Guinea and the Solomons, they didn't have that kind of written record, and we were helping to establish migration patterns and how long people had been there, and helping, along with archaeology and historical linguistics, to build up a national history. This gave them a sense of self-importance, to be studied this way. We argued every new nation needed its own history or its own story. They liked that idea especially because they all had their own ideas about where they came from. Some were a little, uh, crazy (for example, some Bible stories were supposed to have taken place in New Britain – reminiscent of how the Book of Mormon is situated in the U.S.). Everybody had their own ideas of origin stories.

Genomics and Commercial Applications

The commercial aspect of genetics has become an especially hot issue lately. Ken and Judy Kidd have been in some of the same controversial situations and they've made it clear, to everybody that they've been involved with, that there cannot be a profit-making motive if they are going to give out their cell line derivatives (the DNA). I don't know what Sarah Tishkoff finally worked out with the 23&me group, because that group has a clear profit oriented intent.

JR: This is the Google startup, 23&me.

JF: Right. The wife of the founder of Google or something . . .

JR: Yes. Ann Wojcicki.

JF: Yes, they also approached me, but then they backed off when I told them I had made that "no profit" pledge in the consent form. I think nothing has happened with Sarah too, but I'm not sure. At one point they were interested, because she has the best African sample coverage anybody's ever going to get. So in terms of establishing where anyone with an African ancestry might have come from, she'll be able to provide the best estimate, however good that is (and it won't be specific at all).

JR: So how do you think the people at 23&me came to know that people like you and Sarah had these samples? Hank Greely? Who is their representative? How did they figure out where the materials were?

JF: I don't think there are that many comprehensive samplings of populations globally, so the people interested know about everyone else's sample of relevance. It's a small community, we read each other's papers, and meet one another at professional meetings. As you can see from the picture of the people invited to participate in an organizing session of the HGDP, there are perhaps only 30 or 40 people world-wide who could have been involved in that sort of survey at the outside.

Genomics and National Politics in the Pacific

JR: That's something that maybe we can return to at the end, this current state of genomics and commercial dimensions. But I want to stay on this topic of regional differences in terms of what you were able to do and not do. Or would be able to do or not do. One of the questions I have is there is all this variation within groups within the Solomon Islands. So does having this knowledge create controversy in a geographical space that's trying to form itself as an independent nation?

JF: Good question. You would think that the best answer for nation-building would be, "We're all the same." Bougainville's aspirations to secede from Papua New Guinea might be reinforced by our findings. I haven't heard that connection so far, except from one sophisticated political leader, Mel Togolo. He said, "You know, Jonathan, your books could be used to argue Bougainville should be entirely separate from New Guinea." It may be that our findings are all too new, and the word isn't out yet. However, I suspect that, from the Bougainville perspective, it's a case of "old news" – "we already know we're different from them," or in Tok Pisin, "*Mipela oli blakskin, na ol man bilong Niu Ginea emi redskin.*"

The way it's been written up in the press so far has been in terms of the two ancient migrations that we can trace, the first old early settlement, 40 to 50,000 years ago, that corroborates some of the archaeology, and the subsequent much later migration of proto-Polynesian people that left a faint footprint. I think it's probably the neatest thing in the microsatellite paper, and also echoed in the Y and mtDNA papers. The Austronesian genetic signal is clearly detectable, but weak.

So that's the story that's been put out there. I haven't been to Papua New Guinea in the last five years to find out how people feel about that, if anybody's even noticed. I know that there were some reports from Australian overseas radio, as well as a write-up in the major Port Moresby newspaper (the *Post-Courier*), but I don't know what's happened in terms of other reaction, and I don't know how much of a difference it will make. In terms of trying to get word back, I talked to a New Guinean archaeologist at the PNG University there before I left about writing a joint textbook for schools and do something to get our materials into school curricula. But George Koki said, "He's hopeless, you'll never get anything done with him." George was right. The archaeologist I mentioned before, Glenn Summerhayes said he would be happy to see how he could help – he talks a lot to the radio and TV people there – he's always going up in PNG – so he said he would try and think of ways to get information out. I would love to go back and with a video to take with me back to the places I went to show our results – this could even be shown on my computer. I think they'd love to see that. Or it might be good enough for national TV. It might be a somewhat simplified story, but I think we have a story to tell now, with the age and the different migrations coming through.

Genes as Property and Issues of Confidentiality

JR: A related question, which you've been touching on, on one level, is the question of ownership. But by ownership I don't just mean the controversies over people giving their bodies to science, but with all of the sharing of samples that circulate around. When I spoke briefly with Chuck Weitz a couple days ago, I said "If you had a question for Jonathan, what would it be?" He said, "Well I'm real curious to know about who owns the samples," and he meant who are the scientists who can claim ownership and authorship and what are the complicating factors in that?

JF: At one extreme, there's the issue of gene patenting, where ownership is supposed to reside with the "inventor," meaning the researcher who did certain modifications to the original biological or genetic material. I think the U.S. Patent Office policy allowing patenting of genes is fundamentally wrong, as well as politically unfortunate. As I understand patent principles, to be patentable, something has to be a novel invention as well as having a potential use. You can't patent Mt. Everest – it's a natural phenomenon, and not apparently useful. I think gene patenters are trying to patent knowledge, not something new. I hope this policy changes. I know the Kidds and many other laboratory geneticists are upset about this policy. In theory, a lab geneticist with breast cancer wouldn't be allowed to test or analyze her own DNA for the BRCA variants, because they're patented by Myriad Genetics.

More problematic with regard to ownership are the transformed cell lines. And, as I indicated, we can't take cell lines anymore because of the problems associated with that. The Kidds do make it clear to everyone who requests DNA derived from their cell lines that commercial projects cannot apply (like 23&me), since they informed their subjects that there would be no commercialization of their samples. The actual cell lines are held in a sort of receivership by the labs involved, who must then judge applications for the DNA produced from those cell lines. The DNA from the Nasioi cell lines (not the cell lines themselves) has been sent all over the place, so that's in the public domain, along with a lot of the others. But in all cases, the requestors have signed statements that they are to be used for research purposes, not for profit. Still, it's clear that we could not collect cell lines again. I find it odd that gene patenting is currently allowed, while people are generally opposed to the expansion of cell line repositories. If they're properly managed, with oversight, potential abuses of cell lines could be avoided, and their advantages could be utilized more broadly.

A third set of ownership issues surrounds old samples collected for various purposes over the years, now in freezers around the world, possibly to be used for new studies, unrelated to the original ones. Should that be allowed? There are changing ideas about ownership. I heard somebody suggest recently that all samples collected for a project should all be destroyed once the grant expires and once a subsequent publication is out. I think that would be a shame, like destroying museum collections. In the end, I think it depends a lot on what scientists do with these materials in terms of making money, number one, and number two, the whole business of confidentiality, and number three, a reasonable subsequent research investigation.

Finally, there's simply the question of genetic information – whether a researcher's primary results belong to the researcher, or whether at some point they belong to the wider community (of course, individual confidentiality has to be maintained – I'm talking about the scientific knowledge gained). Government policy is clear on this one. Government funded results are "confidential" for a year, after which time they must be made publicly available, on websites or in public databases like GenBank (but still retaining the anonymity of individuals). Therefore, the "ownership" of the results is finally "given away" to the public after an initial grace period for the original investigators to get their analyses out promptly.

JR: And I would imagine that another complicating factor is the particular kind of information that is trying to be gleaned from this material –

JF: Absolutely –

JR: It's genetic. At the fundamental level – we spoke earlier about the pedigrees and family trees that were built around these data, so family members are implicated, be they future kin or deceased kin. So, I wonder, is privacy in terms of genetic testing an issue scientists think about a lot in the U.S., in general?

JF: I don't see how one could interpret what we're doing as in any way stigmatizing a population. However, it might exist in some cases.

Some Ashkenazim have gotten upset about stigmatization because they have a special genetic disease load. Even though I find that argument strange I understand the notion. We wanted to do a diabetes study but it hasn't worked out. If we'd found one group was far more susceptible to diabetes than another, that might have been regarded as something of a stigma. What's the difference between that and recognizing that a particular family is at risk?

Here's a contrary story where it would have been beneficial to know the genetics underlying a disease. I had a great aunt named Stella Meyer in Montgomery who was in love with an albino. Apparently they'd sit for hours holding hands in a big swing on the porch. My father said they never married because they assumed any kids they had would be albinos as well. Since common albinism is a recessive disease, this is false. Their kids would just have been healthy carriers.

We had to get our research designs approved by the Papua New Guinea IRB which was called the Medical Advisory Research Committee (a group of physicians in Port Moresby). We were told that once we'd cleared that permissions hurdle we were free and clear as long as we stuck to the approved protocol. In the Solomon Islands, we had to get the Health Service's approval and then we had to get local groups' more informal approval in each instance.

We also tried to keep local officials informed of our findings, as specified in research permission applications. Lord knows I've sent lots of reprints to the Institute for Medical Research in Papua New Guinea and to comparable institutions in the Solomon Islands. But I don't know what happens to these. In PNG, a lot of our articles and books are now in the IMR library. However, I remember going back to the Solomons and a health service officer said, "Your proposal is fine, Jonathan, but we want to make sure you send us your publications, since you haven't sent us your reports." I said, "But I sent a batch of publications before." They said, "Whom did you send it to?" I said, "I sent it to the head of the Health Service." They responded, "Well he's long gone, we need these for the library." I said, "I'll give you another set." I always go armed with new sets of my old publications. The question is: what is sufficient, in terms of keeping people informed on what you're doing? There's the National Health Service, or in Papua New Guinea, the Medical Research Institute, and there are the local folks whom you're getting the blood samples from. Those are two entirely different interest groups, the professionals and the local people. Concerning the PNG Institute, I've given talks there to the staff on our findings, which was, I think, helpful. They have a different perspective from the villagers, however.

Utilizing old samples is a more problematic issue for us. Obviously, we made use of old plasmas in the mtDNA work, and that's essentially over. I don't know what the current state of that kind of analysis is, but we're involved with it less and less. We're using these materials mostly from the last six years.

Changing Gender Roles in Anthropology and in Fieldwork

JR: You've raised the question of gender differences between men and women a couple of times throughout the discussion of fieldwork and your assessment of what you were studying. I wonder if you have considered how gender influenced your success in the field. Also you mentioned certain anthropologists traveling with their families. Could you have done this work at that time as a woman? And how did traveling or working with your family in tow shape the way your fieldwork proceeded?

JF: In the Pacific, there are certainly examples of early successful women anthropologists, not just Margaret Mead, but also Beatrice Blackwood and her *Across Buka Passage* book, Hortense Powdermaker, and others. So there clearly were examples, going back to the 1920s and 1930s, of women who were successful anthropologists. I don't know if they always lived alone. Mead went with a husband usually, I think. She was certainly successful in different areas. I don't know about Blackwood. So it's not like women couldn't do it, O.K.? Ann Chowning and Jane Goodale are two more recent cultural anthropologists in New Britain who managed successfully. How they negotiated it, I'm not quite sure. I think that because they were Europeans, it meant that they had kind of a distance in colonial times. My guess is they weren't going to be easily attacked. A lot of these groups could be pretty fierce, like the Kwaio. They were still proud of their fighting prowess; a lot of feuding was going on. I don't know of any anthropologist who's been attacked by local people. The closest I know of is this fellow Rutherford. The Aita just said, "Leave him alone and let him stew in his own juices."

With regard the Harvard Solomon Islands Project, the attitude certainly seemed to be at the outset – "We're going to have this team of men only." Bill Howells' wife did come along one year. Now Mary Ann Whelan, who was a graduate student in my cohort at Harvard, never went to the field. She ended up being a physician, and I've reestablished contact with her recently. She said, "What I wanted all along was to become a physician, but I didn't think that was an acceptable thing for a woman to do in the 1960s. So at first, physical anthropology was a substitute for that, but finally I convinced myself that I could do medicine." This was still kind of early in the development of a broad acceptance of female professionalism in the U.S., even though there were these blue stockings from the 1930s who went off and did what they damned well pleased, like Margaret Mead.

So we didn't have any women on board as biomedical or physical anthropological types on the first Harvard Solomon Island Expeditions. There were a couple of women cultural anthropologists involved, but they were parts of married couples. Jill Nash and Don Mitchell were in Nagovisi, and Pierre and Ellie Maranda were a couple in Lau. Roger Keesing brought his first wife with him although she was not much of an anthropologist, but his second wife was. David and Kate Aiken were another example. They were Peace Corps volunteers but cultural anthropologists. So the "couples" situation was an easy way to go. But a single woman, doing a survey like mine, I'm not sure if that's happened. Sue Serjeantson collected her blood samples on the north coast of New Guinea near Madang during that period – that would be interesting to know her circumstances. As I think about it, I do recall one woman cultural anthropologist who was sexually assaulted in New Guinea – she was essentially working alone, and it was her assistant.

Taking Family into the Field

Now, in my case, as with most fieldworkers with families, you can't simply disappear for months on end, especially when your kids are small. I first married in 1971, and did a "short" field trip in 1973 for six weeks. This absence didn't work at all well, so in subsequent trips, I tried to have my family join me for at least part of the time. When I next went back to the field with my wife and daughters in 1978 and 1980, it created a lot of excitement, especially among the women and children in the different areas we stayed. They were used to the young Australian male *kiaps* passing through occasionally on patrol, but not to having women and especially children live there for any length of time. Maybe nuns from the mission on health surveys came in for the day, in trucks. They tended to stay at the mission station and be involved in medical care and teaching.

So the fact that my wife and the kids came along did cause considerable excitement. I remember we entered one village in Nagovisi, where Jill Nash and Don Mitchell had lived before. We arrived around 7 o'clock in the evening after a long truck ride across Bougainville, and there was a big hullabaloo. "Oh, we are happy (*hamamas tumas*) that you are here." It was almost like a political rally, shaking hands, waving, shouting, and so on. I'd already been there once, so it wasn't because of me. But again, it depends on the personalities. My kids and my wife were, on that first trip, trying to find ways to enjoy the experience of that novel situation. My daughter Mira, who was just 6 at the time, thought of it all as simply one big adventure. My wife, Bilgé, who was an artist, was quite concerned about what the kids ate and their health, but she developed her own interests in photographing the vegetation, basketry, shells, and other aspects of the tropical world. I think really, the people picked up the positive attitude, so that was good.

Now, in subsequent expeditions as well, in the mid-1980s (when I was first divorced) and more recently, I had mixed male and female teams. I didn't think about it too much. For example, Tina Lesser was a senior in biological anthropology who wanted to come along. After a lecture I gave with pictures of the Solomons I'd taken, shortly before the end of a course in April, she said, "Jonathan, that looks so exciting, is there any way I can come along?" I thought we could get money for her through Temple, since she had excellent grades, and I said "Fine, let's try to arrange it." She worked hard and helped prepare the data records in advance, and did well in the field. The next year, Ruth Beizer, a Temple graduate student came along (she was considerably older, married with grown children), and I said, "Great, there is no problem – I've got grant money that can cover you."

Mira Friedlaender and teenage boy. Foueda, Lau Lagoon. 1978.

My second wife, who was a physician, also came on that 1986 expedition, when we were just married. That was much less successful, because of various personality issues. By the time our son Benji was old enough to go in 1998 (age 10), we were involved in an acrimonious divorce, and she wouldn't allow me to take him, so he's never been, which is too bad – it would have undoubtedly meant a great deal to him.

Tina Lesser, Dan Hrdy, JSF, and Chuck Weitz resting on the long walk to Aita. Bougainville. 1985.

We probably could have had more women involved in the 1960s on the Harvard expeditions, but it had much more to do with what was going on in the U.S. It also had more to do with the attitude towards female professionalism in biological anthropology and medicine in the U.S. as opposed to what was going on in the Solomons. However, I still think being basically alone in a bush survey, of the sort I did in the 1960s, would have been problematic for a women. Again, I'd be interested to know the nature of Sue Serjeantson's fieldwork – how solitary it was.

Having family members along that aren't directly involved in a survey does add special considerations. You don't undertake long bushwalks or potentially dangerous situations under those circumstances, and childcare duties become more of an issue, since they are difficult to share on a survey. So again, there are always complicating factors that need to be thought through, and many can't be properly anticipated in advance.

JR: And would you say biological anthropology remains more of a male-dominated profession or is it –

JF: No, not any more. There's been a major shift in the last 10 to 15 years in graduate training and who's getting jobs. The majority of degrees are now being given to women, and that's even more the case, and happened earlier, in cultural anthropology. I don't know about archaeology, but I think the same trend is true there. Biological anthropology has shifted more recently. For example, at Temple, when I first came here in 1976, both Chuck Weitz and Len Greenfield were junior professors, so it was just us three guys for many years. We finally got a chance to hire somebody new, (we'd had a couple of chances to hire people over the years that didn't work out), but it was clear by then that we had to hire a woman. It was not a problem to find a good woman candidate because that was who was being turned out, by and large, by graduate programs. There's been a real turnover now as I've retired and the two other men will be retiring in the next few years. We hired a woman (Christie Rockwell) eight years ago, and they just hired another woman who's coming in this next year. So that's just a matter of course.

JR: Do you have any speculations about what accounts for that change?

JF: Well, I think biology, as opposed to physics and chemistry, has been more appealing to women as an area of study, and that also takes in physical anthropology – it has been appealing for a variety of women and it may also have to do with different strains of physical anthropology that have become stronger over the last generation. Primate behavior studies, for example, are famous for being heavily dominated by women. Women get along better with animals than men do. They are much less threatening to animals, I believe. They do, I mean Jane Goodall was only one example . . .

I just remembered there was an issue of minor molestation on an expedition of ours. This was in Ontong Java, which is a Polynesian outlier, a coral atoll. When we were there in 1986, there were three women, two of them with husbands along. There was a married couple's hut and a single people's hut. My second wife and I, and another couple, Frank Richards and Martine Armstrong, who were older than us in their 40s or 50s, shared the married hut. She was a virologist and he was a pulmonary specialist. This little hut was directly on the ground, and had no doors, but had a sheet for a dividing partition. It was a school room that we'd been loaned. Somebody would sneak into the doorway at night and pinch Martine on the leg. Martine would say, "Ow!" Frank would jump up and shout, "Get out!" This was in pitch-black on the beach, you know. The first thing Frank tried to do was to get some fishing line and to block the doorway by stringing it across, making a sort of web, but that wasn't working. The pinching went on for a couple of nights, and then Frank told me something had to be done, so I talked to the leaders of the village. This was a Polynesian stratified society, so there was a hierarchy between the nobility and the ordinary people. I told the chief about the situation and said, "This is troubling—is there something you can do about this? So, the chief, Thomas Keopo said, "Hmm, yes, we know who that has to be. We know who does that kind of thing; we'll take care of it." It's a small community and everybody knows everybody else's business. So, they put him on the next boat, they got him off the island. So, that's an interesting story both in terms of the possible problems, and also in terms of how to negotiate problems with the local population. You have to be able have effective communication and cooperation.

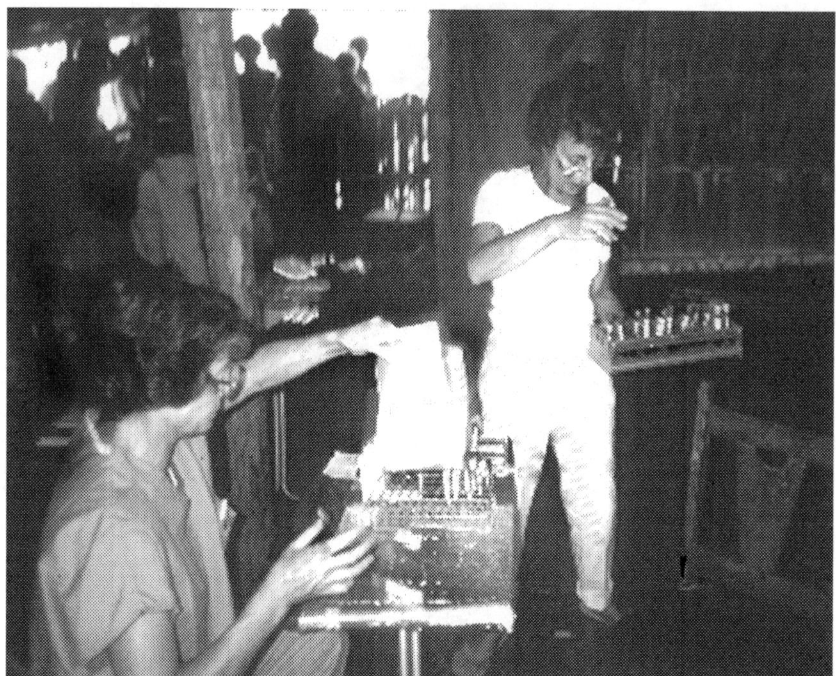

Ruth Beizer and Martine Armstrong working in Luangiua, Ontong Java. 1986.

Things don't always turn out so well, however. At the end of our stay there, in Ontong Java, we had a great going-away party, a great pig feast with women painted with ochre (both locals and team members). You'll see in the slides, there were a lot of photographs taken. We wanted to invite all the people who'd helped us out, who were our interviewers, assistants, and hosts, but it got to be more than a small dinner.

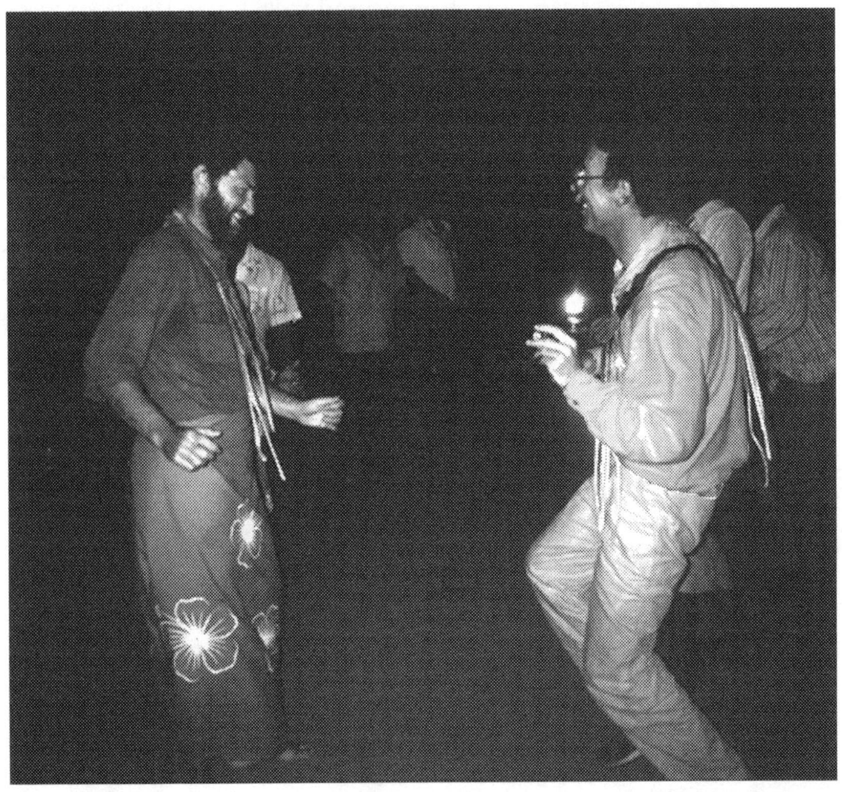

Going away party in Luangiua, Ontong Java. 1986. JSF and Chuck Weitz.

Somebody had a boom box. Chuck and I were dancing together, and with everybody else, for that matter. It was a great time. But the next morning, something clearly was wrong. A pall had fallen over the whole village. So finally, I said to the chief, Thomas Keopo, "Thomas, what's wrong?" And he said, "Well, not everybody in the village was invited to the party. The people who weren't invited are jealous and upset." And I said, "Oh, geez." Of course, there are about 1,000 people in the village, so I don't know how it could have been handled. It had become a big deal, with beer and the roasted pig and the costumes and dancing, so it became public. We all should have anticipated the problem, but no one did. Being socially aware of what was going on was always important, probably primary.

JR: An interesting dimension of the fieldwork experience.

Anthropology Departments and Genomics

JR: To change gears a bit, we haven't spoken that much about the contemporary landscape of the field – this current state of anthropological genomics – and your sense of how that fits within biological anthropology, in general. So I wondered if we could discuss that.

JF: Sure. First of all, I think it's important to say that the development of laboratory genetics in biological anthropology and in anthropology departments has been difficult and remains so. For institutional reasons and also for larger funding issues, there are fairly obvious obstacles. Population genetics studies have the same kind of problems within genetics or biology departments. The thing that's easiest to fund, from the National Institutes of Health, are health-related projects, and with genetics, that means clinical genetics. Genomics researchers have tried hard to make a case that there's going to be a major health payoff when the genome is more adequately understood, which I'm still skeptical about. If you go to a human genetics society meeting you won't see many podium presentations by population geneticists, unless they're somehow talking about health-related issues. The American Society of Human Genetics consists primarily of medical geneticists, so that human population genetics is a small section within human genetics. Look at the contents of any issue of their journal. Within physical anthropology, the same is true – the anthropological geneticists are a small minority – they have their own little affiliated society (American Association of Anthropological Genetics), which is tiny by comparison to the big breadth of physical anthropology, which is still primarily osteologically-trained and oriented. That has a lot to do with the history of the discipline, but also the cost of research and training. A wet lab is an unusual thing to have within an anthropology building. We spent a hundred thousand dollars or thereabout to develop a wet lab here at Temple. Last year, we didn't hire somebody that I liked, Heather Norton, who'd been on our expedition in 2000. One of the reasons is that she would have needed $500,000 dollars in terms of startup costs.

JR: For her lab?

JF: Yes. So instead they're getting somebody who does computer modeling, which is a lot cheaper. In Biology, $500,000 is sort of a standard kind of startup. They're used to that level of cost, and anyway the wet labs are already in their building. So, that's a real stumbling block. There are few anthropology departments that have been able to develop a serious wet lab genetics component. I remember the discussion at Harvard when they were first considering this, "Well, if we give this person a lab, how do we know that they'll get tenure and what will happen to the lab if they don't? It will be money down the drain." So there's that sense of a lack of commitment over an extended period of time. In my own career, as a teacher, it's only when I could send people off to The Coriell Institute for laboratory training, or have Joe come over here –

JR: This is Joe Lorenz you're speaking of –

JF: Right – that's when we began to develop any reasonable training with a laboratory-based genetics component, instead of just doing number crunching or things like that. That's still an issue. Also, Françoise became important in grad training as well – we produced about five good doctoral students from this combination, with the three of us.

At Penn, I think that accommodating Tad Schurr has also been an issue in the anthropology department. Tad was unhappy for quite a while. He thought he was promised a lab when he was hired and I don't know exactly the current status of it, but it's been difficult for him. His lab is in an old biology building removed from the Museum.

To return to Sarah Tishkoff, she's been able to negotiate an endowed chair for five years at the medical school. That means she doesn't have to raise any external money for her salary for those five years. She's also got a good lab. It's not in Anthropology, but it could have been if the money were right. Her undergrad degree at Berkeley was in anthropology and genetics, and she greatly admired Margaret Mead. In terms of funding, she does apply to NSF-Anthropology upon occasion, but her primary funding comes from NIH, which is a much bigger basket, a much bigger funding source.

It's been difficult to have a real tradition within anthropology departments of anthropological genetics that is in any way competitive. After Paul Baker's retirement at Penn State, Ken Weiss was able to build genetics up there, in collaboration with a fine evolutionary biology program. Utah does well with their contacts as well in their medical school, and I don't know what other departments to mention. Yale has had an off-and-on geneticist in its anthro department, now off. Students there interested in genetics tend to be drawn to the Kidds (in the medical school, again, though Judy has a bio anthro degree, and Ken's first job was in the anthro Department at Washington University in Saint Louis).

In terms of my own research, I've always been dependent on other people to do the lab work. Now, a lot of that had to do with my own poor training in laboratory biology, but also it was much more efficient to farm out the lab work. My greatest strength was as a fieldworker and in designing projects. It became increasingly common to have a group of collaborators, so that's the route I went. Some tried to do both, which worked when just a few genes were important to test, or when there were assistants or graduate students to help out in various aspects, but it became rare over the last four decades for single individuals to work alone.

JR: Given the different funding priorities, and the ability for someone like Sarah Tishkoff to get a position at the medical school, what do you think this means for people who see themselves primarily as fieldworkers? What does this suggest about how this research is going to proceed? Where are the data going to come from? How are the people doing the lab analyses going to have connections with the people who provide the data, because one of the things you've stressed over the course of our conversation is your desire to go back to the community and your ability to form relationships. It would seem a change has happened.

JF: This is hard to predict, but some changes are afoot. For example, there is a tendency for groups in different nations to be studied genetically by local scientists. This is most notable in China, India, the Philippines, and Indonesia. A lot of these countries now also prohibit the export of DNA, as well.

JR: What do you think the promise and power of genomics is?

JF: First of all, the development of genetics and genomics in the last 20 years has provoked an interesting response among observers. The best model is what happened with the development of the A-Bomb and the Manhattan Project. In the 1940s and 1950s, there was a sense of this enormous new power of atomic science. Harnessing this enormous source of power was both a source of great pride in (American) science, and also a terrible fear in its use. In a certain sense, but far less accurately, the idea that we know the nature of the genetic material and code, as well as something rudimentary about how genetics influences our development and health, has caused a dramatic change in the attitude towards genetics from the 1980s to the present. I recall an interview of Water Gilbert saying, "With the completion of the human genome project, we will have, as it were, the directions for making a human on a computer disc." While I understand what he meant, it sounded as though they might be ready to clone people. It was hyperbole and frightening to many. James Watson then made a more reasoned statement that the deciphering of the human genome was just the first step, that learning how it *worked* would be rather like learning the meaning of an extremely difficult poem that might take hundreds of years, perhaps thousands.

This powerful specter is clearly one of the reasons that a lot of self-styled representatives from some local groups felt that this was going to be another way that they were going to be exploited by dominant American and European society. "Those people are going to steal and patent our genes," or even, "They're going to clone us." That's where I think a lot of the RAFI excitement came from. One Hopi geneticist, Frank Dukepoo, said in effect, "Our genes are sacred parts of our heritage, and should not be exploited." We were badly bruised by that and that's why, ultimately, the attempt to develop a major federal funding source for anthropological genetics failed, which could have been the Human Genome Diversity Project, because of the political resistance of some local groups especially in parts of the Americas and also in Australia.

I still believe the perceived power of genomics is overblown, both by the practitioners as well as by the outside observers. The practitioners want to be able to say, "We are going to usher in a new era of genomic medicine. Give us billions of NIH funding." I think we've discussed the contrary feeling that this simply is not happening now, and may never be feasible or possible in a general way. One of the people whose critiques I like of modern genomic medicine is David Goldstein at Duke. The problem is that the search for major genes that might have a lot of different, significant effects on things like Parkinson's disease, and other diseases of complex etiology, is not yielding a lot of useful insight right now. What this search is showing is that many genes and a lot of alleles at different loci often have a complex and individually small effect on diseases, maybe accounting only for 1 or 2 percent of the disease susceptibility or less, rather than 30 or 40 % as one might hope. The search for the determining genetic set of particular disease alleles may not lead quickly to such simple notions as designer drugs for particular individuals or major diseases that have been trumpeted about. If we pursue this road, it's going to be immensely costly and a long trek before much of a payoff.

Earlier, I talked about the search for natural selection and the associated difficulties. The latest models for selection detection often assume that almost all the detected variation in the genome is, in fact, neutral, or determined by effects of mutation, age, and demography, and that the "outliers" in these distributions are the candidates for selection. There are now promising strategies for looking for signatures of selection in large genomic studies of linkage disequilibrium and its decay, but major problems in this approach remain. However, I'm skeptical of some of the claims (as by Henry Harpending) for a great deal of identified selection. What he sees as clear signals of selection may be caused by other phenomena. These tests are certainly going to fail when you apply them to our sorts of populations in Melanesia, because a lot of the same signatures that people are saying you can assign to selection effects can also be mimicked by small population sampling or demographic effects. You can only expect those kinds of selection studies will work in large populations, and that makes those inapplicable and uninteresting for me and the kind of groups that I know and study.

JR: So, the flipside, a project that I'm interested to get your opinion on, on tape, is National Geographic's Genographic Project. What's interesting about that project is that it's a non-medical, anthropological genomic project that also has a public participation arm that's captured the attention of a lot of people. Could you talk about your sense of the role of that kind of project and then maybe that will lead us into a discussion of commercial genomic services?

JF: Absolutely. The real problem for all the genetic ancestry attempts is the limit of their power to identify individual and ancestral homelands. This will become even clearer with the publication of Tishkoff's Africa microsatellite paper. No one is going to be able to genetically identify someone as of "Zulu" or "Hausa" ancestry or anything else so specific. That's simply not in the cards for African ancestry. The Genographic project has additional problems as I understand it. They're trying to make it economically feasible to do a few simple tests (a much reduced set of mtDNA and Y markers) on a large number of people, which are going to give them a clear cut result on their ancestry. This isn't going to work even as well as the microsatellites would. Ken Kidd would call the overblown Genographic claims "genetic snake oil."

I had an ex-student who called me up a couple of years ago concerning a commercial ancestral gene test. He said, "Dr. Friedlaender, I took one of your classes in anthropological genetics years ago. I'm just a good old African American guy from Indiana, but I had a Y-chromosome ancestral test done. I know my grandfather was an American Indian, my father's father. But the genetic test results say my Y-chromosome comes from India." I groaned. This was from Mike Hammer's Y-chromosome consortium. I said, "Do you remember what haplogroup you were?"

Well I looked up the distribution of haplogroups and I believe it was haplogroup F that is an ancient variant and has an apparent origin in the Middle East, but spread to India and even back to the Horn of Africa. But my guess is his grandfather or his great-great-great-great grandfather was probably from East Africa or something like that. But you couldn't be more specific in terms of what part of that entire distribution his paternal ancestry was from. Of course, there's also the sociological notion that his grandfather might have been culturally and socially an American Indian, he could have been adopted into it. You just don't know that non-biological part of his story. So there's a biological uncertainty of knowing exactly where in that distribution of Y-chromosomes his ancestor comes from, plus the sociological uncertainty of assignment of an individual.

JR: Also, I understand that with these services results depends on the content and size of the database.

JF: Oh sure, absolutely, that's what I meant. So, for example, my mtDNA haplogroup, if you look, or at least a couple years ago – I'm an old Ashkenazi – my mtDNA haplogroup occurs in about 30% of Ashkenazim, but it is also common in the British Isles, Central Europe, and even Iceland. You have to do considerably more specific sequencing to break it down into subgroups that might be somewhat more specific, but generally it's not ever going to be as specific as people would like.

JR: So what haplogroup is that?

JF: It's a subgroup of haplogroup K. So there are these problems in terms of distributional studies. Now, the Genographic Project would certainly say they're trying to map out more intensive sampling of the mtDNA and Y-chromosome variance, but they're going to have problems in terms of not using fine meshed haplogroup tests, they're not doing whole genomes by any means – just a few mtDNA and Y variants. They're certainly not going to do whole mtDNA genome sequencing for a nominal price. They're overselling their product; they're not going to be able to isolate people's ancestral homelands that well at all. It's probably more informative to rely on facial appearance. Look at Bougainville and my old model of anthropometric results.

A second major issue is the problem of commercialization. They're assuming they're going to be able to collect a lot of genetic information on populations around the world and get a good idea of these gene distributions, but they're not going to pay people for their involvement or donations. Now, a lot of the Genographic materials and a lot of new programs aren't using SNP-chip kind of things, they are using cheek swabs, so that's no so invasive as taking a 10 cc blood sample. Is there a big difference there? You're still collecting people's genetic information. I would argue that you need just the same amount of consent and compensation for one as the other, and I don't think that's been talked about adequately.

JR: So where did Tishkoff get all the samples from?

JF: She did a lot of fieldwork herself, but she also had colleagues in Africa, some of whom she trained who also collected. There were other collaborators as well who pooled their data. It's quite an impressive sample and it's been a problem to pull into publication because it's been so large and complex, but it'll be a major contribution.

JR: Another dimension of that – do you think her status of being affiliated with a medical school, as opposed to being in anthropology, puts more pressure on her in terms of commercialization and . . .

JF: She tries hard to justify her collections in terms of medicine and health benefit. I think that's where that monetary pressure comes in. I do think the relative payoff for medical vs. Genographic sort of work is still skewed, certainly at the moment (I doubt if the Genographic projects will be highly profitable over the long run). If you read her grant proposals and some of her papers, you'll see the medical or health emphasis.

There's one she wrote with Ken Kidd, who was her old mentor, on genetics and medicine, so they were both in medical schools and that was the attempt to bring in population genetic diversity and its applications to medicine. She's also worked on particular genes that have an effect on the phenotype, but not always. One of her papers was on G6PD deficiency, which is a clear single gene disease related to malaria resistance, and the distribution of its variants in the Middle East and Africa. That's interesting in terms of population history, but also related to selection favoring the heterozygote, in a peculiar X-linked situation (so only women can be a heterozygote with the favorable combination). Other papers from her lab have focused on other genes that have a health-related benefit, such as genetic variants that cause lactose intolerance, but this latest African dataset she's working on, these microsatellite genomic screens, has been more pure population history, so it's been a mixture in her work.

Chapter 13.

What Have We Learned?

A Description of Human Genetic Variation

JR: Something that gets spoken of in critiques in this kind of work is that it involves the "molecular reinscription" of race, that there's a certain set of categories that are presupposed which structure how genetic data is interpreted. Could you reflect on that?

JF: This is an easy and accurate critique to make of early studies, especially. Even major contemporary efforts like the HapMap have been based on just a 3 or 4 populations, assuming that is adequate for all human diversity – "The Yoruba who are going to represent all Africans, and these students at Berkeley will represent the Han Chinese . . ." Anyway, it's an inadequate population distribution that's supposed to represent the major axes of human variety.

The population geneticists and anthropological geneticists know better than that. We've now got an overall description of the pattern of genetic variation that does exist across the human species. That has become clear with the recent flurry of papers, beginning with the Rosenberg paper on the Human Genome Diversity Panel out of CEPH in Paris, the Wang paper on Native Americans, ours on Pacific islanders, and some papers on India that have come out, and Tishkoff's Africa paper that will ultimately come out. That pattern is not going to change in the future. The early landmark work that came out 10 or 15 years ago by Cavalli that's called *Human Gene Map* has been greatly superseded now, showing the lumpiness of human genetic variation in many regions, and from here on, there will not be any new huge surprises in that regard.

What's clear is that the genetic diversity within any African population is much greater than what you get as you move out of

Africa because of this notion of migrations or "serial founder effects." A nice commonly used phrase to describe this attenuation of genetic variation out of Africa is that human genetic diversity has been *titrated* outside Africa. Populations in the Pacific have gone through a number of bottlenecks, of founding effects, and each is relatively homogeneous internally. Now the distinctions *among* populations can still be great, in the Americas, in Melanesia, and elsewhere, but Africa is this big storehouse of genetic variety no matter what gene or gene segment you look at, whether it's microsatellites or SNPs or the mtDNA and Y, and that pattern is going to be just reinforced from here on out.

Now, for me, one unanswered question is if there is any faint signal of an ancient Melanesian relationship to Africans. Right now, the answer is that we can't see any convincing evidence. People have continued to think, because of the skin color and hair similarities, that there is some special connection, but we can't find it, try though we might. Melanesians are a very old and distinctive group, long isolated from most other groups, and they only show the weakest of affinities to East and South Asian groups, whatever markers you examine.

I don't know if that's what you're looking for – I got side-tracked again.

JR: Well, yes it is. That's a nice statement.

JF: There's another story that relates to some of the early ancestral genographic work that shows the likelihood of misclassification of individuals' ancestry with these techniques. Ever head of Affymetrix? Well Mark Shriver, at Penn State, is closely associated with Affymetrix, which makes those large SNP chips for identifying variation in large numbers of SNP loci. He was using the STRUCTURE program and an earlier Affy chip, which "only" covered hundreds of thousands of SNPs, to try and talk about people's ancestry in a three-dimensional grid or a triangle. The three dimensions were: how European you were, how African you were, or how Asian you were. He'd just added a fourth dimension, making it a pyramid, for how Native American you were. He had four populations who had been characterized with the SNP chip, and he could put new individuals into this four-dimensional space, depending upon their genetic profile according to the Affy chip. He invited us, and whomever else he thought would come, to a free dinner at the Physical Anthropology meetings in Tampa in 2004, where he was going to make a presentation on the power of this Affy chip. This was trying to get people to use it and send in samples. This was when we had George Koki, a Tolai from New Britain, visiting. There were only a few of us who went to the dinner – a lot of people said, "Don't go. This is just a lot of craziness and new racism – genetic profiling." One of the things Mark did to show was the power of this individual identification for forensics in a Texas case, where there was a question as to whether the suspected perpetrator had a European or mixed European/African ancestry. At the end of his talk, Mark made a general invitation to people afterwards to have their cheeks swabbed and the DNA analysis put in their database. He came up to us afterwards and said to George, "You know George, we'd be happy to have you give a cheek swab," and George, who knows his human genetics said, "Oh no, I'm fine, thanks." So when Mark left I said, "George, I'm interested. Why didn't you want to let him take your cheek swab?" George said, "I would have just looked Chinese," which, in terms of the dimensionality, was exactly what it would have suggested. So, it does depend on the breadth and the accuracy of the databases that people use for these studies, but it all has definite limits.

Public Benefits

JR: What do you think the general public gets out of these kinds of commercial services? I also wondered if you might have a statement to make about what you think is the appropriate use of this kind of information, to the extent that the general public is interested your work or work of people you respect and train. What would you hope they would gain from that?

JF: First of all, my interest has nothing to do with practical application – it's all simply population history and the history of the human species. I think it's all consistent with this notion that yes, there might be some room for a few Neanderthal genes or *Homo erectus* genes floating into modern human populations, but there's no question, overall, that we all primarily have an African ancestry, and relatively recently, not hundreds of thousands of years ago. The greatest diversity is Africa, and a series of founding events occurred in the general framework of 40 to 80 to 100 thousand years ago out of Africa, and that's where the majority, if not the entire, genetic history of modern human patterns comes from. I hope that is useful or intellectually satisfying to people to have a sense for the history of modern human society – the recent common ancestry of our species. I find it so.

I know for my students, it is something that African-American students particularly like because it puts Africa at the center of modern human history. However, it has made some students uncomfortable, I know. I had one student who was from Korea, and after I talked about the genetic Out of Africa hypothesis, he came to my office and said, "Dr. Friedlaender, I had a lot of trouble with that lecture. You're saying our ancestors all came from Africa?" And I said, "That's the way it looks – not last year, but over the last tens of thousands of years." He said, "Well, my minister and I have a lot of trouble with that. I don't think I or my ancestors were African." This obviously had to do with poor race relations between Koreans and African Americans. He said, "My minister says that we were created as a species, according to the Book of Genesis, 4,000 years ago." And I said, "Well, it's true the literal Genesis account is not compatible with the results we seem to be getting from the genetic diversity." So perhaps people will begin to take these genetic messages seriously. I think it's great we're beginning to have more and more information that begins to tie humans together. Africa is the homeland of modern humans, and it's damn clear that our genealogy has a much longer history than 4,000 years ago. So, I think all that is great. However, I think the genetic ancestry services are going to be relatively uninformative.

Religion and Science

JR: Since you brought it up, it occurs to me this might be interesting place for us to discuss religion and the student's story. The question of religion and biology is one that is potent in America. Do you have any reflections on that in terms of the role of various scientists' religious views? Someone like Francis Collins is outspoken about his religious views even as he promotes the Genome Project. Do you think this kind of knowledge promotes a different cosmology, if you will, of understanding the world that possibly is competing with religion or is compatible with religion? This is not an elegantly put question . . .

JF: Well, I'm not going to give an elegant answer either. I think it depends a lot upon the religious perspective you're trying to reconcile with this genetic information. No reconciliation is possible if you're talking about the strict Genesis, fundamentalist, creationist account of the world. Just in terms of my own personal situation, at this point, I'm not religious (as an eleven-year-old, I thought it would be nice to become a rabbi – I lost any sense of religion in college). I think that's important to say up front.

I've always argued, in class, and otherwise, that accepting what I'm teaching about the "facts" of human genetic diversity doesn't have to mean the absolute rejection of a belief in a higher organizing principle or spirit. The founders of the Modern Synthesis were, for the most part, religious, with only one an avowed atheist (Mayr). Richard Dawkins has been making a major effort to debunk religion from an evolutionist's perspective, of course. Evolutionary theory operates without the necessity for a supreme being, for sure. But it doesn't have to be incompatible. There obviously are a lot of fine geneticists – not many though – Francis Collins I would say is in a small minority – who talk about the hand of God in the order of genetics and human design, and all that. There were a number of Jesuits who were involved in paleontological work in France – Pierre Teilhard de Chardin and others, so it's not irreconcilable, but it's tenuous. I find a lot of the attempts to reconcile science and religion, like Sir John Templeton's tortured conferences – I don't know if "misguided" is quite the right word, perhaps "pointless." Mine is apparently a minority stance in the U.S. in this day and age, but that's where I am.

JR: Thank you for thinking about that question –

JF: One thing to add about notions surrounding the argument of the perfection of creation and Intelligent Design is that there are so many obvious failures in life (fetal deaths, high infant mortality, and so forth) – would a supreme being allow all that mess? It's *unintelligent* design! I'm not the first person to say that, but it's the way things seem to work – many mutations and a lot of imperfections leading to a great deal of loss in terms of early death or so on. Darwin understood and experienced this clearly. His own daughter's death at an early age was a major blow and led to his rejection of religion.

Genomic Genealogy Services

JR: Interesting. Could I get you speculate a little bit, from the other side – as someone in the "general" public, what's the appeal of this kind of knowledge? I'm talking about genetic ancestry knowledge. How do you make sense of why it seems to be so desirable to some? There's certainly an enormous amount of media attention to trace your ancestry using DNA and Henry Louis Gates, Jr. has been promoting the African ancestry stories. What is your opinion about the appeal of getting ancestral information in this way?

JF: Well, I think it relates to people's curiosity about themselves. It's almost like fortune telling. I think we're all susceptible to having somebody tell us something about ourselves that we had no idea about. I'm susceptible to that, too. I remember once when I was in Turkey in my early twenties, with my then fiancée, who was Turkish. She said, for fun, "Let's go to the fortune teller." He was a Jew named Dr. Jacob, who'd trained as a psychologist in Vienna and had come back to Istanbul and hung out a shingle as a psychologist – nobody would come (psychology was not fashionable). Then he changed his "profession" to being a fortune teller and was much more successful. Someone would come in and say, "Dr. Jacob can you please help me. My husband doesn't come home until late at night, and we have endless arguments and I don't know what to do." And he would say, "I'll give you this amulet, and you put this under his pillow and say these prayers, but also, be extremely nice to him, cook him his favorite dinner, try not to argue with him, don't berate him, listen to him, sympathize with him, and so on" – which of course was the real message, but in the guise of now being a fortune teller. So we went to see Dr. Jacob as a curiosity, and I didn't believe in fortune telling, and I'd heard these stories about him before. When he looked at my palm and said, "Something you're doing here in Turkey has to do with the

American government." I said, "Hmm, he's right!" Of course, for an American guy to be in Istanbul there was a strong likelihood that he had something to do with the government in those days. I was doing bone analysis on an archaeological expedition directed by George Hanfmann at Sardis that was supported, partially, I believe, by U.S. funds (the Endowment for the Humanities). Then he said, "You've had some near death experience with water." I said, "You know, when I was 18 I did get pulled out from a beach by an undertow and I struggled with that for a while, so yes, you're right about that too!" And in the same way, I kept finding things in my past that could be reconciled with his rather vague general statements. Finally, he said, "You're going to live to be 83 and have three children, two boys and a girl." And I said, "That sounds excellent." So I felt good and reinforced by the whole meeting. We walked out into the street. The traffic in Istanbul is just terrible, and even people on the sidewalks aren't safe from cars, and drivers don't pay any attention to stop lights, since many don't function. I walked right across the street without looking to the sides, and my fiancée said, "Jonathan, you're going to get killed – you're not paying any attention to the traffic!" And I said, "I don't have to, I'm going to live to be 83!" I partially believed it, too.

So I think there's a lot of that same element of "If we look at your DNA, we're going to be able to tell where your most ancient ancestors are from. It's powerful magic." You may be able to reinforce what your family has already told you to some degree, unless things are just a total blank slate. So I think it has that apparent power of insight that we've lost, but it's rather inaccurate, and will remain so. A great deal of historical reconstruction is like that, in fact.

JR: What do you mean, "That we've lost?"

JF: Most people don't know the names of their ancestors beyond their grandparents or great grand parents. Our histories get too complex and diluted after that, and uncertainties creep in. We also know less and less about each ancestral or historical figure. The mist of history creeps in, as they say. However, we all like to think we have a connection to someone special or interesting in the past. In my family, my mother's family claimed they were related to the Rothschilds, for example (my father's father retorted that it was undoubtedly through a female washerwoman in the Rothschild household).

One of my college roommates is from a Jewish background on his father's side, and he had his Y-chromosome variants analyzed by Michael Hammer's group. Low and behold, he's got the Cohen modal haplotype, which is particularly common among men named Cohen, who are supposed to be descendants of the ancient Hebrew priestly caste, the *Cohanim,* and Aaron. So he asked me, "Jonathan, does this mean I'm an actual descendant of Aaron?" I said, "Well, the chances are better that you're a descendent of Aaron or at least some of his male relatives than somebody outside that group, but it's not a hard and fast certainty." He said, "Oh, I see what you mean . . ." But that's an exciting connection to be able to try and make to an important historical figure. So, it's fascinating stuff. Why does anybody do genealogy anyway? It's for the same kind of purpose, but genetic work is done with the promise of a little more notion of scientific exactness, when in fact it may be less exact.

JR: Recently, I don't know if you're aware, the American Society for Human Genetics released a statement at the most recent meeting –

JF: I don't know about this . . .

JR: On the appropriate uses of genetic data for ancestry purposes.

JF: I *don't* know about that.

JR: I'll be happy to send you the bullet point executive summary statements. So, in concluding our conversation, in your professional opinion, we've addressed this a little bit, but what do you think are the kinds of issues that people who choose to engage with this information should be aware of? And do you feel that there's a need for anthropologists to kind of make a statement on the appropriate use of these kinds of services by the general public?

JF: Hmm. Well, I better read that statement, but I think the thing that pops to mind in terms of inappropriate use, that people are worried about, is the notion of stigmatization which we discussed earlier. That's an issue with regard to the distribution of certain harmful genes. Some people are sensitive about that. In the early days, in the 1950s and 1960s, sickle cell anemia was equated with being from a sub-Saharan African population, as if everyone from that background had it. Of course, it's only a portion of people with African ancestry who carry sickle cell alleles, much less the full anemia, and some people outside Africa also carry it as well. That was the kind of overly facile equation. Tay-Sachs, Jewish; Sickle-cell anemia, African; and so on. But beyond that, I'm not sure what issues they raise that I would be concerned about. I am concerned, too, about the over-selling of the power of ancestral genetic services – it's a false promise. Perhaps the greatest practical payoff of population genetics to date is in the field of forensics, which is indeed powerful, since each person has a unique genetic profile.

JR: Yes. It's something to think about. And so it's almost noon and that will probably signal the end of our conversation. That wraps up the interview.

END OF INTERVIEW

Postscript

I was flattered and pleased when Joanna Radin first approached me about doing an oral history, and I hope that you have found this edited version with the added photos interesting and perhaps entertaining as well.

In retrospect, the process made me realize a number of points about my career that I would like to underline.

First off, it is apparent just how fortunate I was to be in certain situations and environments at particular times. My parents strongly encouraged my education and scholarship, which was an extraordinary gift. If I did not pursue science and mathematics training with conviction in secondary school and college, I was influenced to develop a strong skeptical and critical sense at Exeter and Harvard. While I was easily bored or dismissive of many teachers or colleagues, there were a few good ones that caught my attention, sometimes intimidated me, and influenced my ideas and plans. It is clear that I was often attracted to particular individual personalities as much as, or more than, to their ideas. Many early decisions I made were not well thought through, and I was just lucky some worked out so well. In particular, being a graduate student and junior faculty member at Harvard during the post-Vietnam period, with the evolutionary controversies swirling around the work of Mayr, Simpson, Wilson, and Lewontin, as well as learning and evaluating the anthropological approaches of Howells, Damon, and others, made me think that all this was important and worth devoting my professional life to. Having the chance to tag along on the Harvard Solomon Islands Expedition was obviously a major turning point, and I never regretted my commitment to the Southwest Pacific afterwards. Amorous concerns were more important than one might like to acknowledge, sometimes much for the better (as with Françoise), and sometimes for the worse. Balancing extensive fieldwork stays with marriage was difficult in my life, for example. I think that is a common thread in many anthropologists' careers.

Certain aspects of my personality were also important (again for better or worse). I have a somewhat cautious and passive nature typical of second children. Understanding new approaches or concepts was never easy for me – their logic took a while to sink in. While I was often attracted to new paradigms, I usually was equally quick to look for their weaknesses. No one could say I was single-minded in a drive to become a human evolutionist interested in Pacific genetics. However, I was always interested in how things got to be the way they are (whether it was the development of Western civilization, the evolution of art styles, or human biological evolution). My interest in human genetic variation was not something that evolved over the course of my career. It was there early on, along with many others. However, it was only recently that the power of genomics enabled us to realize the potential to describe human population relationships and history, and I took advantage of that, with the critical help of others.

Many of my "decisions" were more in the nature of deciding *not* to pursue certain interests of mine. The first rejection was classical archaeology and then cultural anthropology. Later, I turned away from primate behavior studies because I thought their explanations lacked rigor. Teasing apart hereditary and environmental factors in behavior studies with statistical approaches gave misleading or unsatisfactory results. It is only now that geneticists are beginning to have some success in identifying how certain genes, or sometimes many dozens of genes, can contribute in a significant way to clinical psychological conditions, for example, or can influence essential human characteristics such as speech. This is finally becoming exciting.

Although cautious and critical, I still could be quick to decide on a course of action in the field. Once I had the chance to go to Melanesia, I made a prompt and decisive decision about which island to study, what problems to study, and what information to collect. Bougainville had considerable linguistic diversity, but it appeared to be manageable to survey, unlike New Guinea. Subsequent research decisions followed logically from that, although not always in a linear sequence.

Looking back, I'm pleased that our studies, coupled with those from other regions, have now established the broad outlines of human population relationships, and I am confident that our conclusions will not be significantly altered in the future. In terms of my career, I'm also happy that I chose to become a biological anthropologist. I could probably also have become a decent physician, a classical art historian, or even a Foreign Service officer. I'm sure, however, that I never would have been a good or happy businessman or lawyer.

Jonathan S. Friedlaender

Sharon, CT
Summer 2009

Returning from work. Foueda, Lau Lagoon. 1978.

APPENDIX 1:
Jonathan Friedlaender's Publications

Monograph

1975. *Patterns of Human Variation: The demography, genetics, and phenetics of Bougainville Islanders.* J.S. Friedlaender. Harvard University Press, Cambridge, MA.

Edited volumes/issues

2007. *Genes, Language, and Culture History in the Southwest Pacific. Edited by J.S. Friedlaender.* New York. Oxford University Press.

1996. Invited Guest Editor, *Cultural Survival Quarterly*. "Genes, People and Property: Furor Erupts Over Genetic Research in Indigenous Populations." (Summer issue).

1992. Editor, *The Yearbook of Physical Anthropology*

1990. Editor, Symposium on the Solomon Islands Project. *American Journal of Physical Anthropology.* (special edition, May).

1987. Editor, *The Solomon Islands Project: A long-term study of health, human biology, and culture change.* The Clarendon Press, Oxford University Press.

1976. Giles, E and Friedlaender, JS (eds), *The Measures of Man: Methodologies in Biological Anthropology (Festschrift in honor of William White Howells).* Peabody Museum Press: Cambridge, Mass.

Textbook

1991. Friedlaender, JS; Greenfield, LO; and Weitz, CA. *Fundamentals of Biological Anthropology.* Kendall Hunt: Ames, Iowa.

Research Articles/book chapters (peer reviewed unless noted with asterisk)

2008

Hunley KL, Dunn M, Lindstrom E, Reesink G, Terrill A, Healey ME, Koki G, Friedlaender FR, and Friedlaender JS. Gene and language coevolution in Northern Island Melanesia. *Public Library of Science-Genetics*. October 2008.

Friedlaender, JS, Friedlaender, FF, Reed F, Kidd KK, Kidd JR, Chambers G, Lea R, Loo JH, Hodgson J, Koki G, Merriwether DA, Weber J. The Genetic Structure of Pacific Islanders. *Public Library of Science – Genetics.* January 2008, 4(1), pp 173-190.

Ciarleglio, CM, K Ryckman, SV Servick, A Hida, S Robbins, N Wells, J Hicks, SA Larson, JP

Wiedermann, K Carver, N Hamilton, KK Kidd, JR Kidd, JR Smith, JS Friedlaender, DG McMahon, S Williams, ML Summar, and CH Johnson. Genetic Differences in Human Circadian Clock Genes Among Worldwide Populations. *J. Biol. Rhythms* 23: 330-340.

2007

Friedlaender JS, with contributions from Pilbeam D, Hrdy D, Giles E, Green R. William W. Howells – A biographical memoir. *National Academy of Sciences Memoir.* Pp 1-18.

Friedlaender JS, Friedlaender FR, Hodgson JA, Stoltz M, Koki G, Horvat G, Zhadanov S, Schurr TG, Merriwether DA. Melanesian mtDNA complexity. *Public Library of Science – One.* February 24, 2007.

Friedlaender, JS. Introduction (chapter 1). In: *Genes, Language and Culture History in the Southwest Pacific.* JS Friedlaender, editor. Oxford University Press, NY. Pp 3-9.*

Friedlaender JS, Friedlaender FR, Hodgson JA, McGrath S, Stoltz M, Koki G, Schurr TG, Merriwether DA. (chapter 4). Mitochondrial DNA Variation in Northern Island Melanesia In: *Genes, Language and Culture History in the Southwest Pacific.* JS Friedlaender, editor. Oxford University Press, NY. Pp 61-80.*

Scheinfeldt L, Friedlaender FR, Friedlaender JS, Latham K, Koki G, Karafet T, Hammer M, Lorenz J. Y chromosome variation in Island Melanesia. (chapter 5). In: *Genes, Language and Culture History in the Southwest Pacific.* JS Friedlaender, editor. Oxford University Press, NY. Pp 81-95.*

Norton H, Koki G, Friedlaender JS, Pigmentation and Candidate Gene Variation in Northern Island Melanesia (chapter 6). In: *Genes, Language and Culture History in the Southwest Pacific.* JS Friedlaender, editor. Oxford University Press, NY. Pp 96-112.*

Hunley K, Dunn M, Lindström E, Reesink E, Terrill A, Norton H, Scheinfeldt L, Friedlaender FR, Merriwether DA, Koki G, Friedlaender JS. Inferring Prehistory from Genetic, Linguistic, and Geographic Variation (chapter 9). In: *Genes, Language and Culture History in the Southwest Pacific.* JS Friedlaender, editor. Oxford University Press, NY. Pp 141-156.*

Friedlaender JS. Conclusion (chapter 16). In: *Genes, Language and Culture History in the Southwest Pacific.* JS Friedlaender, editor. Oxford University Press, NY. Pp 230-236.*

Garrigan D, Kingan SB, Pilkington MM, Wilder JA, Cox MP, Soodyall H, Strassmann B, Destro-Bisol G, de Knijff P, Novelletto A, Friedlaender JS, Hammer MF. Inferring Human Population Sizes, Divergence Times and Rates of Gene Flow From Mitochondrial, X and Y Chromosome Resequencing Data. *Genetics.* December; 177(4): 2195–2207.

2006

Scheinfeldt L, Friedlaender FF, Friedlaender JS, Latham K, Koki G, Karafet T, Hammer M, Lorenz J. Unexpected NRY chromosome variation in Northern Island Melanesia. Molecular Biology and Evolution. Aug; 23(8):1628-41. Epub 2006 Jun 5.

Norton HL, Friedlaender JS, Merriwether DA, Koki G, Mgone CS, Shriver MD. Skin and hair pigmentation variation in Island Melanesia. *American Journal of Physical Anthropology.* Jun; 130(2):254-68.

Friedlaender JS. William White Howells (1908-2005). Obituary. *American Anthropologist.* 108 (4): 936-939.

2005

Friedlaender JS, Friedlaender FR, Gentz F, Kaestle F, Koki G, Schurr TG , Schanfield M, McDonough J, Smith L, Cerchio S, Mgone CS, Merriwether DA. Mitochondrial genetic diversity and its determinants in Island Melanesia. In: Pawley, Andrew, Attenborough, Robert, Golson, Jack, Hyde, Robin. *Papuan Pasts: Studies in the cultural, linguistic and biological history of the Papuan speaking peoples.* Canberra: Pacific Linguistics. Pp. 693-716

Merriwether DA, Hodgson JA, Friedlaender FR, Allaby R, Cerchio S, Koki G, Friedlaender JS. Ancient mitochondrial M haplogroups identified in the Southwest Pacific. *Proceedings of the National Academy of Sciences USA.* Sep 13;102(37):13034-9.

Friedlaender JS, Schurr T, Gentz F, Koki G, Friedlaender F, Horvat G, Babb P, Cerchio S, Kaestle F, Schanfield M, Deka R, Yanagihara R, Merriwether DA. Expanding Southwest Pacific mitochondrial haplogroups P and Q. *Molecular Biology and Evolution.* 2005 Jun; 22 (6):1506-17

Friedlaender JS. Why do the people of Bougainville look unique? Some conclusions from biological anthropology and genetics. In: Anthony Regan and Helga Griffin, (eds.), *Bougainville Before the Crisis.* Research School of Pacific and Asian Studies, Canberra.*

Shriver MD, Mei R, Parra EJ, Sonpar V, Halder I, Tishkoff SA, Schurr TG, Zhadanov SI, Osipova LP, Brutsaert TD, Friedlaender J, Jorde LB, Watkins WS, Bamshad MJ, Gutierrez G, Loi H, Matsuzaki H, Kittles

RA, Argyropoulos G, Fernandez JR, Akey JM, Jones KW. Large-scale SNP analysis reveals clustered and continuous patterns of human genetic variation *Human Genomics.* 2(2): 81-89.

2004

Friedlaender JS Commentary: Changing standards of informed consent: Raising the bar. In: Trudy Turner (ed.) *Ethics in Physical Anthropology*. SUNY Albany Press.

Shriver MD, Mei R, Parra EJ, Sonpar V, Makova K, Tishkoff SA, Schurr TG, Zhadanov SI, Osipova LP, Brutsaert T, Friedlaender JS, Jorde LB, Watkins S, Bamshad MJ, Guterez G, Argyropoulos G, Kittles RA Akey JM, and Jones K. Compound effects of allele frequency change, recombination rate, and intermarker spacing on linkage disequilibrium. *Genome Research.*

2003

Robledo R, Scheinfeldt L, Merriwether DA, Thompson F, and Friedlaender JS. A 9.1 kb insertion/deletion polymorphism suggests a common pattern of genetic diversity in Island Melanesia. *Human Biology.* Dec; 75(6): 941-9.

Friedlaender JS Population genetic research in the South Pacific. *Cell Lines.* June (Coriell Institute, Camden).*

2002

Friedlaender JS, Gentz F, Green K, Merriwether DA. A cautionary tale on ancient migration detection: mitochondrial DNA variation in Santa Cruz Islands, Solomon Islands. *Human Biology.* Jun; 74(3): 453-71.

Yanagihara R, Nerurkar VR, Scheirich I, Agostini HT, Mgone CS, Cui X, Jobes DV, Cubitt CL, Ryschkewitsch CF, Hrdy DB, Friedlaender JS, Stoner G. JC virus genotypes in the western Pacific suggest Asian mainland relationships and virus association with early population movements. *Human Biology* Jun; 74(3): 473-88.

Cann HM, de Toma C, Cazes L, Legrand MF, Morel V, Piouffre L, Bodmer J, Bodmer WF, Bonne-Tamir B, Cambon-Thomsen A, Chen Z, Chu J, Carcassi C, Contu L, Du R, Excoffier L, Ferrara GB, Friedlaender JS, Groot H, Gurwitz D, Jenkins T, Herrera RJ, Huang X, Kidd J, Kidd KK, Langaney A, Lin AA, Mehdi SQ, Parham P, Piazza A, Pistillo MP, Qian Y, Shu Q, Xu J, Zhu S, Weber JL, Greely HT, Feldman MW, Thomas G, Dausset J, Cavalli-Sforza LL. A human genome diversity cell line panel. *Science.* 2002 Apr 12; 296 (5566): 261-2.

2001

Jobes DV, Friedlaender JS, Mgone CS, Agostini HT, Koki G, Yanagihara R, Ng TCN, Chima SC, Ryschkewitsch CF, Stoner GL. New JC virus (JCV) genotypes from Papua New Guinea and Micronesia (type 8 and type 2E) and evolutionary analysis of 32 complete JCV genomes. *Archives of Virology* 146 (11): 2097-113.

2000

Kidd JJ, Pakstis AJ, Zhao H, Lu RB, Okonofua FE, Odunsi A, Grigorenko E, Tamir BB, Friedlaender JS, Schulz LO, Parnas J, Kidd KK Phenylalanine hydroxylase locus, PAH, in a global representation of populations. *American Journal of Human Genetics.* Jun; 66(6): 1882-99

Ryschkewitsch CF, Friedlaender JS, Mgone CS, Jobes D, Agostini H, Chima S, Alpers MP, Koki G, Yanagihara R, and Stoner GL. Human Polyomavirus JC variants in Papua New Guinea and Guam reflect ancient population settlement and viral infection. *Microbes and Infection,* 2: 987-996.

1999

Jobes DV, Friedlaender JS, Mgone CS, Koki G, Alpers MP, Ryschkewitsch CF, and Stoner GL A novel JC virus variant found in the highlands of Papua New Guinea has a 21-base pair deletion in the agnoprotein gene. *Journal of Human Virology,* vol 2, number 6, pp. 350-358.

Merriwether DA, Kaestle FA, Zemel B, Koki G, Mgone C, Alpers M, Friedlaender JS Mitochondrial DNA variation in the Southwest Pacific. In: Papiha SS, Deka R, Chakraborty R, editors. *Genomic diversity: Applications in human population genetics.* New York: Plenum Publishers.

Merriwether DA, Friedlaender JS, Mediavilla J, Gentz F, Blumberg BS, Mgone C, and Ferrell R. Mitochondrial DNA variation is an indicator of Austronesian influence in Island Melanesia *American Journal of Physical Anthropology* 110:3, pp.243-270.

Weiss KM and Friedlaender JS. *The origins and structure of contemporary genetic variation in the United States.* Special report prepared at the request of Francis Collins, Director, National Institute of Human Genome Research.*

Friedlaender JS. Biotechnology and ethics: comment on “Genome: Moral Choices and the Polity” *High Plains Applied Anthropologist.* 17:1. Spring.*

1997

Friedlaender JS. A Perspective on Race. *Anthropology Newsletter*, November Issue.*

1996

Friedlaender JS. Indroduction, "Furor Erupts over Genetic Research in Indigenous Groups" *Cultural Survival Quarterly*, Summer issue*.

1995

Friedlaender, JS Funding Patterns for Biological Anthropology *American Anthropology Newsletter,* May Issue.*

1994

Kamboh, I., and Friedlaender JS A common deletion polymorphism of the apolipoprotein A4 gene in Solomon Islanders" *Atherosclerosis.*

1993

Kamboh MI, Friedlaender JS, Ahn YI, Ferrell RE A common deletion polymorphism in the apolipoprotein-A-IV gene and its association with lipoprotein-lipid levels. *Circulation 8*8 (4): 267-267 Part 2 Oct 1993.

Friedlaender JS Update on the Human Genome Diversity Initiative. *Evolutionary Anthropology.* Fall issue.*

1990

Friedlaender JS. The Solomon Islands Project: an Introduction. *American Journal of Physical Anthropology*

Zerba KE, Friedlaender JS, and Sing CF. Heterogeneity of the blood pressure distribution among Solomon Islands Societies with increasing acculturation. *American Journal of Physical Anthropology.*

Armstrong MYK, Hrdy DB, Carlson JR, and Friedlaender JS. Prevalence of antibodies interactive with HTLV-1 antigens in selected Solomon Islands populations. *American Journal of Physical Anthropology.*

Kottke A, Friedlaender JS, Zerba KE, and Sing CF. Lipid and apolipoprotein levels in six Solomon Islands Societies differ from a United States Caucasian population. *American Journal of Physical Anthropology.*

1989

Friedlaender JS and Page LB. Population biology and aging: the example of blood pressure. *American Journal of Human Biology*, 1: 355-365.

1987

Mitchell DD, Nash J, Ogan E, Ross H, Bayliss-Smith T, Keesing RM, Gillogly-Akin K, and Friedlaender JS Ethnographic description and recent histories of the Solomon Islands Survey groups. In: JS Friedlaender (ed),

The Solomon Islands Project: A long-term study of health, human biology, and culture change. Clarendon Press, Oxford, pp. 14-27.*

D. D. Mitchell DD, Nash J, Ogan E, Ross H, Bayliss-Smith T, Keesing RM, and Friedlaender JS

Profiles of the Solomon Islands Survey samples. In: J. S. Friedlaender (ed.), *The Solomon Islands Project: A long-term study of health, human biology, and culture change.* Clarendon Press, Oxford, pp. 28-60.*

Page LB, Rhoads JG, Friedlaender JS, Page JR, and Curtis K. Diet and nutrition in the Solomon Islands. . In: J. S. Friedlaender (ed.), *The Solomon Islands Project: A long-term study of health, human biology, and culture change.* Clarendon Press, Oxford, pp. 65-88.*

Friedlaender JS and Page LB. Epidemiology in the Solomon Islands Survey. In: J. S. Friedlaender (ed.), *The Solomon Islands Project: A long-term study of health, human biology, and culture change.* Clarendon Press, Oxford. pp. 89-124.*

Rhoads JG and Friedlaender JS. Blood polymorphism variation in the Solomon Islands. In: J. S. Friedlaender (ed.) *The Solomon Islands Project: A long-term study of health, human biology, and culture change.* Clarendon Press, Oxford, pp. 125-154.*

Dow M, Cheverud J, Rhoads JG, and Friedlaender JS. Statistical comparisons of patterns of biological and cultural-historical variation. In: J. S. Friedlaender (ed.), *The Solomon Islands Project: A long-term study of health, human biology, and culture change.* Clarendon Press, Oxford, pp. 265-282.*

Friedlaender JS and Rhoads JG. Longitudinal anthropometric changes in adolescents and adults. In: J. S. Friedlaender (ed.), *The Solomon Islands Project: A long-term study of health, human biology, and culture change.* Clarendon Press, Oxford. pp. 283-306.*

Friedlaender JS and Page LB, Blood pressure changes in the Survey populations In: J. S. Friedlaender (ed.), *The Solomon Islands Project: A* *long-term study of health, human biology, and culture change.* Clarendon Press, Oxford. pp. 307-326.*

Friedlaender JS. Conclusion. In: J. S. Friedlaender (ed.), *The Solomon Islands Project: A long-term study of health, human biology, and culture change.* Clarendon Press, Oxford. pp. 351-380.*

Bowcock, AM; Bucci C; Hebert JM; Kidd JR; Kidd KK; Friedlaender, J. S.; Cavalli-Sforza, L. L. Study of 47 DNA markers in five populations from four continents. *Gene Geography*, 1: 47-64

M. M. Dow, J. M. Cheverud and J. S. Friedlaender. Partial correlation of distance matrices in studies of population structure. *American Journal of Physical Anthropology*, 72:343-354.*

1986

Cavalli-Sforza LL, Kidd JR, Kidd KK, Bucci C, Bowcock AM, Hewlett BS, and Friedlaender JS DNA markers and genetic variation in the human species. *Cold Spring Harbor Symposia on Quantitative Biology*; LI, 411-417.

Page LB and Friedlaender JS. Blood pressure, age, and cultural change; a longitudinal study of Solomon Islands populations. In: M. J. Horan, G.M. Steinberg, J.B. Dunbar, E.C. Hadley (eds.), *Blood Pressure Regulation and Aging. Proceedings from a Symposium.* Biomedical Information Corporation, New York. Pp. 11-26.

Hrdy DB, Carlson JR, Friedlaender JS. Absence of antibodies to HTLV-III on Bougainville (Papua New Guinea). *Medical Journal of Australia*, 144: 723.

1983

Stevens RG, Kuvibidila S, Kapps M, and Friedlaender JS, and Blumberg BS. Iron-binding proteins, hepatitis B virus, and mortality in the Solomon Islands. *American Journal of Epidemiology*, 118: 550- 561.

1982

Sokal R and Friedlaender JS. Spatial autocorrelation analysis on biological variation on Bougainville Island. In: Michael Crawford and James Mielke (eds.), *Current Developments in Anthropological Genetics: Ecology and Population Structure.* vol. 2. Plenum Press, New York. pp. 205-215.

Friedlaender JS and Rhoads JG. Patterns of adult weight and fat change in six Solomon Islands societies: A semi-longitudinal study. *Journal of Social Science and Medicine*, 16: 205-215.

1980

Friedlaender JS. The people of the Pacific. In: Jean Hiernaux (ed.), *La Diversite Biologique Humaine.* Masson, Paris. pp. 275-311.*

1978

J. Cadien, M. Hassett and J. S. Friedlaender. Linkage disequilibrium in Bougainville Island. *American Journal of Physical Anthropology*, 48: 297-304.

1977

Page LB, Friedlaender JS, and Moellering R. Culture, human biology and disease in the Solomon Islands. In: G. A. Harrison (ed.), *Population Structure and Human Variation.* International Biological Programme, vol. II. Cambridge University Press. pp. 143-164.

J. S. Friedlaender *et al.* Longitudinal physique changes among healthy white veterans at Boston. *Human Biology*, 49: 541-558.

1976

Friedlaender JS and Oliver DL. Effects of aging and the secular trend in Bougainville males. In: E. Giles and J. S. Friedlaender (eds.), *The Measures of Man.* Peabody Museum Press: Cambridge.*

Friedlaender JS. Genes: The physical basis of heredity. In: A Damon (ed.), *Human Biology and Ecology.* New York. Norton.*

1975

Friedlaender JS. Models of population structure and reality. In: F.S. Salzano (ed.), *The Role of Natural Selection in Human Evolution.* Burg Wartenstein Conference #67. North Holland/American Elsevier. pp. 121-132.*

Rhoads JG and Friedlaender JS. Language boundaries and biological differentiation on Bougainville: Multivariate analysis of variance. *Proceedings of the National Academy of Sciences, USA*, 72: 2247-50.

1974

A comparison of population distance and population structure techniques. In: J. F. Crow and C. Dennison, (eds.). *Genetic Distance.* New York: Plenum.*

Mazzur S, Blumberg BS, and Friedlaender JS Silent maternal transmission of Australia antigen. *Nature.* 228-259.

1971

Friedlaender JS. Isolation by distance in Bougainville. *Proceedings of the National Academy of Sciences, USA*, 68:704-707.

Friedlaender JS. The population structure of south-central Bougainville. *American Journal of Physical Anthropology, 35*:13-25.

Friedlaender, JS, Sgaramella-Zonta L, and Kidd, KK. Biological divergences in south-central Bougainville. *American Journal of Human Genetics, 23*:253-270.

1970

Friedlaender JS and Steinberg AG. Anthropological significance of gamma globulin (Gm and Inv) antigens in Bougainville Island, Melanesia. *Nature,* 228-229.

1969

Blumberg BS, Friedlaender JS, and Sgaramella-Zonta L. Hepatitis and Australia antigen: Autosomal recessive inheritance of susceptibility to infection in humans. *Proceedings of the National Academy of Sciences, USA, 62*: 1108- 1115.

Friedlaender JS and Bailit HL. Eruption times of the deciduous and permanent teeth of natives on Bougainville Island. *Human Biology 41*: 51-65.

Rowlett RM., Rowlett ES, Boureus M, Friedlaender JS, *et al.* A rectangular early la Tene Marnian house at Chassemy (Aisne). *World Archaeology I. 1*:105-135.

1966

Bailit HL and Friedlaender JS. Tooth size reduction: A hominid trend. *American Anthropologist 68*:665-672.

APPENDIX 2:
Fieldwork History

2003 (July-August). Fieldwork in Papua New Guinea (West New Britain and North Bougainville) with George Koki.

2000 (July-August). Fieldwork in Papua New Guinea (New Britain and New Ireland) continuing the 1998 work, with George Koki, Andrew Merriwether, and Heather Norton.

1998 (May-July) Fieldwork in Papua New Guinea (Eastern Highlands and New Britain) on JC virus epidemiology, diabetes, and population genetics and history, with Dan Hrdy and George Koki.

1994 (June). Preliminary trip to Papua New Guinea and Solomon Islands to arrange permissions for further fieldwork.

1986 (June-November). Fieldwork as P. I. in the second follow-up Solomon Islands Expedition - head of a team of 7 U.S. medical-anthropological researchers. Included exercise physiologists, virologists, pulmonary specialist, and serologists, as well as graduate students in anthropology – Weitz, Beizer, Armstrong, Richards, Beyerly, Lewis.

1985 (June-September). Initiation of fieldwork as P. I. in the first follow-up Solomon Islands Expedition - same general description as above applies – Weitz, Lesser, Hrdy, Pearson,.

1980 (June-November). Completion of fieldwork as P. I. in the first follow-up Solomon Islands Expedition - three year project on acculturation and health, with John Rhoads and Kevin Mohr.

1978 (January-August). Initiation of fieldwork as P. I. in Solomon Islands-same description as above applies.

1973 (October-December). Surveys of biological variation in north Bougainville (Buka) and eastern Indonesia (Timor).

1970 (June-August). Further studies on Bougainville, Territory of New Guinea, with Howard Bailit and Glenn Rappaport.

1966-67 (August-May). Fieldwork for dissertation - a study of micro-evolution in south -central Bougainville Island, Territory of New Guinea.

1966 (June-August). Physical Anthropologist on the Harvard Solomon Islands Expedition, as one of 12 team members, Albert Damon Director.

1963 (June-August). Osteologist on Harvard-Cornell Excavation of Classical Sardis, Turkey, George Hanfmann Director.

1958 (June-July). Excavation at Hell Gap, Wyoming, under direction of Cynthia Irwin-Williams and Henry Irwin, Harvard University.